"A bracing call to move every parish community from a maintenance model to a mission model… or die! I heartily recommend it to every parish priest and his parish council."

Terrence Prendergast, S.J., Archbishop of Ottawa

"Fr. Mallon has 'walked the walk' and is now sharing with all of us the frustrations, the victories and the humour in transforming sleepy Catholic parishes into places of dynamic encounter and mission. Well worth reading for anyone interested in more dynamic parish life."

Ralph Martin, President of Renewal Ministries and author

"A book that transmits extremely well the passion for the New Evangelization at the heart of parish life. Truly inspiring, practical and challenging! I believe that this is where the Lord is leading his Church."

† Gérald C. Cardinal Lacroix, Archbishop of Quebec, Primate of Canada

"This is a book for Catholics who want to bring the full power of the Christian faith to bear in their parishes. With a keen understanding of the Church's true missional identity, Fr. Mallon sets forth a transformative yet very practical vision for outward-focused parish renewal. This book will inspire you to expand your own vision of what can be, and will energize and equip you to turn your parish into a place where God makes new disciples every day."

William E. Simon, Jr., President of Parish Catalyst

"Mallon's much-needed book combines theological and pastoral insights in a way that is just as thought-provoking and stimulating for the theologian as it is for leaders in the Church."

Fr. Luigi Gioia, Professor of Systematic Theology, Pontifical University of S. Anselmo, Rome

"*Divine Renovation* is not a comfortable read: this radical book points to a daily reconversion and rebuilding. It comes from real-life experiences as a pastor. As the author states in the book, the mission of Christ has a church, not the other way around!"

Peter Togni, composer

"*Divine Renovation*, rooted in our fundamental identity in Christ, and packed with stories, ideas and practical initiatives for creating healthy and vibrant parish communities, is certain to inspire. The fresh vision and approach carved out challenge parishes to break free of the status quo and engage the whole community in missionary discipleship."

Edith Prendergast, RSC, Director of the Office of
Religious Education, Archdiocese of Los Angeles

"Thank you, Fr. Mallon, for your scholarship and synthesis, honesty and guidance, rooted in clearly articulated Catholic theology and effective parish leadership and practice. *Divine Restoration* is a must-read for all who hope to build up the Church."

Leisa Anslinger, author and Co-director of Catholic Life and Faith

"Fr. Mallon has acquired an immense amount of experience in renewing struggling parishes. His book is an essential guide to defining the identity of one's parish and changing the culture."

Fr. Michael White, Pastor and author of Rebuilt

"Let's face it. Lukewarmness – even coldness – is noticeable at too many parishes. Despite an indescribable proximity to the God of the universe in the Eucharist, too many Catholics live a kind of half-life. Well, here is an antidote. Fr. Mallon diagnoses the causes of mediocrity, introduces the reality of intentional discipleship, and provides real-world strategies to help Catholics deeply connect with Jesus and one another. Welcome to the journey from pew-sitting to world-changing."

Patrick Coffin, Radio host, Catholic Answers Live

"Fr. Mallon is a gem in the Church, a true blessing to all of us. He presents here a powerful, practical and real-world call to action that can transform parishes, lives and souls. Buy one for yourself and another for your pastor."

Patrick Lencioni, President, The Table Group and bestselling
author of The Five Dysfunctions of a Team *and* The Advantage

"Fr. James Mallon is a gifted communicator with a passion to help build vibrant Catholic parishes, which spread the good news of Jesus and grow 'missionary disciples'. He is also a friend and I wish him every success with this book."

Nicky Gumbel, Vicar of Holy Trinity Brompton
and Pioneer of Alpha

"This book is a tour de force – a must read! Fr. James speaks from experience: vibrant parish renewal is not only essential, it is possible!"

Very Rev. Scott McCaig CC,
General Superior, Companions of the Cross

DIVINE
RENOVATION

From a Maintenance to a Missional Parish

FR. JAMES MALLON

NOVALIS

© 2014 Novalis Publishing Inc.

Nihil Obstat: Most Rev. Anthony Mancini
Archdiocese of Halifax-Yarmouth
18 June 2014

Cover design: Martin Gould
Cover image: evirgen/iStockphoto
Layout: Audrey Wells

Published by Novalis

Publishing Office
10 Lower Spadina Avenue, Suite 400
Toronto, Ontario, Canada
M5V 2Z2

Head Office
4475 Frontenac Street
Montréal, Québec, Canada
H2H 2S2

www.novalis.ca

Cataloguing in Publication is available from Library and Archives Canada.

Printed in Canada.

We acknowledge the financial support of the Government of Canada through the Canada Book Fund for business development activities.

5 4 3 2 1   18   17   16   15   14

Table of Contents

My mission of being in the heart of the people is not just a part of my life or a badge I can take off; it is not an "extra" or just another moment in life. Instead, it is something I cannot uproot from my being without destroying my very self. I am a mission on this earth; that is the reason why I am here in this world.

Pope Francis, *Evangelii Gaudium* (no. 273)

Introduction

································

HOUSE OF CARDS

"We don't need to know about Jesus. What we need is cards!" With this, she pounded the table and a hush fell over everyone in the hall. Jaws fell open and hands still clutching the next card to be played hung suspended, frozen in the air. In addition to looking shocked, people's faces held a look of righteous appreciation that she had voiced what they had all wanted to say themselves.

The week before, when it became public that I was indeed going to sequester the parish hall on Monday nights to run a ten-week program of evangelization called the Alpha Course, the uproar was so great that an emergency meeting of the parish council had to be called. In spite of words of advice to back off, I, as a 31-year-old priest pastoring my very first parish, stubbornly pushed ahead. There was no other option. Little did I know that this would be the first of many matches I would have with the game of cards over the next ten years of my priesthood.

God blessed our small parish immensely in those early attempts to run Alpha and reach out to the unchurched in our community. Within a year, this small parish would be hosting evenings with over a hundred people gathering in the hall on a Monday night to listen to a presentation of the Gospel message with an invitation to respond. Lives were being transformed. The Lukewarm were catching fire, and people who had been away from church were encountering Jesus in a powerful way, experiencing the Holy Spirit and returning to the community of faith. The great card confrontation had been worth it.

Although we had offered the card social group the first pick of any day or hour other than Monday nights, they opted to vacate the premises and go somewhere else. Not a few heads turned at this: after all, the social had been going on since the fourteenth century, and included some of the original members, or so it seemed. The mystery of why they could not switch to another night was solved one year later.

During my second summer at this parish, I was given a second, smaller parish in a community about 8 miles down the road. It was a church in decline. Attendance was waning. There was no outreach, no ministries other than liturgical ones, and a few generous members who looked after the buildings. They were barely making ends meet by hosting community suppers in the church hall. The first task was to address the catechetical program, which required about 30 kids ages five to sixteen to be stuffed into an overcrowded area and sit through classes that scrambled each week to find a babysitter/catechist. We wanted to separate the junior high kids into their own group and make it more of a youth group experience rather than a classroom one. The only night that worked was Tuesday, and Tuesday night was card social night … with the exact same crowd I had evicted from Monday night at the other parish. The mystery was solved: the reason they could not change their night was that they played cards in a different place every night of the week!

From 2004 to 2010 I was pastor of a relatively well-to-do parish in the well-to-do part of town. It had traditionally been the jewel in the crown of the diocese and had always housed the

Archdiocesan Vicar General and a gang of curates. Until very recently, it was still viewed by pre-retirement priests as the place to be before you hung up your hat. As a result, nothing new had really taken place there for 30 years. Buildings were crumbling due to deferred maintenance, and the church of living stones, the people, was not in much better shape. No adult faith formation, no development of ministries and no development of leadership had taken place. In many ways, it was living off the fumes of the past. The one saving grace was that there were no card socials. However, there were Beavers, Cubs and Scouts who used our building four nights a week, and had been doing so for 30 years.

Once again, we began a series of discussions with the community groups that were using our buildings at no cost to see if we could get even one night to use our hall to run Alpha. Over the six years I was there, we eventually regained control of our buildings, and would go on to run over a dozen multi-week faith formation programs for 70 to 80 people at a time. Needless to say, this dozy parish began to wake up, and amazing things began to happen.

In 2005, one year after I moved to this new parish, once again I was given a second parish. This parish, a mile away, could be described in exactly the same way as the other, with the exception that 90% of its facilities had been leased to a boys' school, in addition to hosting a community basketball league that had no real connection to the parish except that one of the teams played under the name of the parish. Whatever space was not used by these groups was jealously guarded by, you guessed it, two afternoon card socials.

Finally, I moved to my current parish of Saint Benedict three months after the building of the brand new, state-of-the-art facility. This parish had been formed from an amalgamation of three previously existing parishes, and the people, some willingly and others not so, had just moved under the same roof and had been together for a few months. I was to be in place as pastor before the first "ministry year" would get under way. "Great," I thought, "a clean slate. No community groups using our buildings. Lots of space to initiate programs of evangelization and adult faith formation so that we can build a church of living stones to fit the beautiful physical structure."

To my horror, within a week I realized that verbal promises had already been made to community groups to have our available space. I had to move quickly. We tried to compromise, we tried to do both, but we could not. Although we would not launch any initiative for another four months and would use this time to prepare, the Scouts needed a long-term commitment from us, so they decided to move. The other group was … a very large card social. We compromised. We would share the space until December, but in January, when we launched the Alpha Course at Saint Benedict, they would have to move to another time or location. The first time we gathered to share the space, there were a few shocks in store. The first was that 160 people came forward to be trained as leaders for Alpha. The second was that when I walked into the hall, I met angry glares from the 60 to 80 sixty- to eighty-year-old card players, many of them the very same people I had "evicted" from that small country parish ten years earlier.

In the chapters that lie ahead, I will be proposing that much of the confusion within our Church today, including confusion about the purpose of our buildings, is rooted in an identity crisis. We are an essentially missionary Church. I will be laying a theological foundation for this identity, and proposing a model for a renewed parish life. I pray that Church leaders and anyone who cares about the future of our Church will find here a blueprint for a process of Divine Renovation of this Church we love so well.

1

HOUSE OF PRAYER

Remembering Our Identity and Purpose

The key to regaining the buildings of every parish I've ever led was to address the very reason they were turned over to community groups to begin with. It's all about identity.

There is much talk in our Church today about crises. We are told that we have a vocations crisis, a family crisis, a marriage crisis, a financial crisis, a faith crisis, a sexual abuse crisis, a leadership crisis and a [insert your own here _____] crisis. While there may be much valuable discussion around these issues, I contend that our deepest crisis is an identity crisis, and that these other crises are but symptoms of this deepest crisis of all: we have forgotten who we are and what we are called to do as a Church. When this happens, we soon forget not only what our buildings are for, but why we exist as a Church to begin with.

The Temple

This present age is not the first time the People of God have needed to recall their true identity. Over the last few years, I have had the pleasure of leading groups on pilgrimages to the Holy

Land. I love doing it and it is always an unforgettable experience. On our first full day in Jerusalem, we walk down the Mount of Olives, from which you have an amazing view of the Temple Mount and the Dome of the Rock. Before ascending to the Garden of Gethsemane, we pause at the Church of *Dominus Flevit*, the site associated with Jesus' weeping over the city of Jerusalem. (Luke 19:41-44) It is not uncommon to hear tour guides telling the story of how Jesus cleansed the temple of money changers because he was angry that commerce was taking place within the sacred precincts. This is a most common understanding of this action of Jesus, but it is misunderstood. It has more to do with card socials and Scout gatherings than we might imagine.

Fr. Robert Barron, in his beautiful *Catholicism* series, echoes the research of biblical scholar N.T. Wright in speaking about the intentionality of Jesus presenting himself as the Jewish Messiah as he enters the city of Jerusalem. Descending the Mount of Olives riding a colt and entering the city from the East through the Golden Gate, says Barron, would be the equivalent of entering Washington, D.C., in a black stretch limo, with U.S. flags mounted on the front of the car, accompanied by a police escort. The point is that everything was planned and intentional. One of the tasks the Messiah was to fulfill was the restoration of the temple. In Mark's Gospel, after Jesus enters the city to the sound of Messianic acclamations, he immediately enters the temple. Then something odd happens. Saint Mark tells us that Jesus then took a look around, checked the time, realized it was late and left with the Twelve to spend the night in Bethany.

It is not until the next morning that Jesus enters the temple and begins to drive out those who are selling and buying. He upsets the tables of the money changers "and would not allow anyone to carry anything through the temple." (Mark 11:15-16) This was not a spontaneous, passionate outburst by Jesus. It was not a moment of righteous indignation at finding a marketplace in his Father's house. It was a cool and collected Jesus who intentionally made a symbolic gesture. He was not shocked at what he found in the temple. He had been going there his whole life, and buying and selling animals was a necessary part of the worship of the people, as the temple was where sacrificial offerings were made. It is not even anger towards the money changers who added an exchange rate when changing currency from multiple nations into the unique temple currency, the only money with which the sacrificial animals could be bought. Notice that Jesus' action does not just interrupt those making money, but even those who were buying or even trying to enter the inner courts of the temple. Jesus shuts down the entire temple for a period of time and invokes the authority of the prophets. The first quote Jesus gives the astonished crowds is from the prophet Isaiah (Isaiah 56:7); he then makes a reference to Jeremiah's prophecy against the first temple (Jeremiah 7:11): "'My house shall be called a house of prayer for all the nations'? But you have made it a den of robbers." (Mark 11:17)

The Jeremiah reference, when viewed in its original context, would seem to identify the robbers with those charging exorbitant amounts to people who had no other options, just like hot dog vendors in sports stadiums today. However, the key to understanding Jesus' actions is the first quote, from Isaiah, where God reminds the Jewish people that the temple was intended to be a house of prayer for all people, that God's exclusive choice of Israel was intended towards the most generous inclusion of all nations:

> And the foreigners who join themselves to the Lord…
> these I will bring to my holy mountain,
> And make them joyful in my house of prayer;
> their burnt offerings and their sacrifices
> will be accepted on my altar;
> for my house shall be called
> a house of prayer for all people. (Isaiah 56:6)

Most scholars agree that this part of the Book of Isaiah (chapters 56–66) was written in the sixth century BC, and that this prophecy comes from the time of exile before the temple was rebuilt in 520 BC, the original temple of Solomon having been completely destroyed by the Babylonians. It is clearly God's intention not only for the temple, but for the nation of Israel itself, to be a conduit of salvation for all people. We find hints of this great universal vocation throughout the Scriptures, but especially in the prophets and, in particular, in the Book of Isaiah. Isaiah chapter 49, in what is known as the Second Song of the Servant, was written during the exile and speaks of the restoration of the people of Israel, but goes on to expand Israel's vocation:

> "It is too light a thing that you should be my servant
> to raise up the tribes of Jacob
> and to restore the survivors of Israel;
> I will give you as a light to the nations,
> that my salvation may reach to the end of the earth."
> (Isaiah 49:6)

Mindful of this call, he who was declared in that very temple from the lips of Simeon (Luke 2:29-32) to be the embodiment and fulfillment of this prophecy now beheld a temple that did not reflect the radical inclusion of all nations through the exclusive choice of Israel. Rather, he beheld a people who had forgotten their vocation, who had robbed the Gentiles of their inclusion into God's covenant. They had decided that it was enough to keep it all for themselves. They were content with the status quo, they were content with their worship and ritual, and they had forgotten their purpose – their identity that the prophets of Israel had pointed out, often at their own cost.

The very architecture of the temple communicated this theology of exclusion. Gentiles could ascend to the sacred Temple Mount and be present in what was known as "The Court of the Gentiles," but were forbidden to enter the gates of the temple. From there, access to the Holy of Holies, the inner sanctuary, was limited by varying degrees of proscription. After the Court of the Gentiles was the Court of the Women, then the Court of the Israelites, to which only Jewish men could be admitted. Next was the Court of the Priests, and lastly the Holy of Holies, into which only the High Priest could enter once a year. The Holy of

Holies originally housed the Ark of the Covenant in Solomon's Temple, and was separated by a veil, the same veil that was torn in two when Jesus died on the cross. By his death and resurrection, Jesus allows the temple of his body to be destroyed and rebuilt so that in his person, he manifests the new temple of God, where earth is joined to heaven. In this temple there are no more walls of separation. (Ephesians 2:14) There is now no Jew and Greek, no male and female. (Galatians 3:28) All are priests and have access to the Holy of Holies. Jesus fulfills in his person the destiny of Israel. All of the ancient prophecies of radical inclusion are fulfilled exclusively by this only Son of God, the Son of David, Jesus the Messiah. The mission of inclusion is handed on to the New Israel, the ones who are called out by Jesus, his *ekklesia*, to go and make disciples of all nations. But then, we too would eventually forget this and become satisfied with keeping it all for ourselves.

Déjà Vu

The identity crisis in our Church today is not unlike the one that existed at the time of Jesus. It is said that it's not so much that the Church of Christ has a mission, as that the mission of Jesus Christ has a Church. We, however, have so forgotten our essential missionary calling that we have contented ourselves with maintenance and serving ourselves. That the Church exists for the sake of mission has been asserted by popes and theologians continuously for the last 50 years, but most Catholics perceive mission as something that a select few carry out in far-off places, and most parishes, crippled by a culture of maintenance, focus at best on meeting the needs of parishioners. Like Israel at the time of Jesus, we have become robbers of the people God has appointed us to reach, that his "salvation may reach to the end of the earth." (Isaiah 49:6)

April 14, 2012, was the 100th anniversary of the sinking of the *Titanic*. My home city of Halifax was deeply affected by these commemorations, as it had played a key role in the rescue operations. As I write these words, I am aware that the cemetery that holds the remains of those victims who were recovered is a short distance away. On the night of the anniversary, I watched the old black-and-white movie *A Night to Remember*. It reminded me that many of the lifeboats launched from the stricken vessel that night were no more than half filled. In fact, in the eighteen lifeboats that launched from the ship, there were a total of 472 unused spaces. After the ship disappeared below the water, around 1,500 people floundered in the icy waters while the lifeboats sat at a safe distance and watched. Only two of the eighteen lifeboats went to rescue survivors. They transferred passengers to maximize free space, and it is a recorded fact that some of the first-class passengers complained about terrible inconvenience. By the time those in the lifeboats had recalled their purpose and had gone among the victims, only nine people were found alive, and three of these eventually succumbed to hypothermia.

As I watched the movie, it struck me that this was a metaphor for the Church. We exist for mission. Like Jesus, we have been sent to "seek and save" those who are perishing, and there are plenty of seats available in the lifeboats. Yet, so often as a Church, we sit at a safe distance, more concerned with our own needs and comfort. Perhaps if a few people swam over to us, we would help them, but going to them? This is not just a question of our comfort zones being challenged – it is totally outside of our frame of reference, because we have so thoroughly forgotten our identity. Lifeboats exist to rescue people. So does the Church. We maintain our lifeboats, we paint them, we serve the people in them and keep them in good order and hold card socials, but we do not use them for the purpose for which they were created. Any crew member who would dare to disrupt life on the lifeboat will quickly hear a chorus of complaints from the passengers who are adverse to being inconvenienced in any way. We lament the tragedy of the loss of faith, secularization, church closures and so on, but it does not occur to us to pick up the oars and row.

The Mission

So, if we exist for mission, what is the mission of the Church? To answer this question, we turn to the last verses of Matthew's Gospel, to the passage known as the Great Commission. (Matthew 28:19-20) Here, the wavering disciples are told to "Go therefore and make disciples of all nations, baptizing them in the name of the Father and of the Son and of the Holy Spirit, and teaching them to obey everything that I have commanded you." Translations of this text vary slightly, but what is obvious is that Jesus gave his nascent Church four tasks: go, make, baptize and teach. Of these four imperatives, we find in the original Greek that one of them is a finite verb and three are participles. A finite verb is always the grammatical hinge of a sentence, and participles are verbal nouns that, although they qualify a sentence, ultimately make sense only in reference to the finite verb. So it is with the Great Commission. One of these verbs is the grammatical centre of the sentence and thus, also, the theological centre. Over the years, when speaking at conferences, I have asked groups to choose which of the four verbs is the hinge of the Great Commission and, therefore, the heart of our purpose, the very task that gives us our identity. I have asked groups of lay people, priests and even bishops. I have asked large groups and small groups, and all with the same result. The right answer is always chosen by the least amount of people, and not just by a few but by an insanely small minority. Once, from a group of 600, only two people chose the right answer. Once, from a group of over 3,000 people, only about 20 people chose the right answer. These disproportionate results reflect the identity crisis that afflicts our Church and reveal a deep, unconscious bias against the very task that the Lord placed at the heart of his mandate.

Which do you choose: to go, to make, to baptize or to teach?

Here's the answer:

The finite verb is "make" – literally, "make disciples" (*matheteusate*). This task is the very heart of the Great Commission, and it is around the making of disciples that all the other missionary aspects of the Church revolve: the going, the baptizing and the teaching. Think about this: in recent centuries, the Catholic Church had the distinction of being a great missionary Church. We went. We have a rich didactic tradition and are famed for our schools and universities and curricula. We teach. We surely know how to baptize and celebrate all the other sacraments, but our one pastoral weakness, the task we struggle with the most, is that which lies at the very heart of Christ's commission to the Church: to make disciples.

Making Disciples

What do we mean by making disciples? In Church culture, we often use terms such as "disciple" or "apostle" without understanding the meaning of these words, but "disciple" is so key to our mandate from Jesus that we ought to know its meaning. The word in Greek for "disciple" is *mathetes*, which, in turn, comes from the verb *manthanein*, meaning "to learn" (think of the term "math"). To be a disciple is to be a learner. To be a disciple of Jesus Christ is to be engaged in a lifelong process of learning from and about Jesus the master, Jesus the teacher. The English term "disciple" comes from the Latin *discipulus*, and provides the connotation that this learning process is not haphazard, but intentional and disciplined. To become a disciple is to commit to such a process of growth.

But how many of our parishioners does this term honestly describe? We all have people in our churches who are passionate about their faith, committed and hungry to grow and learn, but they are, sadly, a small minority who often are considered a little odd by "normal Catholics." When I speak to pastors, they will often admit that this designation describes about 6 to 10% of regularly attending Catholics – at most, 20%, if a parish is particularly vibrant. We have a real problem before us. It is the membership of our churches who are called to be making disciples, but most have not yet become disciples themselves. A further obstacle to this task is that being an adult learner in the faith is viewed as entirely optional and non-essential. We value it for children and teenagers, but somehow think that adults do not need to learn, grow or mature. Catechesis in Catholic circles usually means what we do with children. Although the laity of our Church is more educated and professional than at any other time in history, the corresponding literacy in things of faith, theology, scripture and the spiritual life lags far behind.

Over the last 50 years, our society has witnessed what can arguably be called the most accelerated social change in human history. As we have moved through several paradigm shifts in the last generation, the pastoral practice of the Catholic Church in the West remains, for the most part, unchanged from what existed prior to this state of flux. Culture supported faith and church attendance. Demographics supported our pastoral development through the birth of children and the movement of migrants. We just had to build it and people would come. I do not believe we were particularly good at making disciples 50 years ago, but it was not obviously to our detriment. As long as we would go and open churches, there were always new communities of migrants and new babies. As long as we baptized and taught in our schools, we pumped out good "practising Catholics." In a sense, we got away with not making disciples, because the culture propped it all up. Fast forward through the 60s, the sexual revolution, mass media, new media, post-modernism, materialism, relativism, individualism, hedonism and every other "ism" we can think of and all of a sudden the fault lines are revealed for all to see.

Hundreds of thousands of faithful, believing Catholics carry the enormous burden of children and grandchildren who have abandoned "the faith." These faithful Catholics carry the extra burden of blaming themselves for this situation, unsure of what they did wrong: after all, they did for their children what their parents did for them. Pointing fingers is, well, pointless. The fact is that the rules have all changed. We no longer have the cultural props we had before, and the social current has turned against us. The only solution going forward is to return to what Jesus asked of us 2,000 years ago: to not just make believers, or "practising Catholics," but to make disciples. To make *disciples*. That's it! This is the heart of the matter and the lens through which we are to evaluate all activity of the Church – all pastoral programs, all expenditures and all use of our buildings.

Evangelization

How do we make disciples? If a disciple is one who learns, who yearns to grow, who hungers for knowledge, how does this happen? We know that just because someone "believes" in Jesus or goes to church does not necessarily mean they have this hunger. Something must happen to awaken this hunger: that something is evangelization. We know that "to evangelize" literally means to announce good news, but what is this Good News? I suspect that many of us could fill pages describing the Good News of Jesus or the Good News about Jesus. It is multi-layered and complex. A part of us resists the temptation to oversimplify things and ends up giving in to the temptation of unnecessarily complicating them. We can speak of the message of "God with us," of God's Kingdom or Reign, of God's mercy, of God's unconditional love, of the forgiveness of sins, of God's love being revealed on the cross, and of the defeat of death through the resurrection of Jesus. We can speak of the truth that we are never alone, that God desires to dwell in us, to consume us and have us consume him, but in the end it is possible to simplify the message into one word: Jesus. In Jesus, we have the very embodiment of God's salvation presence, love, mercy and life. We know in the Gospels that he who was the proclaimer of the Good News of the Kingdom becomes the Good News and the embodiment of that Kingdom. To receive this Good News, to be evangelized, is not only to hear these wonderful truths, to know about them, but to come to know him – to not just believe in him, but to love him and to be in love with him. Only then will our hearts sing and our song be heard. Only when we come to encounter him as alive and real, he who is the Way, the Truth and the Life, do we then desire to walk his way, hunger for his truth and seek to live his life.

The difficult truth for us as pastors, leaders and people who care about our church is that so many of our people have never come to know him personally, and therefore have no hunger for him. We still have the shadow of duty and fear as a religious motivation hanging over us. Scripture tells us, however, that where this is active, perfect love has not been discovered. (1 John 4:18) It is most often not a willful reduction of faith to simple *knowledge about* Jesus, but a lack of awareness that it is even possible to know him and to be known and loved personally by him. We are often like people who live in a black-and-white world who cannot begin to conceive of the reality of colour. The fact that so many Catholics are utterly convinced that they are missing nothing shows that the weekly experience of faith and "religion" acts as a kind of vaccine to the full power of the Christian faith. Many who are no longer held in the clutches of duty, guilt or fear walk away, rejecting a hollow version of the real thing. As a result, we have all too often capitulated as leaders and formed pastoral methodologies designed to feed those who have no hunger. We give in to pressure from distracted and bored parishioners to preach shorter and shorter homilies, aware that many would be quite pleased if we just dispensed with the whole thing completely and got to the communion bit so that the mad dash to the parking lot could commence.

What is to be done? The very thing that our popes from the time of Paul VI to Francis have been telling us. There must be a New Evangelization (we will be speaking about the development of this teaching in the next chapter). Jesus Christ must be proposed anew! We must break through the invisible suits of armour that so many in our pews wear. We must labour to create spaces for people to come to know Jesus as the living Lord, awaken that hunger and then begin to form them, to make them disciples. We must rediscover our identity and place the heart of the Lord's mandate for his Church at the heart of everything we do, so that at the heart of every parish there will be a community of growing, maturing believers who are committed to a lifelong process of disciplined learning, who are discovering their God-given talents, who are prepared to serve and eventually to become apostles. We must labour so that a Church of disciples may eventually, someday, be considered normal.

From Disciples to Apostles

Being a Church of disciples, however, is just a part of our calling. This Church of disciples must "go" and "make disciples" of all nations, of all peoples. We are mandated by the Lord to proclaim this Good News not just to lukewarm or fallen-away Catholics, but to all who do not know Christ and his Church. We are called to go out to the fringes of society, to the poor, the rich, the vulnerable and those who hide in their gated communities. We are called to go. Jesus said, "As the Father has sent me, so I send you." (John 20:21) The Greek word that means "to send" is *apostellein*. An apostle is one who is sent. To take up the Great Commission of Jesus means that we have been sent, that we are apostles. That this sending constitutes the nature of the Church is affirmed when we speak of the Church as being apostolic. This is the earliest meaning of this term. Later it would be associated with the ministry of the Twelve and their successors, and their role in preserving the content of the Church's faith. From the mouth of Jesus himself we see its first meaning. We are a Church that is sent. The Latin equivalent for *apostellein* is the verb *mittere*, which gives us the noun *missio* and the English word "mission." Thus, an apostle is a missionary. That the Church is apostolic means that it is missionary by nature: it is who we are; it is our deepest identity. "How are they to proclaim him unless they are sent?" says Saint Paul. (Romans 10:15) Disciples must eventually become apostles.

Several years ago, I was sitting in a coffee shop in the Montreal airport with some friends, discussing parish renewal and evangelization, when an image of the Church came to me. The Church is like a photocopier. It exists to photocopy paper, to make copies. It does this by drawing the paper into itself. This is evangelization. Then it prints, copies, staples and punches holes. This is discipleship (baptized, taught, formed). Then it spits out the paper with the imprinted word that can go and change the world; after all, history has proven that the pen is mightier than the sword. This is missioning. The Church is at its best when it experiences this kind of cycle. She evangelizes and makes disciples and sends them out as missionaries to go and evangelize, to make more disciples who can be baptized and taught, and eventually sent out. When the Church is healthy, she does this. When the Church is not healthy, when she is turned into herself, she has forgotten her great calling to be *lumen gentium*, a light to the nations, just as Israel had forgotten at the time of Jesus. In this state of forgetfulness, the Church becomes like an overheated and jammed photocopier that sits in a corner, collects dust and is eventually forgotten.

Something must be done. Drastic action is required. Over the last four years, in my present parish of Saint Benedict, after overturning a few figurative card tables, we did regain control of our facilities. Since then, we have seen almost 2,000 people participate in Alpha, with 20% to 30% being non-churchgoers. We have run hundreds of different faith formation events or programs and have seen hundreds of lives changed and transformed as people encountered the person of Jesus Christ, in the power of the Holy Spirit. Through these experiences, they have come to know God as their Father and have come alive in their experience of God's family, the Church. All this through the grace of God, which has enabled us to rediscover our new identity through Pope John Paul II's call for the New Evangelization, whose roots are in the Second Vatican Council.

2

REBUILD MY HOUSE

From Vatican II to Pope Francis

Do you remember where you were on March 13, 2013? I bet you do. It was the day that Jorge Bergoglio was introduced to world as Francesco. Although rumoured to have been a close second in the previous conclave that elected Pope Benedict, Cardinal Bergoglio was a relative unknown and was on no list of the pundits for the 2013 election. I remember where I was when I heard the news, and I remember my first words: "Who?" and "Francesco!" Although he would go on to explain his choice of name based on his love for the poor, my first thoughts were that this man was declaring himself to be a reformer after the saint who heard the Lord say to him, "Francis, rebuild my house, which as you see is falling into ruin." I like to believe that he chose this name for both reasons, and his actions so far as pope would confirm this hope.

Since that momentous day, Pope Francis has exploded onto the international scene. He speaks to all Christians with clarity and urgency, challenging us to recall our identity and to be a Church that goes out and a Church that makes "missionary disciples." In doing this, he continues the call of his predecessor, who spoke often of the New Evangelization and called for the re-evangelization of the West.

The Second Vatican Council

There is no doubt about the priority of evangelization in Church teaching over the last number of years. To truly understand the call to the New Evangelization, we must begin by looking at something that happened over 50 years ago: the Second Vatican Council (1962–1965). This Council would produce sixteen documents, each an original synthesis of traditional Catholic doctrine and new theological insight. Without any academic attempt to support my statement, I would like to claim that the central theological insights of all sixteen conciliar documents can be summed up in the following phrases: *the universal call to holiness* and *the universal call to mission*. Holiness and mission are not new in the teaching of Church, but the stress on the universal nature of these things was relatively new. The idea that the call to holiness and mission is rooted not in ordination or in religious profession but in baptism had been so forgotten that it was revolutionary. We are called to holiness because we are baptized. We are called to mission, to evangelize, to share the Good News because we are baptized.

Pope Paul VI

Ten years to the day after the Council was closed, Pope Paul VI released a groundbreaking document called *Evangelii Nuntiandi*, which means "Announcing the Good News." Its title in English is "Evangelization in the Modern World." This document enunciated a theology for mission and evangelization that is the responsibility of all Christians. Since the close of the Council, it remains the most profound call for the Church to rediscover her identity.

Let us begin with how Pope Paul VI defines evangelization:

It has been possible to define evangelization in the terms of proclaiming Christ to those who do not know Him, of preaching, of catechesis, of conferring Baptism and the other Sacraments. (EN, no. 17)

We see right away that he chose a broad definition of evangelization. It includes all of the tasks that make up the Great Commission, but also includes most of the activities of the Church: preaching, catechesis, teaching, sacraments, and proclamation, or kerygma.

Pope Paul also reminds us that we must avoid the temptation of thinking that the witness of our lives alone is sufficient to evangelize. As he says, "the Good News proclaimed by the witness of life, sooner or later has to be proclaimed by the word of life." (EN, no. 22) This is a very important principle for us today, as it emphasizes the proclamation or kerygmatic dimension of Paul VI's definition. There is much confusion today about the necessity of using words to achieve the goal of evangelization. We have all heard that saying attributed to Saint Francis of Assisi: "Preach the Gospel at all times and if necessary, use words." In spite of the popularity of this phrase, it appears to be a kind of ecclesiastical urban myth. A search of the Franciscan Omnibus of Sources will not turn up this quote. Saint Francis appears never to have said this, and, in any case, it is erroneous. Saint Paul tells us that "Faith comes from what is heard." (Romans 10:17) Certainly, however, there is a primacy to the witness of life. We instinctively cringe when we encounter someone who is not living it but is spouting it. However, it is not an *either/or* situation, it is *both/and*, and *both/and* is a sound Catholic principle. The witness of life must come first, but it must lead to the word of life being proclaimed. Without actions, our words are not believed by our cynical postmodern, post-Christian society, but without words, our actions are not understood. Saint Peter says, "Always be ready to make your defense to anyone who demands from you an accounting for the hope that is in you" (1 Peter 3:15), and so does Pope Paul, when he insists that evangelization must be "made explicit by a clear and unequivocal proclamation of the Lord Jesus."

> There is no true evangelization if the name, the teaching, the life, the promises, the kingdom and the mystery of Jesus of Nazareth, the Son of God are not proclaimed. (EN, no. 22)

Although he gives a broad definition of evangelization throughout the document, he makes it clear, then, that

> evangelization will also always contain – as the foundation, center, and at the same time, summit of its dynamism – a clear proclamation that, in Jesus Christ, the Son of God made man, who died and rose from the dead, salvation is offered to all men, as a gift of God's grace and mercy. (EN, no. 22)

In this beautiful one-sentence definition of the Good News, Pope Paul prepares the way for a development that would emerge in the writings of Pope John Paul II, Pope Benedict, Pope Francis and magisterial documents around the topic of the New Evangelization. The Church's pastoral methodology must be broad, but evangelization *qua* evangelization is essentially keryg-matic and leads to an encounter with the person of Jesus. It does not just communicate information about him or his teaching, but consists in the very encounter that makes one become a disciple.

Pope John Paul II

Within three years of the writing of this still pivotal docu-ment, after the 33-day ministry of Pope John Paul I in 1978, Karol Cardinal Wojtyla of Krakow would put on the fisherman's ring and continue to advance the notions of the universal call to holiness and mission that he encountered at the Second Vatican Council. *Evangelii Nuntiandi* was an apostolic exhortation, writ-ten after a synod of bishops who gathered in Rome in 1974 to discuss the meaning, definition and relevance of evangelization. Karol Wojtyla worked at the Synod as the General Secretary and played a major role in the drafting of the document. Within eight months of his election as Pope John Paul II in 1978, the man who had played no small role in the formulation of key documents of the Council and in the writing of *Evangelii Nuntiandi* itself would coin the phrase "the New Evangelization" during his first papal visit to Poland on June 9, 1979. He used the term then, but did not define it until four years later. He did this during an address to CELAM, the Latin American Bishops' Conference, in 1983, saying that the New Evangelization would be "new in its ardour, in its methods, and in its expression."

The theme of evangelization appeared continuously throughout his ministry and his writings. From his encyclical letter *Redemptoris Missio* ("The Mission of the Redeemer," in English), published in 1990, he said this:

> I sense the moment has come to commit all of the Church's energies to a new evangelization and to the missions *ad gentes* [to the nations]. No believer in Christ, no institution of the Church can avoid this supreme duty: to proclaim Christ to all peoples. (RM, no. 3)

Saint John Paul unequivocally states that the proclamation of Christ is not only the summit of all evangelizing activity, but is the supreme duty of the Church and every individual believer. None of us can avoid it. He builds on this theme in his Apostolic Letter *Novo Millenio Ineunte* (On Entering the New Millenium) from 2001 to mark the close of the Great Jubilee year.

> This passion will not fail to stir in the Church a new sense of mission which cannot be left to a group of "specialists" but must involve the responsibility of all the members of the people of God. Those who have come into genuine contact with Christ cannot keep Him for themselves, they must proclaim him. (no. 40)

Evangelization is now a moral obligation. It's almost a selfish thing to not evangelize. If we find something wonderful and we keep it for ourselves, then we would be morally culpable.

Fr. Bob Bedard, founder of the community of priests called the Companions of the Cross, used to say that evangelization was "one beggar telling another beggar where to find bread." Jesus is the Bread of Life and the Living Water, and we live in a world filled with hungry and thirsty people. In the name of respecting those who hunger and thirst, we all too often give physical bread and water but almost hide the fact that we do it in his name, not to mention that we rarely offer them Jesus himself. This great division within the Church's missionary activity, between justice and charity on the one hand and evangelization on the other, would be taken up by Pope Benedict.

Pope Benedict XVI

Josef Ratzinger, present at the Second Vatican Council as a theological advisor to Cardinal Frings, participated at all sessions of the Council and played a key role in helping the German bishops overturn the documents and agenda that had been prepared for the bishops by the Roman Curia. He was also personally involved in drafting or redrafting many of the conciliar documents. As the pope's right-hand man throughout John Paul II's pontificate, Josef Ratzinger witnessed first-hand the unfolding of the call to the New Evangelization. He would go on to formalize it as Pope Benedict through two major developments: the establishment in June 2010 of the Office for the Promotion of the New Evangelization, and through the convocation of the 13th Synod of Bishops on October 2012 to discuss the topic of "The New Evangelization for the Transmission of the Christian Faith."

Although these two developments are concrete manifestations of the magisterial response to the New Evangelization, his writings and the writings of curial documents during his pontificate contain the language of an evangelization that is new in its ardour, methods and expression. They extend the development and refining that had begun to take shape in Pope John Paul II's development of Paul VI's writings. The distinction between evangelization and catechesis increases, with evangelization being identified more with proclamation that leads to encounter. Under Benedict, a relatively unfamiliar term, at least in official Catholic documents, begins to appear more and more often. Benedict begins to speak of the necessity of the *personal* encounter and *personal* relationship with Jesus.

In an address to the bishops of the Philippines in 2011, he reminded them that "Your great task in Evangelization is therefore to propose a personal relationship with Christ as key to complete fulfillment." Personalist language also appears throughout what is known as the *Lineamenta* document for the synod, released two weeks before this address to the Filipino bishops. This document was distributed to create discussion throughout the world and provide input from bishops and local churches. This feedback would help form a working document for the synod itself. The *Lineamenta* defines the goal of evangelization as the "realization of a personal encounter with Jesus Christ in the Spirit, thereby leading to an experiencing of His Father and our Father." (no. 11) Evangelization is always Trinitarian, but not in an abstract, theoretical manner. It is about experiencing a person or persons, and the goal of evangelization is to bring people to Jesus Christ so they can then be filled with the Holy Spirit and come to know God the Father. The Holy Spirit who fills us is the Spirit of adoption, who speaks to our spirits so that we cry out, "Abba! Father!" (Romans 8:15) It is totally Trinitarian. This is the goal of evangelization.

For many traditionally minded Catholics, the recurrence of terms such as *evangelization* and *personal relationship* with Jesus seems, well, not quite Catholic. In my first months at my present parish, when I would speak in this way, many parishioners would say, "Father, this just doesn't sound very Catholic." That the average Catholic struggles even today with evangelization is seen in the reason for the synod topic given in the *Lineamenta* document: "That despite the fact that the expression [the New Evangelization] is widely known in the Church it has failed to be accepted fully and totally." (no. 5) The document says this in spite of the fact that 30 years had passed since Pope John Paul II first spoke about it.

What more can we do to demonstrate that this language is quintessentially "Catholic"?

> Being Christian and "being Church" means being missionary; one is or is not. Loving one's faith implies bearing witness to it, bringing it to others and allowing others to participate in it. (no. 10)

So just as we were beginning to make peace with the term "evangelize," along comes this even more evangelically Protestant–sounding language from the Pope and Vatican documents: *personal relationship* and *personal encounter*. Again, hear the *Lineamenta* document: "People are able to evangelize only when they have been evangelized and allow themselves to be evangelized, that is, renewed spiritually through a personal encounter and lived communion with Jesus Christ." (no. 22)

Perhaps our reticence to use such language is rooted in our suspicion of the individualism that is rife in our culture. However, while this *term* may be foreign to our spiritual tradition, the notion of an individual having an encounter with the living God is most certainly not foreign, and is at the heart of our Catholic mystical tradition. Is mysticism or mystical union the same as personal relationship with Christ? Surely it is: if someone has a mystical experience with God, it is likely personal. That is what the mystics in our tradition speak about when they describe a deeply intimate and personal encounter with God. While it is true that we do not hear the term "personal Lord and Saviour" in Scripture, the concept of Jesus as Saviour who speaks to every human heart does exist. We must remember that the whole concept of the individual, as we now understand it, is relatively new in our culture. It's less than a hundred years old, and it is not invincible when it comes to criticism. Rampant individualism has wreaked havoc in our culture, and the ascent of the rights of the individual over that of the community has not necessarily led to a healthier Church or society. Nevertheless, that is the culture we have to work with, and it is the requirement of evangelizers to speak to the culture.

And then there was Francis.

Pope Francis

Point number 4 of his handwritten notes from his speech to the conclave on March 9, 2013, four days before he was elected pope, reads as follows:

> Thinking of the next Pope: a man who, through the contemplation of Jesus Christ and the adoration of Jesus Christ, may help the Church to go out from itself toward the existential peripheries, that may help it to be the fecund mother who lives "by the sweet and comforting joy of evangelizing."

Cardinal Bergoglio began his speech with a quote from Pope Paul VI, and all four points of his speech were about evangelization and the necessity for the Church to overcome a crippling self-referential tendency. This all-too-present inclination induces illness and evil within the Church, he claimed. Since his election, he has embodied this call for the Church to go out, to rediscover her essential missionary identity through his own actions first, and also through his words. In doing so, he probably is the first pope in history to command a mess to be made:

> I would like to say something. What do I expect as a consequence of the Youth Day? I expect a mess. There will be one. There will be a mess here in Rio? There will be! But I want a mess in the dioceses! I want people to go out! I want the Church to go out to the street! I want us to defend ourselves against everything that is worldliness, that is installation, that is comfortableness, that is clericalism, that is being shut-in in ourselves. The parishes, the schools, the institutions, exist to go out! If they don't go out, they become NGOs, and the Church can't be an NGO. (Address to Argentinian Youth at World Youth Day, Rio de Janeiro)

Pope Francis would deliver the same message three days later, in an only slightly more subtle way, when he spoke to the leadership of CELAM, the Latin American and Caribbean Bishops'

Conference. In this address, which we will visit in later chapters, he names in a provocative manner the "temptations" that prevent or hinder the Church from doing what it is supposed to do: to create "missionary disciples." To credit the term "missionary disciple" to Pope Francis is only partly accurate, because it is a term that appears from one end to the other of what is known as the Aparecida document, published in 2008, one year after the gathering of the bishops of Latin America and the Caribbean at the famous Brazilian shrine in the town of Aparecida. The theme for that conference was "Disciples and Missionaries of Jesus Christ, so that our peoples will have life in him." The extensive document that would emerge from this gathering, and be the inspiration for a new "Continental Mission" throughout the region, was very much guided by the hand and heart of Cardinal Jorge Bergoglio of Buenos Aires. In spite of the fact that Pope Francis published the Apostolic Exhortation *Evangelii Gaudium* in the first year of his pontificate, I believe that neither he nor his papal exhortation can be understood without knowledge of the Aparecida document.

Aparecida

I first encountered the term "Aparecida" when I travelled to northern Mexico in 2009 to do workshops on evangelization and Alpha with local churches in the city of Chihuahua. During this conference, the associate pastor of the parish, who taught Church history at the local university, gave an amazing talk on the Continental Mission that was called for from "Aparecida." These were new terms for me. I quickly learned that Aparecida was the national shrine of Brazil and a popular pilgrimage site. I also learned that Pope Benedict met there in May of 2007 with the bishops of Latin America and the Caribbean to call the Church in that continent to recall its identity. The result was a commitment to a Continental Mission that would impact all sectors of the Latin American Church and bring about renewal. Since that time, I have travelled to Mexico several times and have been a part of a conference on evangelization in Aparecida itself.

What I have repeatedly found among the ordained and lay leadership of the Church in Latin America is a profound commitment to authentic renewal and a clear grasp of what is truly at stake. During that first trip to Chihuahua, I encountered clergy and lay leaders who were not only asking questions that our own clergy in Canada were not asking, but also men and women who were proposing answers. I expected to find a disheartened Church attempting to recover from the domination of certain forms of liberation theology of previous decades, but found young leaders asking bold questions and proposing bold solutions.

The Aparecida document is a document of the Magisterium of the Church. Although it is a call to action for the Church in South America, it would be a real mistake to ignore its importance for the universal Church, and not only because the man who would become Pope Francis had a strong hand in shaping it. I believe that the insights of this document have given the Church in Latin America a six-year lead in the process of renewal that was proposed to the universal Church through the publication of *Evangelii Gaudium* (The Joy of the Gospel), the call to action after the gathering of many of the world's bishops under Pope Benedict.

The document itself is expansive, addressing every aspect of the Church's missionary endeavour, proposing concrete goals for various Catholic institutions towards their role in implementing the Continental Mission. It addresses the need for the Church's mission to include a "preferential option for the poor," to work against poverty, injustice, ecological degradation and exploitation of any kind. In spite of the scope of this document, however, the central theme dominates throughout: to remind "the faithful of this continent that by virtue of their baptism, they are called to be disciples and missionaries of Jesus Christ." (no. 10) These words are a quote of Pope Benedict from his Inaugural Address to the bishops at the beginning of the conference the year before. The cycle is complete. They highlight a theme that goes back to the heart of the Second Vatican Council itself. They clarify that, although the tasks that the Church must take up are many, none trumps the call of the Lord to make disciples and to lead these disciples to become apostles, or missionaries. The juxtaposition of the terms "disciples" and "missionaries," or the term "missionary disciple," occurs 121 times in this document.

If, in magisterial documents from Paul VI to Benedict, we have witnessed a focusing of the definition of evangelization on proclamation, conversion and personal encounter, this development is complete in the document of Aparecida. Although we find this throughout the document, there are two places I would like to focus on. The first is in section 5.4, entitled "Those Who Have Left the Church to Join Other Religious Groups." In this section, we see the recognition of research that was carried out before the gathering by Dr. Jose Luis Perez Guadalupe, a researcher and professor at the University of Peru. This research amounted to hundreds of "exit interviews," a mere fraction of the number of Latin American Catholics who have left the Catholic Church to join Evangelical Protestant groups. The interviewers found four reasons why the majority of Catholics left the Church; the bishops incorporated this research into the Aparecida document. They report the following:

1. The faithful had never experienced "a personal encounter with Jesus Christ" (that was "profound and intense") within the Catholic Church but had in other churches. This encounter had come about due to "a kerygmatic proclamation and the personal witness of evangelizers that leads to a personal conversion and to a thorough change of life." (no. 226a) They had not encountered this in their experience of the Catholic Church.

2. The presence of meaningful community life where people are "accepted ... and feel valued, visible, and included in the Church." They had not experienced this in their Catholic context, but did when they joined the other churches.

3. Biblical and doctrinal formation, not as "theoretical and cold knowledge" but something that brings about "spiritual, personal and community growth" and brings people to maturity.

4. Missionary commitment that moves Church members from
   the pews to go out to meet those on the periphery to bring
   people home to the family of God.

What is so heartbreaking about the truth of so many testimonies is that there is nothing in our Catholic theology or tradition that need hinder any of these essential elements that have resulted in such a huge exodus from the Catholic Church in Latin America. The document itself testifies to this fact:

> In our pastoral experience, often sincere people who leave
> our church do not do so because of what "non-Catholic"
> groups believe, but fundamentally for what they live; not
> for doctrinal but for vivential reasons; not for strictly
> dogmatic, but for pastoral reasons; not due to theological
> problems, but to methodological problems of our Church.
> (no. 225)

The difficult reality is that these methodological deficiencies consist, no less, of the essential tasks of evangelization, discipleship, fellowship and mission. We can have a wonderful theology of all these key aspects of Church life, but if they are not incarnated into actual Church living, they remain abstractions. Thus the powerful call in this document for a total "pastoral conversion."

I believe that chapter 6 of the Aparecida document is its most important section, as it not only lays out a theology for the formation of "missionary disciples," but provides a detailed outline of the necessary formation process. This is the second part of the document, which authoritatively crystallizes the narrowing of the definition of evangelization that began with the writing of *Evangelii Nuntiandi*. Section 6.2.1 proposes "five fundamental aspects in the process of forming missionary disciples," and begins with the "Encounter with Jesus Christ" and links it directly and explicitly to the *kerygma*. It is clear that the kerygma must be distinctly heard, and goes as far as saying that "Without the kerygma, the other aspects of this process are condemned to sterility, with hearts not truly converted to the Lord." The second "aspect" of formation is conversion that transforms our lives and leads to a decision to follow Jesus as Lord. This decision will bring a person to the sacrament of baptism or reconciliation. The third aspect of formation is discipleship. The bishops speak here of how each believer "constantly matures" in knowledge and love of Jesus the master, and "delves deeper into the mystery of his person." Catechesis and sacraments, it is noted, are of "fundamental importance for this stage." The remaining aspects are *Communion* and *Mission*. No surprises here. Communion is vital, meaningful community where an "encounter" with other disciples takes place. It is a place of encouragement, support and maturation. All of these aspects, if authentic, lead spontaneously to mission: the mission to proclaim Jesus to others in joy, to love and serve the needy and to build the Kingdom of God.

Below is a schema that outlines in a linear fashion the process proposed by the Aparecida document for the formation of missionary disciples. Every stage of this process takes place within a vital and caring community of faith.

MAKING MISSIONARY DISCIPLES

Pre-Evangelization	Evangelization	Discipleship	Apostleship
Opening	Conversion	Maturing	Serving
Relationship	Proclamation	Catechesis	
Belonging	Encounter	Sacraments	Going out:
Inviting	Personal	Equipping	Evangelization
Prayer	relationship	Renewing	and Social
Witness of Life	**Decision**		Justice

I wish I could continue to unpack the treasures found in this document. At different moments later in the book we will look at other sections of this document, but for now we must move on and look briefly at what must be one of the most down-to-earth papal documents ever written. I am speaking, of course, about *Evangelii Gaudium*. I will look at it only briefly in this chapter, as its rightful place is throughout this entire book. For anyone who is familiar with the Aparecida document, the only thing that is surprising in *Evangelii Gaudium* is its informal style. The central themes of the CELAM document appear throughout *Evangelii Gaudium*, which stresses that "In virtue of their baptism, all the members of the people of God have become missionary disciples," and repeats this iconic term throughout the text. The Aparecida document and related texts, such as Pope Benedict's opening address at the conference, are referred to eighteen times in the exhortation, and the central call for pastoral conversion in the Latin American Church is explicitly applied to the Universal Church: "we need to move 'from a pastoral ministry of mere conservation to a decidedly missionary pastoral ministry.'" (EG, no. 15)

It is clear that in the 50 years since the Second Vatican Council, we have slowly unpacked and laid out the true innovation of the Council. It was not about liturgical language or postures. It was not about Church governance, the decentralization of authority or empowering the laity to exercise liturgical ministries. It was about recalling the Church's deepest identity. From the Council fathers and the three popes who were part of those historic days – Paul VI, John Paul II and Benedict XVI – to Bergoglio, our Francis, who calls us to rebuild his house today, all have played an essential role in pointing out what lies ahead for us. In the days following the election of Pope Francis, I found an image on the Internet that showed Saint John Paul, Benedict and Francis, with a caption for each under the photograph. Under John Paul were the words "This is what we believe." Under Benedict, the ever-ready German systematic theologian, were the words "This is why we believe it." And under Francis, the one who calls us to rebuild, was the command "Now go do it."

3

HOUSE OF PAIN

The Experience of a Maintenance Church

As I mentioned in the previous chapter, at the conclave that eventually elected him pope, Cardinal Jorge Bergoglio had written by hand a four-point reflection on the type of pope the Church would need. It described a pope who would help the Church remember her true identity: to be a Church "called to come out from itself and to go to the peripheries." He warned that if the Church does not do this, if it "does not come out from itself to evangelize, it becomes self-referential and gets sick." This "self-referentiality," he warned, is a "grave" evil wherein the Church no longer glorifies Christ, but seeks to glorify itself. The Church succumbs to the "worst evil" and becomes a "worldly Church that lives in itself, of itself, for itself." The Church has, therefore, become a house of pain, because our Church is sick. The root of this sickness is our deep forgetfulness of our deepest identity: that we are missionary, that we are a Church "called to come out from itself."

When any person suffers a deep amnesia, there are always consequences from this loss of identity. The awareness of this identity loss results in an experience of pain. This is also true within the Church, the House of God, built upon the cornerstone of Christ and having the apostles and prophets for its foundation. (Ephesians 2:20) It is a spiritual edifice made up of living stones: the faithful members of our Church. (1 Peter 2:5) If we are confused about our deepest identity, there will be pain: institutional pain, and pain in the individual members. If the Church is to be rebuilt, it must first be healed. The first step in healing is acknowledging the pain.

Whenever we go to the doctor with some kind of concern, we do so because pain or discomfort has told us that something is wrong. The doctor then asks us to describe the pain. How does it hurt? Where does it hurt? Confessing pain and hurts is not just some fruitless exercise, or worse, a sign of lack of discipline and spiritual backbone. Rather, it has deep biblical roots in the tradition of lamentation. We find both communal and personal lamentations in many of the psalms, in the Book of Jeremiah (20:7-18) and, of course, in the Book of Lamentations. These biblical writings are blatant and brutally honest declarations of how and where it hurts. We, as a Church, do well to learn from and emulate them.

For these things I weep; my eyes flow with tears.
(Lamentations 1:16)

In the seventeen years that I have been a priest in the small patch of the world that is eastern Canada, I have witnessed no lack of pain in those who are "the living stones" of God's house. To begin with, there is the all-too-common pain of seeing so many family members and others walk away from the Church, from faith in Christ and even from faith in God. This pain is especially acute in the lives of so many of our parishioners who have witnessed the wholesale apostasy of their entire family. Bewildered, faithful people ask, "What did I do wrong?" as they struggle with children and grandchildren who are indifferent or hostile to the Church and faith. So many tears have been shed. Saint Monica has never had so many spiritual children seeking her intercession for their wayward sons and daughters.

Hear, all you peoples, and behold my suffering;
my young women and young men have gone into
captivity. (Lamentations 1:18)

Countless times have I presided at the funeral of faithful parishioners who had a deep relationship with Christ, and were authentic disciples and servants, whose children had all abandoned the faith. The intimate rituals of our funeral rites, that so beautifully express the faith and devotion of the deceased, are too often politely tolerated by family members who seem lost and unfamiliar at the funeral Mass and, understandably, anticipate getting to their own, more meaningful, ritual when the church stuff is finished. These experiences are painful reminders of the fact that the biological family and the family of faith are no longer aligned. At such times, I have experienced deep sadness and deep pain.

Our faithful people have every right to ask us shepherds what they did wrong, because they honestly do not know. They did for their children what their parents did for them. There is nothing more natural than this. The problem was that no one told them the rules had all changed. Like a rugby match that, without warning, has become a soccer match after half-time, so many suffer from the experience of being penalized without knowing why. Everything they did for their children would have sufficed if it had still been 1956, but that age might as well have been a thousand years ago. Our people need to have this pain addressed, and they need to find the Lord's peace.

Among the many tasks of the shepherd is that of keeping watch and warning the sheep of approaching dangers. We shepherds need to acknowledge our failure to recognize the signs of the times and to sound the alarm, even at the risk of disturbing the peace. We shepherds were supposed to be keeping watch, giving warning of the approach of an enemy and calling for urgent preparation, but we have failed, and this, too, is painful.

Her gates have sunk into the ground;
he has ruined and broken her bars. (Lamentations 2:9)

The pain within our Church is present as a result of the loss of so many of our institutions that framed our identity and were a source of pride in the largely immigrant Catholic communities of North America. Our hospitals, schools and universities, Catholic only in name, or with every vestige of Catholic identity stripped away, decorate our cities like the ruins of some ancient civilization. As we walk or drive past them, they are constant reminders of the decline of the Church as an institutional force for social good when the hungry were fed, the abandoned were cared for in our orphanages, the uneducated were instructed in our schools and universities, and the sick and the elderly were cared for in our hospitals and homes for the aged. These corporal and spiritual works of mercy were motivated completely by a spirit of faith that, at the time, seemed invincible. Now the convents that housed the many faithful sisters of so many congregations lie as empty as the institutions they once vivified.

Institutional decline is not the gravest challenge we face as a Church. Indeed, a case can be made that, throughout history, the Church has been spiritually strongest when she has been institutionally impoverished and even socially marginalized. Many of these institutions were a response to the needs of the past; their demise was often a result of their achieving the very thing they set out to do. Universal literacy, health care and social welfare are things we take for granted today, but their absence in the past was the cause of so many of our institutions being courageously built and staffed. Nevertheless, the pain remains.

This pain continues to be felt in the Western world through the institutional collapse of the parish structures of many dioceses. Parish closures, amalgamations, twinning and clustering are familiar to Catholics all over the Western world. Of my fourteen years as a pastor, eleven of them have been taken up with amalgamating parishes and dealing with the at times literal collapse of our infrastructure. We can rationalize these changes. They are for the best, administratively and financially. They help us deal with the priest shortage, or at best, they help us subordinate the infrastructure of the church to its mission. However, no matter the rationale for these actions, and no matter the range and manner of actions taken, it hurts.

The Church truly is people and not buildings – it is about living stones, not bricks and mortar – but it hurts because it reminds us of the institutional decline we are facing. We know there are legitimate reasons to make these changes and that they are the necessary and right things to do in our present situation. No amount of "spin," however, will ever remove the deep-down conviction that it is always "tragic" to close a church, and that closing a church is, in the end, a consequence of the Church not being healthy, not growing. This realization is also painful. This, I believe, is the deepest pain when a congregation faces the loss of identity in a parish amalgamation or the closure of their parish. This deeper pain is greater than the immediate pain of the loss of an institution that has shaped and formed their lives, the loss of stability and familiarity, and the subsequent pain of changing towards something new and unfamiliar and even unknown.

> My eyes are spent with weeping;
> my stomach churns,
> my bile is poured out on the ground
> because of the destruction of my people.
> (Lamentations 2:11)

What reservoirs of pain exist within the heart of all the faithful, priests, laity and religious over the devastating scandals of sexual abuse of children by priests? As if this was not enough, what pain have we experienced over the complicit tolerance of such behaviour by so many in leadership in our past, often for the sake of protecting the institution? Is this not a classic example of what Bergoglio pointed to when he spoke of "the worldly Church that lives in itself, of itself, for itself"? Even though we know that the crime of sexual abuse was perpetrated by a small minority of individuals, and even though the reason of so many examples of failed episcopal oversight are complex, we know the pain corporately, for if one part of the body suffers, all suffer.

Victims and their families who still bear the imprint of such a dreadful breach of trust are still members of the household of God. They continue to carry a deep pain within themselves and experience it anew every time a new crime from the past is brought to light, every time a failure of leadership is exposed. Pain is experienced by the faithful parishioners who see the dismantling of their churches and church buildings to cover the cost of settlements for victims. No matter how convinced we are of the justness of this recourse to selling church property, we experience the ongoing suffering of the innocent. The people who suffer the loss of these buildings, built by their ancestors or by their own resources, are innocent. Innocent victims of abuse who will "benefit" from such closures can often be alienated again, especially in small communities. Parish priests who must administer such actions, and bishops who must make these decisions, also suffer as innocents facing the consequences of actions and decisions taken often decades before.

Finally, the loss of credibility of the Church and the shame that rests upon the head of every priest because of the misdeeds of a few translates into a dull, chronic ache. Even though secular studies have revealed that the abuse of minors among clergy in the Catholic Church is slightly lower than the general male population (no cause for boasting), and that institutional "cover-up" or failure to address sexual abuse as either a sickness or a crime also exists in other churches, in sports institutions and in schools, many people today, when they think about a priest, almost immediately associate a priest with a "pedophile." It is an association that has many roots, the least of all being the truth, but it does exist and it is painful. I remember a young father in one of my parishes who told me in the wake of yet another scandal, "Fr. James, when you are transferred to another parish, not only will I not trust the new priest, I will distrust him. He will have to prove himself to be worthy of building trust." In truth, many of our faithful people confess to this association even if they know that it is unfounded, undeserved and unwanted.

I know this pain myself, and it has haunted me most of my adult life. When I was in my early 20s and a seminarian, the sexual abuse crisis in Canada, beginning with the Mount Cashel Orphanage in St. John's, Newfoundland, broke open. The pattern that we have become all too familiar with first manifested over 25 years ago, as cases of abuse and mishandling began to emerge all over Canada. I remember that summer, sitting on a bus and hearing the bus driver tell a joke about a priest-abuser.

When the Boston *Globe* broke the news of widespread sexual abuse of children by priests and consequent mishandling of allegations, it set off a second wave that would spread across the United States and eventually into Europe. Many of us in Canada were asking why we were living through this again. Wasn't anyone paying attention to what happened in Newfoundland? Had no one learned from these painful mistakes? Living in Halifax, Nova Scotia, only intensified this experience and the pain. If you draw a line on a map from St. John's, Newfoundland, to Boston, Halifax is right in the middle. We relived the whole experience, with the Boston TV stations being beamed right into our living rooms. Then there was the worst day of my life: September 30, 2009. It was one of those "Do-you-remember-where-you-were?" days. Bishop Raymond Lahey of the neighbouring Antigonish diocese, mere weeks before, had been heralded for settling a class action law suit to give compensation to victims of child sex abuse in his diocese – cases that stretched back 50 years. Now this same man was arrested, and subsequently convicted, of importing child pornography. I have never experienced the intermingling of individual and corporate pain as I did that day.

> All who pass along the way clap their hands at you;
> they hiss and wag their heads. (Lamentations 2:15)

I remember in the weeks that followed experiencing a deep sense of shame over my identity as a priest. No amount of reasoning could remove the pain of this. On many occasions, I felt ashamed to wear my Roman collar on the street. I and many of my brother priests had to endure smirks and comments whispered behind our backs. Priests were the butt of jokes of late-night comedians, and it seemed that every time a priest was portrayed in a movie or TV show, he was an abuser of some kind, or at best, an uncaring, self-serving person.

I remember one particular moment in the days following the arrest of Bishop Lahey. That weekend, I was presiding at the wedding of a young couple whose lives had been touched by the tragedy of priestly sexual abuse. The bride's father had been sexually molested by a priest of the neighbouring diocese decades before. When charges had been brought against this priest, the pain of the memories was so great that the bride's father had taken his own life. She had grown up without a father as a consequence of the abuse he had suffered. This priest's victims were among those who were to be compensated by the class action suit settled by Bishop Lahey.

News of Bishop Lahey's arrest had broken on Wednesday afternoon that week, and on Friday afternoon I was preparing for the wedding rehearsal for this young couple, with all their family and friends present, including the victim's widow. I was terrified. I was almost paralyzed with fear, apprehension and shame. In truth, I wanted to turn and run. I will never forget what happened next. I came out from the sacristy, greeted the young couple and went to the bride's mother, who was seated at the end of one of the front pews. I knelt beside her and said, "I'm so sorry. This must be a very painful time for you and your family." She smiled a sad smile and placed her hand on my head. Tears were in my eyes and I was trembling. She said, "I forgive the priest who abused my husband, and I am in the process of coming home to the Church. You don't need to carry the sins and failures of others." It felt like this woman, who had suffered so much and had every right to be angry at what I represented, was giving me absolution of a collective sin that I as priest somehow carried, and that through her kind words the pain would be bearable, and the wound would be healed.

The memories of those days are now distant and less acute. Mercifully, new allegations of priestly abuse from the past are rare, and the ones we do hear about have been in the public eye for many years now. And yet, the pain is still there, like a dull, thudding headache, and the lasting damage caused on so many fronts by the tragedy continues to be an ever-present source of pain.

> The thought of my affliction and my homelessness
> is wormwood and gall!
> My soul continually thinks of it and is bowed down within
> me. (Lamentations 3:19-20)

And then there is the pain of priests who labour in the trenches, desperately trying to hold on to the passion that made them choose to "give it all up" and become a priest. Over the last four years, I have had the grace to travel throughout North America, Europe and Latin America to speak with priests and Church leaders about Church renewal. The men and women I meet at these conferences are those who keep the flame of faith alive in their hearts, who still yearn and strive for renewal, but this striving has cost them dearly. When I think back on my seminary classmates as we entered formation for the priesthood, there were two things that defined us and many priests of the so-called John Paul II generation. The first was that most of us could articulate a strong "conversion moment" that changed our lives, a life-changing encounter with Jesus. Very few of us had dreamed of being priests since we were children. Most of us had strayed from the fold, and some with great aplomb. Our personal experience of conversion and transformation shaped our sense of calling to the priesthood. We were not going to be maintenance priests. We had experienced personal renewal in our lives and believed that we would be instruments of this renewal within the Church. Second, we all had a very clear sense of what needed to happen to bring about this renewal. As proud John Paul II priests, we believed that the path to renewal in the Church would be found in personal holiness and orthodoxy. If we could be holy priests and preach true doctrine and have the right type of catechetical resources in our parishes, all would be well and we would see revival.

Armed with these convictions, we were launched into the brick wall of parish life at a hundred miles per hour. It was not pretty. Most of us had to learn to navigate within a Church culture that was not that interested in conversion and transformation. Those who could not adapt to the new reality did not last as priests or would never become pastors. Personal holiness was expected of the priest, but there was no way that such a calling had anything to do with the average churchgoing Catholic. I will never forget the response of a man in my first parish after my attempts to get him to do Alpha. He said, "Look, Father, I'm just not that religious." It was as if he was saying to me, "Don't you get it? I come to church once a week. I fulfill my end of the bargain. Now you do your job and leave me alone."

Regarding the other key of renewal, orthodoxy, there was a limited result from pursuing it, but nothing near the revival that had been dreamed of, that the masses would be overcome by the *splendor veritatis* of the Catholic faith and the Church would be renewed. Some were so disposed, and responded. The quality of the catechetical resources within my parishes improved, but what we did not realize was that we were speaking to a post-modern culture, for whom the question "Is it true?" is not their principal concern. As a result, huge amounts of energy put into renewing content of programs mostly ended with preaching to the choir. Most Sunday Catholics remained untouched, and our churches remained unhealthy and in decline.

I was recently at the celebrations of the 100th anniversary of the seminary that formed me for the priesthood. At the celebratory lunch, I was with some of my old classmates speaking about these realities. One of the priests, a good and holy man, said, "James, I feel like I am the president of a middle-class social club. This is not why I became a priest." For the person in leadership, there is a kind of gravitational pull towards a Church that is about maintenance, a Church that is self-referential and enclosed within itself.

A Church whose sole purpose, like a club, is to serve the needs of those who claim membership. It was not the kind of ministry that inspired us to seek to be priests.

The game may have changed at half-time, but we are still too often insisting on playing the new game according to the rules of the past. We have witnessed in the last 50 years the most accelerated social change in human history, yet in the world of our churches, we insist on pastoral methodologies that presume bygone ideal cultures of the past. What results is an experience of being trapped. Being caught between an experience of a call and desire for renewal and the weight of Church culture towards maintaining the *status quo* is painful. Those in pastoral leadership know that our methods no longer work, yet are bound by layers of expectations that demand the continuation of the old, while, at the same time, having to juggle the new realities.

A concrete way in which we experience the tension between reality and expectations in the Church is around the place and time of Masses. For many Catholics, this is where the rubber hits the road, as the church is the place where you go to Mass. I think of the parish priest who is subtly threatened by his parishioners not to dare to touch a weekend Mass schedule, lest "my favourite Mass time is changed." I remember once in a parish when I had to amalgamate two churches that both had very underattended Saturday afternoon vigil Masses (you could fit everyone into the smaller church and it would still be only half full). When I cancelled one of the Masses, I discovered to my great surprise that many of the parishioners expected me to keep both going, for that was my job. A parishioner came to register his distress over the situation, telling me that he had ceased to give financially to the parish and was urging others to do likewise until I re-established the other Saturday Mass. What he was basically saying was this: "I don't care about the parish. I don't care about the mission of the Church. I don't care about you. I just want my favourite Mass time, and if you don't give it to me, I will hurt you." This is a common experience for many of our priests who have a genuine pastoral desire to gather the people of God at the celebration of the Eucharist, but are forced to scatter this same people across an array of unnecessary times and locations because of "convenience." As a result, our energies are dissipated, our gatherings are really scatterings, and we are stretched ridiculously thin, attempting to cover an obsolete schedule of Masses.

We experience this tendency when bishops, for similar reasons, are not free to reform the infrastructure of dioceses. The migration of peoples from urban areas to the suburbs, the drop in the practice of the faith, and the lack of priest personnel are all urgent reasons to consider restructuring a diocese. Too often, rather than restructuring so that the infrastructure serves the mission, we subject the mission of the Church to the infrastructure. In spite of the new reality, we try to keep everything going and everything open. We give priests a second, a third and sometimes a fourth parish. We bring elderly priests out of retirement for the second or third time, and we ship in priests from other countries who have no experience of our culture and have difficulty communicating with the people they have come to serve. We watch all this happening, knowing that at some point it will all fall down.

There is an old military maxim that says, "He who defends everything defends nothing." In the attempt to keep it all going, precious resources – financial and human – are used up. The priest is often caught in the middle between an exasperated bishop who is just trying to pull another rabbit out of his hat, his own sense of duty, and demanding parishioners who want him to know that they expect nothing to change, in spite of the fact that they are now parish number two on the priest's shoulders. About six years ago, I was at an ordination in our archdiocesan cathedral. After the laying on of hands, one of the priests behind me whispered, "Fresh meat!" It was kind of funny at the time, but it spoke to a dimension of priests' experience of pain, that we are a piece of meat being fed into a hungry machine. We did sign up to offer our lives in sacrifice, but not to a hungry, self-referential machine "that lives in itself, of itself, for itself."

Knowing that the ship is heading for the rocks and feeling powerless to change the course is painful. It is the pain of doing palliative care and funerals not just with our parishioners, but for our parishes, that too often are slowly or rapidly dying. It is the pain of wondering what my life was given for and being forced to develop a personal theology that rationalizes the lack of fruit, the lack of health and the ongoing decline. With all dreams of renewal fallen away, pastoral ministry consists in just being a fool for Christ and standing at the foot of the cross so I can find some sense of meaning in my suffering. All of this amounts to the pain of witnessing a Church in decline, a Church that is sick, a Church that slides towards the insanity of doing the same thing again and again, expecting different results. The pain is intensified for those who love the Church and truly believe that it does not have to be this way – that it is God's will that the Church be healthy and grow.

> The steadfast love of the Lord never ceases,
> his mercies never come to an end;
> they are new every morning;
> great is your faithfulness.
> "The Lord is my portion," says my soul,
> "therefore I will hope in him." (Lamentations 3:23-24)

What are the options for the person in leadership in such a situation? The first is to quit and stay. This person chooses to let go of every vestige of passion, zeal or idealism. They have given up hope and yet, bound by fear, they remain at their post. This sadly describes some of our priests and lay people in pastoral ministry. They are putting in time until retirement because they have no other option. In J.R.R. Tolkien's great work, *The Lord of the Rings* trilogy, we see this dynamic in the person of Denethor, the high Steward of the ancient Kingdom of Gondor. He is a steward, not the King. The line of kings had ended centuries before to leave the Kingdom under the management of a steward, but Gondor was maintained by an almost supernatural hope that the King would return to reclaim his throne once again, a hope that Denethor has lost. Sadly, there are too many in leadership positions within our

Church who have succumbed to the temptation of Denethor. They have lost hope that renewal will ever be possible, and have resigned themselves to the inevitable decline and death – yet they remain at their posts, inflicting pain on the members of their parishes who still have a vision and a desire for renewal. Pope Francis named this reality in *Evangelii Gaudium* as a form of "worldliness." He said, "This way of thinking also feeds the vainglory of those who are content to have a modicum of power and would rather be the general of a defeated army than a mere private in a unit which continues to fight." (EG, no. 96)

A preferred option is to stay and fight, to hold on to the vision, zeal and passion that enticed you to get into it to begin with. This is a true fight, like those gasping for breath as they attempt to keep their heads above water. But what a struggle, and at the heart of the matter is the struggle for hope. Denethor made mistakes that led to his utter loss of hope. First of all, he had forgotten that he was but a steward, not a king, and not *the* King. In truth, he had forgotten about the King who was promised to return. We in the Church are also but stewards awaiting the return of the King. We are managers whose very role is defined by the fact that the King is coming back to claim what is his own. This should not lull us into some kind of passivism, so that we wash our hands of any responsibility, but at the same time this sense of responsibility must be infused by a clarity that it is his Church, and that he is the sovereign "Lord and giver of life." I think of the words of Saint Augustine, who said, "Work as if everything depended on you, and pray as if everything depended on God."

The second mistake is that Denethor had a distorted and edited view of reality. Those familiar with the story know that Denethor had been using one of the lost *Palantir* stones. These were magical stones that let him see what was happening all over what Tolkien called "Middle Earth." The problem was that the evil Lord Sauron controlled what Denethor saw. Through this edited version of reality, Denethor was manipulated into his loss of hope. We, too, can easily fall prey to viewing what is always an edited reality as being the whole story. When we regard the work of grace in the life of any individual or within the Church itself, we stand before a great mystery. Jesus likened the unfolding of the Kingdom of God to seed scattered in a field that grows mysteriously. (Mark 4:26-29) The sower has participated, but has no control over the growth that takes place even while he sleeps. The mystery of God's grace is always at work in the life of every Christian and in the life of the Church, and it always involves suffering, as it always involves the process of dying and rising. It is the great story of the defeat of Good Friday flowing into the empty tomb and bursting forth on Easter Sunday morning. It is the story of the Church. Saint Paul says we are "always carrying in the body the death of Jesus, so that the life of Jesus may also be made visible in our bodies." (2 Corinthians 4:10) Dare we hope that so much pain and dying can move us to a place where we can experience Easter Sunday?

The biblical tradition of lamentation teaches us that denial of our pain and sorrow is not an option. This has been a difficult chapter to write and, no doubt, difficult to read, but the truth of our pain needs to be spoken. When we do this, in the context of our faith, our pain can become suffering. Pain, in and of itself, does not lead to life, but takes it. Suffering is pain-grappled-with, pain-wrestled-with. Only a self-conscious appraisal of our pain can move it to the realm of suffering, and suffering can be redeemed. This was the experience of the Israelites, who had witnessed the destruction of their nation, of their great city of Jerusalem and even of their temple. Pain expressed through lamentation led them to the hope of redemption and restoration. They knew that they did not have the whole picture. They were brutally honest about their plight, but every biblical lamentation, from the psalms to the writings of the prophets to the Book of Lamentations itself, ends in hope: hope for rebirth, hope that the Lord's love has not been exhausted.

> Restore us to yourself, O Lord, that we may be restored;
> renew our days as of old. (Lamentations 5:21)

Jorge Bergoglio concluded the third point of his pre-conclave speech notes, after he had identified the great calling of the Church and the great evil within the Church, by stating, "This should illuminate the possible changes and reforms to be realized for the salvation of souls." Redemption from our suffering does not lead us to illumination only, but also to action, to make changes and reforms. In the Book of Lamentations, the entire discourse ends in a similar vein. It is a plea – not just for illumination or for the Lord to act, but for the Lord to help us to act so that we can recall and rediscover our true identity as the Church of God, move from our exile, and come out of ourselves.

4

CLEARING OUT THE JUNK

What We Need to Jettison if We Are Going to Rebuild

When rebuilding a house, there is always a certain amount of demolition and removal that needs to take place. Structures that no longer give life or serve the purpose of the building need to be removed. So it is in the Church. In the House of God, the things that need to be cleared out can literally be structures that no longer serve the mission or that prevent the mission from being fulfilled. They can also be attitudes, ideas or theological perspectives that hinder our ability to fulfill the missionary mandate given to us by Jesus.

In Chapter 2, I briefly mentioned that Pope Francis spoke to the leadership of CELAM, the Bishops' Conference of Latin America and the Caribbean, in the middle of his meetings with youth from all over the world during World Youth Day 2013. This was a deeply symbolic visit, as it focused on the theme of the 5th General Conference, held in 2007 in Aparecida. This was the place where the bishops of Latin America and the Caribbean gathered in 2007 to take on the great task of pastoral conversion so that the Church would give rise to an army of "missionary disciples" that, in the words of the bishops, "our people may have life in

Him." Francis returned to Aparecida – not physically, but as a firm point of reference for this significant address. What followed was an evaluation of the key points of that gathering, a review of the commitment to the pressing task of pastoral conversion known as the Continental Mission, and a not-too-subtle critique of the bishops' conference, that they were "lagging somewhat" in the implementation of this renewal.

Temptations

In the fourth part of his talk, Pope Francis spoke about "temptations against missionary discipleship." He named three categories of temptation that he said were the work of "the evil spirit." These were manifested by "certain contemporary proposals which can parody the process of missionary discipleship and hold back, even bring to a halt, the process of Pastoral Conversion." He spoke of the first temptation as making the Gospel message an ideology. For Pope Francis, Gospel becomes ideology when an attempt is made to interpret the Gospel "apart from the Gospel itself and apart from the Church." He went on to name four specific expressions of this temptation:

1. "Sociological Reductionism": This is manifested by defining the Gospel and the Church by purely sociological categories, making the Church an instrument of "market liberalism" or Marxist ideology, as found in many expressions of what was known as liberation theology.

2. "Psychologizing": Pope Francis here identified the trend in the decades following the Second Vatican Council in many houses of formation and retreat centres, whereby an "immanent, self-centered" psychology replaced "the encounter with Jesus Christ" as the foundation of our Christian life.

3. "The Gnostic solution": Gnosticism in its various forms, ancient and contemporary, proposes salvation through the attainment of secret knowledge (*gnosis*). It is essentially elitist and creates a class of "enlightened Catholics" who identify themselves by

their allegiance to a certain "higher spirituality" or fixation on particular disputed pastoral issues. Pope Francis does not get more specific than this, but one can think of certain expressions of liturgical traditionalism that fit this description.

4. "The Pelagian solution": For Pope Francis, this is a form of "restorationism" that is closely associated with moral and disciplinary rigorism that seeks to recover a lost past.

He would also speak about this in *Evangelii Gaudium* as a "self-absorbed promethean neopelagianism" exercised by those "who ultimately trust only in their own powers and feel superior to others because they observe certain rules or remain intransigently faithful to a particular Catholic style from the past." (EG, no. 94) He is brutally explicit in this section of *Evangelii Gaudium* about how exactly this temptation blocks the work of the Gospel:

> A supposed soundness of doctrine or discipline leads instead to a narcissistic and authoritarian elitism, whereby instead of evangelizing, one analyzes and classifies others, and instead of opening the door to grace, one exhausts his or her energies in inspecting and verifying. In neither case is one really concerned about Jesus Christ or others. (EG, no. 94)

In his address to CELAM, Pope Francis briefly mentioned the last two of his temptations against making "missionary disciples" as "Functionalism" and "Clericalism". Functionalism is the reduction of the Church to a mere business, a kind of NGO that leaves no room for mystery. What Pope Francis describes as clericalism, however, is worth quoting:

> Curiously, in the majority of cases, it has to do with a sinful complicity: the priest clericalizes the lay person and the lay person kindly asks to be clericalized, because deep down it is easier. The phenomenon of clericalism explains, in great part, the lack of maturity and Christian freedom in a good part of the Latin American laity.

He goes on to say that although he could outline more "temptations" to the Church against making missionary disciples, those he has named are the most "influential" on the life of the Church.

In this chapter, I would like to focus on two of these temptations that Pope Francis speaks of as being the bulk of the "junk" that needs to be cleared out before authentic renewal can take place in the Church. I have identified these two based on my own experience as a pastor over the years and as a result of theological reflection over these same years. They are the temptation of Pelagianism and clericalism, which lurk within our Church as unspoken theologies that shape our perception of what is normal, how we perceive ourselves and how we live what we perceive.

Pelagianism

Pelagianism was a heresy in the early Church named after a Celtic monk named Pelagius. He lived in the Christian city of Rome and later in Carthage in North Africa in the years around AD 390–418. Pelagius taught that God's grace was not necessary for salvation, since human nature had not been truly corrupted by original sin. Our human weakness was due more to the environmental effect of bad example. Jesus' saving act was to give us an example of pure love that could be imitated. For Pelagius, God's favour could be obtained by moral rigorism or ascetic practice alone, and could be achieved outside of God's grace.

Pelagius' most vigorous opponent was Saint Augustine. Augustine was well known at the time for preaching a doctrine that emphasized the supremacy of God's grace over free will; Pelagius, while living in Rome, blamed this teaching for much of the moral laxity he observed in that city. For him, all that was needed was for every believer to pull up his or her proverbial socks and will to do the good commanded by God. There were many debates and discussions among popes, bishops and theologians over this issue, which resulted in Pelagius' teachings being condemned and Pelagius himself being excommunicated from the Church.

Grace and Free Will

Saint Augustine's theology of grace had won the day, and it is still at the foundation of the Catholic understanding of the mysterious intertwining of God's grace and human free will. In brief, we believe that human beings, while not being totally corrupted by the rebellion of Adam and Eve, have been deeply damaged. This damaged human nature, which has been passed down to us from our first parents, leaves us unable to achieve what is good without God's help. We call this condition "original sin." This is a term familiar to most Catholics, but what most Catholics do not know is that original sin is not a sin *per se*, but refers to our fallen human condition, which leaves us prone to commit actual sin. It tells us that in and of ourselves, we are separated from God. As Saint Paul wrote, "All have sinned and have fallen short of the glory of God." (Romans 3:23) It is this condition that leads us to commit sin and leaves us unable to do the good we desire to do.

This doctrine tells us that we are broken, that we are outside of a saving relationship with God, and that there is nothing we can do about it. Even if, by some superhuman display of discipline and strength, we can deny ourselves and do what is good, it could never be good enough. The highest human standard will always fall short of God's standard. This is the problem, the bad news. The Good News is that God has not left us to our own devices, but has sent his Son as our Saviour. We recall the words of the famous passage of the Gospel of John: "For God so loved the world that he gave his only Son, so that everyone who believes in him may not perish but may have eternal life." (John 3:16) This is the heart of the Good News, what Pope Francis, in his famous interview with the Jesuit magazine *America*, called the "first proclamation": "Jesus Christ has saved you."

Discussion of Pelagianism would have remained an academic exercise if it had not continued to raise its head throughout the history of the Church. Even in the centuries following the condemnation of the teachings of Pelagius, there arose an adaptation of his teachings that came to be known as Semi-Peligianism. This school of thought taught that God meets us halfway. We take a step towards God, and God takes a step towards us. It's 50/50. This teaching was also condemned by the Church as not being authentic to the faith handed down by the Apostles. As Saint Paul says, "It is God who is at work in you, enabling you both to will and to work for his good pleasure." (Philippians 2:13) The Greek text literally says that God gives us the "to will" and the "to act." This tells us that the very desire to draw close to God is already a result of God at work in our life, that there is nothing we can do to draw close to God that is not the result of his grace already at work in our lives. This means that we stand before a mystery, the mystery of the God who has first loved us, a God who, always leaving us free, is able to grace us in a way that does not violate our freedom. Rather than being 50/50, it is 100/100. It is a classic both/and proposition typical of the Catholic faith. Jesus is fully human and fully divine, the Scriptures are fully human and fully divine, so is the Church, and so is the interplay of grace and free will. There is nothing we can do by ourselves that will merit God's grace, but with God's grace at work in our lives, manifested by "faith that works in love" (Galatians 5:6), we receive the gift of being right with God, the gift of salvation, and it all flows from the cross of Jesus Christ. The Good News just keeps getting better.

The Liturgy

If, as pastors and teachers, we are to address this issue with our people, we need to have a proper understanding of the concept of merit in the Catholic tradition. This term has gained new prominence in Catholic vocabulary since the publication of the new English translation of the Roman Missal and does represent a pastoral challenge, or, more positively, a teaching opportunity. This more literal translation of the texts uses the term "merit" more often than the older translation, especially in the collects, the opening and closing prayers, and the prayer over the offerings. In Eucharistic Prayer II, we find the prayer "that ... we may merit to be coheirs to eternal life." This is a literal translation of the Latin "*aeternae vitae mereamur esse consortes*," but communicates a different sense than the old translation, "make us worthy to share eternal life." It places the concept of merit firmly before us and recalls the Catholic–Lutheran debates of the sixteenth century around the relationship of faith and works. In response to Luther's assertion that we are saved by grace through faith alone, the Council of Trent defined as the Catholic position that we are saved by grace through faith *and* works, but the only works that are efficacious towards salvation are those that arise from God's grace. Otherwise, we find ourselves back in the Pelagian camp, earning our salvation through what we do.

The Council of Trent presents a beautiful theology of God's work in our lives. Grace, manifested in faith and love in the life of the believer, is what saves us. We cannot agree with Luther's *sola fidei* (faith alone), but we can firmly proclaim that we are saved by grace alone. I remember many years ago giving a talk on God's grace to an ecumenical group predominantly made up of Evangelical pastors. At the end of the talk, a wonderful, faith-filled man who was a Baptist theologian told me that it was one of the best talks on grace he had ever heard. I smiled and told him that it was straight from the Council of Trent. While he got the irony, most of our people know and care little for the great theological intrigues of the sixteenth century. Already predisposed to a Pelagian mindset, they hear the word "merit" again and again, and this does constitute a challenge. The liturgy itself, if we look closely enough, provides the antidote. In the prayer over the offerings from the Eighth Week in Ordinary Time, we ask of God's mercy "that what you grant as the source of merit may also help us to attain merit's reward." Perhaps we need to heed the directives found in the Roman Missal itself, that from time to time the content of the liturgical prayers could be the subject of our preaching and teaching.

Jansenism

Human beings have always found the graciousness of God to be scandalous and unjust. I think of the parable of the workers in the vineyard, who work all day and are angry that those who worked only one hour receive the same wage as they do. (Matthew 20:1-16) It is a very human thing to believe, deep down, that we earn our reward based solely on what we do. This is the measure of human justice. God's ways, however, are not our ways.

Resistance to the radical Good News of God's mercy and grace manifested itself again in the history of the Church in a new form of moral rigorism in the seventeenth century called Jansenism. Jansenism, named after a Dutch priest-theologian named Cornelius Jansen, who died in 1638, began as a movement that stressed the opposite of Pelagianism. Jansen was a student of the writings of Saint Augustine, especially those in which he opposed the teachings of Pelagianism. Whereas Pelagianism placed the emphasis on human free will – to the point that God's grace was not necessary – Jansenists put such emphasis on God's grace that they nullified the necessity of human free will. Although this was the starting point of this system of thought, by the middle of the seventeenth century, Jansenists had embraced a moral rigorism that they believed to be the necessary evidence of God's favour and grace. Their theology had such a low opinion of human free will that it ended in being elitist, embracing the same kind of absolute asceticism as the Pelagianism they condemned.

The nuns of the convent of Port Royal in Paris, a Jansenist stronghold in the seventeenth century, were described by a contemporary as being "as chaste as angels and as proud as devils." Jansenism taught, for instance, that it was not enough to be free from mortal sin to receive Holy Communion. The true Christian will have been so suffused by God's grace that the person will be completely free of sin. So, in order to be "worthy" of the Eucharist, a communicant had to be completely free of sin in order to receive. As Jansenism spread throughout the Church of Western Europe, the practice of abstaining from the Eucharist became common-place; frequent reception of Holy Communion would not begin to be restored until the papacy of Pius X, over 200 years later. Having set out to emphasize the role of God's sovereign grace, Jansenism would, in time, become a movement proposing moral perfection and rigour. Its negative view of human nature would take its position so far out that it would find itself on the very same ground as the Pelagianism it originally sought to condemn.

Although formally condemned by the Catholic Church, Jansenism would eventually move from the continent in the 1800s to the seminaries of Ireland, and would go on to inform and deform generations of priests, who would bring this version of Catholicism to the world in the great wave of Irish missionary activity in the nineteenth and 20th centuries. The world of Catholic theology and spirituality is vast, but who of us in the Western Catholic Church have been untouched by an image of God as distant, cold and unapproachable, and a view of the Christian life as mercilessly demanding moral perfection?

Good News?

Pope Francis has repeatedly described the Church as a hospital for sinners and not as a kind of club for the perfect. It is clear that the Good News of salvation resounds and is received as Good News only if we have truly grasped the bad news of our fallen condition. The news that I am cancer-free really will mean nothing to me if I have never realized that I was cancer-ridden. Such good news will be experienced as such only if I have truly accepted the bad news of my sickness. Consequently, Pelagianism paralyzes the believer's ability to receive the Good News precisely as Good News, for, in the end, Jesus inspires me by his beautiful moral teachings and his exemplary life. In the end, I can save myself. Moral rigorism and asceticism replace grace and mercy.

This was true of Pelagianism, and it was also the fruit of Jansenism. The perennial human temptation to self-justification, to self-righteousness, won out. It is not God who makes us righteous; we make ourselves so. A Pelagian or Jansenist Church is one that does not truly know the radical, scandalous mercy of God. Either we do not need to be forgiven, or forgiveness is not an option. Either way, we forgot the experience of forgiveness, and excuses suffice. Never having tasted the sheer, naked mercy of God, we are not filled by his mercy, and therefore are not merciful. Having made ourselves right with God (righteousness), we become self-righteous and isolated in our own moral superiority. Worse than all of this, however, is that never truly grasping the Good News, we never experience the *evangelii gaudium*, the joy of the Gospel, and are condemned to a miserable, joyless, merciless moralism that is destined to leave us disillusioned with the bitter taste of our own inevitable failure and collapse. Sounds familiar, doesn't it?

I believe that most churchgoing Catholics have been so deeply impacted by Pelagianism that they really do not grasp the fundamental message of the Good News of Jesus Christ. How many times have I heard Catholics say something like "If anyone deserves to be let into heaven, she does …"? How many times have I sensed confusion about God's mercy, and hints of despair amid jokes about buying one's way into heaven by doing good deeds? I remember about eight years ago being at a funeral of a parishioner. A brother priest preached on the text from John 14:6, where Jesus says, "I am the way, and the truth, and the life." This priest told the people that Jesus was not the way to God in an exclusive sense, but in the sense that he showed the true way to live life through his loving example. How often have funerals become not a proclamation of the Good News of salvation through Jesus Christ, but a proclamation of the righteousness or goodness of the deceased, with Scripture readings chosen to eulogize the deceased rather than proclaim the grace of God's merciful love?

Pope John Paul II, in an address to American bishops, said, "Sometimes even Catholics have lost or never had the chance to experience Christ personally; not Christ as a mere 'paradigm' or 'value', but the Living Lord: 'the way, and the truth, and the life'

(John 14:6)." This hints at the very human tendency to reduce the Christian faith to some form of moral rigorism, or mere ethics. In previous generations, our moral rigorism may have focused on issues of sexual morality. In recent decades, the Gospel message has often been reduced to an amorphous and ubiquitous concern for social justice. In the end, however noble, these are all moral issues that need to be contextualized by the reception of the Good News of salvation. They are always and will always be secondary issues, and can never supplant the first proclamation, or kerygma – lest, as Pope Francis said, the Church fall like "a house of cards."

The Good News

The Catholic philosopher Peter Kreeft once asked a group of university students what they would say if they were to die that very night, appear before God and be asked, "Why should I let you into heaven?" He collected their answers. They had one thing in common: they were all the wrong answers. They were all about the kinds of things we do for God, and made no mention of what God has done for us through his Son, Jesus Christ. Unfortunately, I have encountered this understanding, or lack thereof, on countless occasions in my years as a priest. It is a form of neo-Pelagianism whose starting point is the absence of a conviction that we cannot save ourselves. Rather than receiving our Saviour through faith and living this faith out in love through good works, all of which are grounded in the free gift of God's grace, we strive to be, well... "nice."

Deep down, many believe that unless we are some kind of moral reprobate like Hitler, we all really deserve salvation, because most of are just really nice people. Salvation is something owed to us, not because of what God has done, or really even what I have done, but what I have not done (really, really bad things). So this neo-Pelagianism is manifested in two ways. First, in the traditionally minded Catholic who sees the Christian life as a kind of scorecard with its own economy of salvation. I do certain things for God (go to Mass, be nice, say my prayers once in a while), then

God lets me into heaven. Second, in the post-modern Catholic who bases his or her understanding of grace and salvation not on Scripture or the teaching of the Church, but on his or her sense of absolute autonomy and fundamental niceness. God is my buddy who asks nothing of me except to be "true to myself" and will obviously let me continue to party in heaven.

Three Things

Three things are the consequence of the neo-Pelagianism of our time. If salvation is getting my card punched so I can meet the basic requirements for salvation, it will breed a culture of minimalism. This is not covenant faith. It is not life lived in relationship with the God who says, "I am your God and you are my people." This is fundamentally paganism under a thin veneer of Christianity. In the ancient world, the gods were manipulated to provide favours by external acts that bore no reference to the disposition of the heart. Salvation, eternal life and answers to prayers are too often external favours sought after by fulfilling external obligations. When the minimum requirement is satisfied, that is where it stops. Covenant faith, rooted in a personal covenant relationship with God in the midst of a covenant community, can never do enough or get enough. It is a religion of extravagance rooted in a God who proclaims his insatiable thirst for us, whose thirst can be satisfied only in him. It is only this kind of faith that can yearn for authentic holiness. It is only this kind of faith that seeks to give all and do all.

Second, as already mentioned, people who believe themselves to be justified by their own actions or "niceness" will never know the sheer audacity of God's mercy. Amazing grace will simply be a melody that sounds good on bagpipes. The Good News of salvation will never be fully grasped, and, consequently, the joy that is the hallmark of the authentic Christian life will never be known or communicated to others. The joyful song of praise to God for the gift of salvation never rises from the lips of the one who has no need of such a gift. I honestly believe that this is the reason why so many lips remain silent in our churches on Sunday morning. Too many people literally have nothing to sing about.

Third, if we cannot move beyond the bare minimum of religious observance perceived to earn our own personal salvation, and if the authentic Good News is undiscovered, why are we surprised that many in the Church show evidence of little enthusiasm for the call to the New Evangelization? Obviously, only the evangelized can evangelize. Only those who have received the Good News as good news can proclaim it to others. Good news is never a burden to share with others – indeed, it is the most natural thing in the world. It becomes a burden only when we cannot share it. In the end, with neo-Pelagianism being so present among the faithful, and even among those in ministry, it is entirely understandable that we would suffer from a deep identity crisis about our missionary nature.

How do we take out the junk of Pelagianism? We recall the words of the Latin American bishops in the 2007 Aparecida document, which says, "Without the kerygma, the other aspects of this process are condemned to sterility, with hearts not truly converted to the Lord." It is the kerygma that opens hearts; it is the kerygma of the Good News of salvation that needs to be articulated clearly for people to hear and understand. We remove this junk by making a clear commitment to the first proclamation as both distinct from what we know as catechesis, and as integral to it. *Evangelii Gaudium* states,

> This first proclamation is called "first" not because it exists at the beginning and can then be forgotten or replaced by other more important things. It is first in a qualitative sense because it is the principal proclamation, the one which we must hear again and again in different ways, the one which we must announce one way or another throughout the process of catechesis, at every level and moment. (EG, no. 164)

This proclamation ought to be present in every homily, in every class and in every talk. This is what we were told in a 2010 instruction to priests issued by the Congregation of the Clergy under Pope Benedict, which reminded priests that the "kerygma be given pride of place." Referring to John Paul II's Encyclical Letter "The Mission of the Redeemer," the Congregation reminded priests that "a renewed kerygmatic proclamation of Jesus Christ crucified and risen" has "a power and a special anointing which comes from the Holy Spirit and which cannot be minimized or over-looked in the missionary enterprise."

"I am a sinner whom the Lord has looked upon." This was Pope Francis' response to the question "Who is Jorge Mario Bergoglio?" in his famous interview in *America* magazine. He said that this was not just a figure of speech or a literary genre, but was the clearest, most authentic description he could offer. It is his fundamental identity, and it is our fundamental identity.

Clericalism

What do you think of when you hear the word "clericalism"? Perhaps you think of priests in clerical garb, even a cassock. Do you think of Pharisaic clerics who are obsessed with the minutiae of religious observance? Perhaps you think of a kind of old boys' club that is suffused with a sense of superiority and privilege. If so, then you may already have been shocked by how Pope Francis defined clericalism in his address to the leaders of CELAM at World Youth Day in 2013. Describing clericalism as one of the temptations against the Church forming missionary disciples, he said that "in the majority of cases, it has to do with a sinful complicity: the priest clericalizes the lay person and the lay person kindly asks to be clericalized." In these words he provides the best definition of clericalism I have ever found.

During my very first years as a pastor, we had started running Alpha as a way for the Catholics of my parish to hear the kerygma, experience Jesus personally and have a new, vital experience of Christian community. Lives were slowly being transformed, and many who experienced this transformation were inviting their fallen-away friends and family members, and even non-believers, to attend. I personally invited many of my parishioners. As I can be as stubborn and determined as anyone, many eventually yielded and took Alpha to get me to leave them alone. This worked for the widow pleading her cause to the unjust judge, so I figured that this approach was biblical, at least. Then one day, an older man who had so far resisted my "invitations" drew a line in the sand. (I mentioned my conversation with him in Chapter 3.) He had had enough and said, "Look, Father, I'm just not that religious." With those words he shut me down. I was stunned. Since that time, those simple words have been the source of much theological reflection. What was he really saying?

Appropriation

It occurred to me that he was pushing back, with a sense of indignation, because I was breaking a kind of unspoken agreement about his involvement at church. He would carry out the bare minimum of his religious duty, and I would leave him alone and not expect anything else. He was content in this because, for the most part, ordinary Catholics were just not "that religious." People who were "that religious" were those who became priests or nuns. Since that conversation, I have run into this attitude again and again. The Second Vatican Council may have spoken about the universal call to holiness and mission, but for the average Catholic, holiness and mission is not their job. It is the priest or nun who can be holy and can evangelize. Ordinary Catholics just do not do these things; they are fundamentally unable to do these things. It took me several years before I could put a name to this disconnect between official Catholic theology and popular theology: clericalism.

In the end, clericalism's association with distinct garb or the abuse of power is rather superficial. Clericalism is nothing but the appropriation of what is proper to the baptized by the clerical caste. In this caste I include religious professionals, both clergy and religious. In the last decades, this professional clerical class has also come to include the professional class of lay people who minister within the Church in an official capacity. If, by virtue of their baptism, all Catholics are called to holiness and mission, to the task of witnessing to Christ, to evangelizing, to maturity – in short, to being missionary disciples – clericalism is ultimately a suppression of the baptismal identity. Priests and nuns become the super-Christians who have the superpowers to do what ordinary Christians cannot. This elevation leads to two outcomes: the isolation of the clergy and the immaturity of the baptized. Saint Augustine said, "With you I am a Christian, for you I am a bishop." The Christian, no matter his or her ministry in the Church, needs first to be a Christian among others, and, only then, for others.

The isolation of clergy left alone to be holy and to do the work proper to all members of the Church has been, and is, death-dealing and unsustainable. Clergy were trapped by inhuman expectations held up by such a gulf of double standard that none could pass from here to there. It became obvious to me years ago that the pushback and resistance I received from parishioners when calling them to holiness and mission was none other than indignation that I had broken the unwritten rule about leaving them alone in their mediocrity. Holiness and evangelization was my job. How dare I ask it of *them*? I was to be their spiritual surrogate, to do for them what they were unable or unwilling to do for themselves.

Symbiosis

The system creates a mutual interdependence, as Pope Francis indicated in his description of clericalism. Once this relationship exists, the layperson who desires to be left unchallenged in his or her immaturity must continually prop up the status of the priest or religious as being "other," that which he or she could never be. In such a system, we can hold up priests and nuns and the wonderful work they do and stand at a distance and applaud them. This is safe, but it must be so if the average layperson is to consider his or her own immaturity as normal and acceptable. In this isolation, the priest is not permitted to show any cracks of humanity, or the game will be up. Priests and religious, out of both positive and negative motives, accepted this status of being so set apart that they could not betray the pretense, and so were often left in isolation.

This was the culture that contributed to the sexual abuse crisis that has caused so much damage in our Church. The denial that allowed abusers to reoffend was understandable when an entire way of being Church was at stake. Such awful things could never happen. They were impossible to believe. The laity, therefore, did not so much turn a blind eye as they were blinded by a religious culture that could not admit human defects in its leaders. Clergy were likewise immobilized by a great need to protect the reputation of the Church at all costs, because to allow the extent of the rot to come to light was to call into question the entire system.

Similar dynamics are at play still today when we see the double standard in many dioceses over accountability of priests versus the laity who work in the Church. Lay employees are regularly evaluated and held to acceptable standards of professional accountability. Accountability for priests takes place only when a critical mass of letters of complaint crosses the bishop's desk. As a result, assistance and help are usually given to priests only after the fact, after some kind of failure that could have been prevented if a system of evaluation and accountability was in place. Although it is less common now, I cannot help but think of how alcoholism among priests was tolerated by clergy and laity alike, and how many priests never received the help they so desperately needed. There is only one way to live a healthy, life-giving life as a priest, and that is to be first and foremost a Christian among other Christians before being a priest for the people.

Sorting Through the Confusion

Think of our language. In the past, it was common to speak of someone being ordained to the priesthood or entering religious life as "joining the Church." This is an appropriation of what belongs to the baptized by the religious professional. When I served as vocations director for my Archdiocese, one of my responsibilities was to meet with candidates discerning priesthood or religious life. When someone would tell me, for instance, that they felt "called" to the priesthood, I would ask them to describe for me how they experienced this call. It was not uncommon for a candidate to respond by speaking about a desire for a deeper prayer life, to learn more about theology, to serve others, and to help others come to know Jesus. I remember the first time it struck me that what this candidate was describing was not a call to priesthood but a call to live out his baptismal calling. Everything he described as pointing towards the priesthood was entirely normative of ordinary Christian living: to mature in prayer and the spiritual life, to grow in knowledge, to evangelize and to serve others. I did, not of course, end the discussion there, but would go on to point out to the candidate that what he described should be the desire of every Christian.

What did I listen for as a sign of the call to priesthood? Since the Second Vatican Council, priestly ministry has clearly been defined as embracing the threefold mission of Jesus: the prophetic, the priestly and the kingly. Concretely, this means that the priest's first task is to preach the Word of God; his second task is to celebrate and minister the sacraments; and his third task is to lead God's people. Not many candidates would describe their sense of calling to the priesthood as a burning desire to preach God's Word, or as a yearning to celebrate the Eucharist or minister to the faithful in the sacrament of reconciliation, let alone lead and guide a community of faith. It's quite simple, really. In the past, our categories made no space for any Christians who wanted to live out their baptismal calling to the full. We did not know what to do with them. If someone was "that religious," off to the seminary or the convent they must go, because ordinary Catholics just don't do those things.

Out of the Ordinary?

What do ordinary Catholics do, then? Well, pray, pay and obey. They were to be utterly passive in carrying out the mission of the Church beyond anything in the realm of the temporal. Catholics would build and fix buildings, organize and carry out fundraising activities, make sandwiches, put something in the collection and "practise" their faith by "hearing" Sunday Mass. Spiritual maturity, discipleship, knowledge and familiarity with the Scriptures were traditionally foreign to most Catholics. To this day, ask the average Catholic to open a meeting with a prayer and they will quake in their boots. In spite of the pleading of modern popes, beginning with Pius XII in his 1943 encyclical *Divino Afflante Spiritu*, in which he virtually begged Catholics to get to know and love the Scriptures, for most Catholics, 50 years after the Second Vatican Council, the Bible is undiscovered territory. Despite having the printing press with us for 500 years and nearly universal literacy for 100 years, we are still bound by a mindset of a past age, when picking up a Bible and reading it was not an option for the average person. The clericalism of the past left most Catholics in spiritual infancy, and did not even begin to equip them for the work of ministry.

But hasn't all this changed? Certainly, in the years following the Second Vatican Council, there was an attempt to break away from the clericalism of the past. Ironically, however, these attempts to declericalize the Church led us more deeply into the trap it was trying to spring. I say this because in the years following the Council, the "empowerment" of the laity turned to the only categories of ministry that were known in the life of the Church: clerical categories. Inadvertently, we taught our people that the fulfillment of their baptismal identity was to perform ministries that were essentially clerical in nature. Being a lector at Mass or giving Holy Communion were considered the summit of Christian ministry. In some cases, in the years after the Council, this attempt to break a clerical mould saw laypeople being invited to pray parts of the Eucharistic Prayer, preside at "communion services" while the priest sat among the people, or give out Holy Communion at Mass while priests sat down and meditated on how they were empowering their people. In spite of presumed good intentions, once again we were witnessing an appropriation this time by the laity of what was proper to the ordained – or, rather, an imposition by the clergy upon the laity of what was proper to clerical ministry. Tragically, the true lay vocation was still ignored, and clerical forms of ministry continued to be modelled as "normal."

As a result, the fresh call of the Second Vatican Council to rediscover the universal call to mission died a rapid death. The "lay apostolate," referred to in the conciliar documents again and again, virtually disappeared within the life of the average parish fifteen years after the close of the Council. "Lay ministry" replaced the "lay apostolate." The significance of this substitution is great. If the deepest crisis in our Church is an identity crisis because we have forgotten our fundamental identity as a missionary Church, the imposition of clerical categories as a supposed fulfillment of the call to renewal in the conciliar documents deepened the identity crisis and led the Church to be even more turned in upon itself. Words are hugely significant. The "apostolate" is the going forth, the sending out (*apostolein*, in Greek). The use of this term by the Council fathers reminded us that the fundamental orientation of the baptized is to go out, to be missionary. The disappearance of this term and the substitution of the term "ministry" connoted a redefining of the baptismal calling to be *ad intra* rather than *ad extra*.

No one has to go out anymore; we can all just stay in. Most Catholics can continue to be passive spectators, but the really committed can do the readings and even give out Holy Communion. This is the very definition of a Church turned in on itself, contented with serving itself, blind to the contradiction it lives. As *Evangelii Gaudium* points out, this mindset leaves the lay vocation "tied to tasks within the Church, without a real commitment to applying the Gospel to the transformation of society." (EG, no. 102) The call to professional lay ministry all too often created another category among the clerical caste. As parishioners grew and became more and more involved, they, too, could eventually achieve the status of being professional lay ministers. According to this mindset, the Pilgrim People of God would reach eschatological fulfillment when we all became professional lay ministers and spent all our time ministering to one another within the Church.

In our parishes of today, in spite of all the years forming lay ministers, most Catholics remain unawakened, passive consumers of "religion lite." In most cases, we have raised up another group within the clerical caste – those people who will do what the average Catholic cannot do. Most Catholics remain hugely ignorant of the fundamentals of their faith, unable to find their way around a Bible, and with an experience of prayer that remains largely unchanged from when they were children. More distressing than this is the fact that so often it does not seem to bother anyone all that much, or at least not enough to do something about it.

Pope Francis, in his definition of clericalism, said that it was "a sinful complicity: the priest clericalizes the lay person and the lay person kindly asks to be clericalized, because deep down it is easier. The phenomenon of clericalism explains, in great part, the lack of maturity and Christian freedom in a good part of the Latin American laity." We who are not of the Latin American Church recognize ourselves in this description. The years following the Council saw even so-called liberal priests clericalizing the laity, and the laity were quite content to settle for this, because it is easier. After all, who would not choose giving out Holy Communion to a group of like-minded people in an enclosed space instead of having to "go to all the nations and proclaim the Good News"? The cost of this entrenchment is the continued isolation of the "cleric," who now has a few extra clerical laypeople around him, while most of the people stand at a distance, comfortable and unchallenged in their immaturity.

I write these words as the pastor of a parish that has sixteen paid laypeople on staff, six of whom are directly involved in overseeing much of the ministry that takes place in my parish. In any large church, lay pastoral staff, not just administrative staff, are essential if the Church is to be healthy. This staff enables hundreds of our parishioners to serve in myriad ministries that allow our parish to function and go beyond our four walls. I will say more about this later, but these staff share, as the Second Vatican Council says, in the ministry proper to the pastor, and do not as such model what is normative for the lay vocation, which is to be sent into the world, not into the Church. They fulfill their task not primarily by doing all the work of ministry while others watch, but by equipping others to do the ministry proper to their vocation, to be missionary disciples "out there" in the world, and not just in the church basement.

If the ministry of paid lay staff creates passivity among the average parishioner and confirms in their minds that they could never do such things themselves, we have advanced the clerical model of ministry. I know that it is controversial to say, but in my years of ministry I have preferred to hire lay people who do not have professional degrees in theology or ministry. Ordinary people with ordinary faith seem to be much more capable of inspiring normal Catholics to take a second look at what God may desire to do in and through them.

Redefining Pastoral Care

Saint Paul described his ministry as one of "warning everyone and teaching everyone in all wisdom, so that we may present everyone mature in Christ." (Colossians 1:28) The Greek word *telos* can be translated as "perfect," "complete," "finished" or "mature." Saint Paul is speaking not so much about his labours to bring about moral perfection in those he serves, but to advance them along the road of constant growth and maturation. In many places calling himself a father, he says that this is why he toils and struggles. (Colossians 1:29) In this, he is no different from any parents who desire not just to comfort and care for their children, but to feed them and see them grow and, ultimately, see them mature.

It would not be "cute" for a parent to come home and find their 25-year-old son, in his right mind, sitting on the couch sucking his thumb. Why, then, do we have such tolerance for lifelong parishioners who are stuck in such a place spiritually? Let me be clear that I am not advocating an abandonment of anyone who has not reached maturity, but an abandonment of accepting whole-scale immaturity as being so normal that we no longer notice it. A church that makes missionary disciples has at its very heart a desire and capacity to bring people from immaturity to maturity. A parish church that is doing this well will and must always have a considerable proportion of members who are in their spiritual infancy. If it does not, then there are no spiritual babies being born and that church is sterile. However, a church where the majority of members are spiritual infants has abandoned the central task of pastoral care, which is to labour and strive for all to be brought to maturity in Christ.

If this is so, then part of the solution to this clericalism is to redefine how we think of pastoral care. In most Church circles, "pastoral care" usually refers to care given to those who are sick, dying or grieving. This is and remains an important pastoral action of the Church. However, these activities usually exhaust the meaning of pastoral care in most Church cultures. The term *pastor* is simple the Latin term for "shepherd." The image of shepherding God's people is found in the oldest strata of the Scriptures – the writings of the prophets – and was used very often by Jesus, who spoke of the lost sheep and called himself "the Good Shepherd."

Biblically, the primary task of the shepherd was not to care for the weak, the sick and the dying, nor was it to offer protection: "The Lord is my shepherd, I shall not want. He makes me lie down in green pastures; he leads me beside still waters." (Psalm 23) These words are not given to us just to evoke bucolic nostalgia. They remind us that the first task of the shepherd was to lead the sheep to food and drink. To feed the sheep so they can grow and mature. In Ezekiel, the prophet rails against false Shepherds of Israel for their many failings, chief among them that they "do

81

not feed the sheep." (Ezekiel 34:3) Pastoral care for the Prophet Ezekiel and for Jesus also involves looking for the lost, even leaving the 99 in the wilderness, but the primary task is labouring to feed the sheep so they can be brought to strength and maturity.

Equipping the Saints

In Saint Paul's letter to the Ephesians, we hear these words:

The gifts he gave were that some would be apostles, some prophets, some evangelists, some pastors and teachers, to equip the saints for the work of ministry, for building up the body of Christ, until all of us come to the unity of the faith and of the knowledge of the Son of God, to maturity, to the measure of the full stature of Christ. (Ephesians 4:11-13)

This passage echoes the truth that we have already looked at: that the end game of pastoral care is to bring people to maturity. It also speaks of the different gifts and charisms that God gives to the Church as a whole, and the reason for these gifts. I would like to focus first on the reason for the gifts, especially as it relates to the office of pastoring. Saint Paul explicitly tells us that these charisms exist "to equip the saints for the work of ministry." Thus, the primary task of the pastor is not to do all the work of ministry himself, but to equip the saints to do the work of ministry. A clerical culture that binds the priest to the role of the super-Christian will demand that only the priest does the work of ministry, and many priests are happy to accept this definition. We see this in parishes that have virtually nothing going on. The few activities that do take place must have the direct oversight of the priest. No one else is equipped for the ministry of leading others to maturity, let alone leading ministry that goes out to the fringes.

In my present parish, which by the standards of my area is very large, we see about 2,000 people in the pews on any given weekend. We have over 90 ministries running, very few of which I have direct oversight for. As a pastor, I constantly seek to focus on the three fundamental tasks of the priest: to preach the Word of God, to celebrate the sacraments and to lead the Church. All other ministry not only *can* be pushed out but *ought* to be pushed out to others. As parishioners mature in their Christian life, they ought to be called into service according to their gifts and equipped to serve in that ministry. In this way, they become missionary disciples who are equipped and released into ministry – a ministry that they are not just doing as a favour to the priest, but one over which they have taken ownership in communion with the priest. If all ministry within the parish was clerically centred, two things would happen: I and my assistant priest would burn out very quickly, but more importantly, very little pastoral care would take place in proportion to the size of the church.

I constantly call my parish staff, ordained and lay, to avoid the clerical trap. The goal in their ministry is to call forth and equip others to do the work of ministry so that the Church may be built up. If they do it all themselves, then they, too, have fallen into a clerical model of ministry. What follows from our approach, when we get it right, is a multiplication of ministry that, like a pot that boils over, satisfies the demands for the in-house ministry so necessary to run any parish, so that more and more ministries come into being that are essentially missionary and go out into the community. In this model, as parishioners mature in Christ and become missionary disciples, they yearn to serve. Eventually, *ad intra* ministry reaches critical mass so that the desire to serve spills out into the community to become an apostolate. There needs to be a structure of accountability to maintain such a model, and we will speak about this later, but a principle of low control is also necessary, or it will never flourish. We are speaking essentially of a Church coming to the point that ministry proper to the laity is allowed to flourish without clerical control: serving the poor, feeding the hungry, evangelizing, and forming small Christian communities where people are cared for, loved and helped to move towards maturity. Only a Church filled with an army of missionary disciples can change the world.

The first part of Ephesians 4:11-13 (quoted above) also reminds us of the distinction between office and charism. The ordained have the office of apostle, prophet, evangelist, pastor and teacher. They are ultimately responsible that these ministries flourish in the Church, but these responsibilities do not always coincide with the charism. Charisms are given among *all* the members of God's people; for the Church to be strong, all must be called to identify their charisms and serve from them. An essential part of leadership in the Church today is for the priest to be secure in his call to preach God's Word, to celebrate the sacraments and to lead, while calling and allowing the charisms that are spread among the People of God to be exercised. One of the consequences of the post-conciliar clericalism was the juxtaposition of the clergy against the baptized, as if to speak of the uniqueness of the priestly vocation was to diminish the lay vocation, and to equip the laity for ministry was to threaten the role of the priest. Saint Paul is clear that all parts of the Body are necessary. Roles and responsibilities are distinct, but all are necessary.

Risky Business

The origins of clericalism have deep roots in our tradition. In the early Church, it was a very risky thing to be a Christian. Jesus warned us about the cost of following him, and was clear that this would involve persecution – even to the point of imprisonment and death. The witness of so many martyrs, clergy and lay, is evidence of this. After the Peace of Constantine in 315, Christianity was no longer persecuted by the state. Tolerance of the Church slowly changed to embrace after the emperor himself became Christian. All of a sudden it was the religion of choice for the upwardly mobile. Inevitably, as has always happened in the Church, social respectability led to spiritual decline. Being Christian just wasn't as exciting as it used to be. It became relatively easy to be a follower of Jesus, and the demands of the Gospel were slowly domesticated to be palatable to the ruling classes, who embraced what was quickly becoming the state religion.

At this point, we begin to see figures such as Saint Anthony of the Desert emerge, and with him the beginning of the anchorite movement: men and women who embraced the austerities of semi-hermetical lifestyles. They were driven to live the Christian faith in a bold and daring way. These Desert Fathers (and a few Mothers) inspired the beginnings of Christian monasticism. Within 150 years of Anthony's death, a young Saint Benedict would withdraw from his life as a student in Rome, appalled at the pagan behaviour of so many supposed Christians. He would spend the rest of his life framing a new "school for the service of the Lord" in the form of a monastic movement that would spread all over most of the known world of that time. Within 400 years, his movement and the monastic houses it founded would become the foundation of modern Europe. From this point on, there was born a schism in the heart of the Church whereby those who sought to be authentic disciples "joined the Church" through religious life or ordained ministry, and ordinary Catholics who were "just not that religious" went to church.

After about 1650 years (from the Peace of Constantine in 315 to the cultural revolutions of the 1960s), this Christian culture has now ended. We now find ourselves in a situation like that of the first Christians. It is once again unpopular to be a Christian. It is risky, costly, difficult, fulfilling and exciting. It is a time of rediscovering the essential identity of all the baptized to be missionary disciples, called to know Jesus and make him known. It is time for all who follow Jesus to heed the call to maturity and to be equipped for service within the community of the Church that takes them far from the altar from which they are sent every Sunday.

The Church's deepest identity is to be a missionary Church, called to form baptized believers into missionary disciples who go forth, through the grace of God, to build God's Kingdom. We have reflected on two of the major obstacles to forming missionary disciples: Pelagianism and clericalism. As Pope Francis said, there are many more temptations that could be named. We must, however, move on. Now that we have looked with honesty at the acute need for renewal in our Church, and have cleared the floor of the junk that hinders our ability to truly receive and live the Gospel, we can begin to lay a foundation and prepare a welcoming and warm home. Now we can go out from ourselves, inviting some to return and others to enter for the first time.

5

LAYING THE FOUNDATION

How to Transform the Culture of the Parish Community

When I led my first pilgrimage to the Holy Land, I told the tour company that our visit to Galilee should include a visit to the ancient city of Tsipori, 2 miles northwest of Nazareth. This is not a common stopover for Catholic pilgrimages, and even our tour guide was surprised to be taking our group there. Although there is no conclusive evidence in the Gospels, it is entirely reasonable to believe that Jesus spent a great deal of time in this city, which was known as Sephoris during his lifetime. Sephoris was the capital of Galilee during the time of Herod the Great, and had been destroyed by the Romans after a rebellion of the locals the year before Jesus was born.

The Gospels tell us that the people of Nazareth knew Jesus as a "carpenter" (Mark 6:3). The term in Greek, *tekton*, has a much wider meaning than woodworker. It generally means "builder," or even a "worker". Every time I visit Tsipori and walk on those stones and view the ruins of that ancient city, I can't help but imagine a teenage Jesus working with Saint Joseph – not just working with wood, but building and laying the foundations of the city, once destroyed, that would again flourish in the lifetime of Jesus. These foundations can still be seen today.

Jesus taught very clearly at the end of his Sermon on the Mount what everyone who has been in the construction business from ancient times until today has always known in theory and from experience. A building, no matter how grand and beautiful, is only as good as its foundation. The house built on sand will fall in the face of the storms of life, and the house built on rock will withstand all that is hurled against it. (Matthew 7:24-27) The foundation that Jesus proposes is listening to his words and acting upon them. The foundation is not just about believing or trusting, but includes actions.

Culture

When we examine the question of Church renewal, of rebuilding the Church of God, we begin this enterprise with a clear sense of purpose of what we are building and why. In earlier chapters, we have examined the need to recall and reclaim the lost identity of the Church as being essentially missionary. We have spoken of the pain that needs to be acknowledged before we can move forward in the rebuilding process, and of the junk that needs to be cleared out of the theological subconscious. Now we need to lay a foundation. The foundation of any human organization is the culture of that organization. The Church is no exception.

Although the Church is the spotless Bride of Christ, the Body of Christ, and, therefore, of divine essence, she is also fully human. We stand on solid ground, therefore, when we propose that anything that allows a human organization to be healthy will likewise contribute to the health of the Church. Saint Thomas Aquinas goes farther, telling us that "grace builds on nature." Therefore, it is not just a question of being attentive to the human *and* the divine. The foundation of the work of Grace (the divine) is the human, and so the human dimension of the Church takes priority in the process of rebuilding. If the human foundation of the Church is not healthy, then no matter how intense or sincere our spiritual commitment is, the foundation will be a fragile blend of clay and iron.

Values

The human foundation of the Church, whether at the universal or local level, is the human culture of that Church. When speaking about the culture of a diocesan church or a parish church, we are not speaking about its ethnicity, but rather of the values embraced by that human community. The culture of any organization is reflected in what is truly valued. These values are seen not primarily by what is said, but by what is done or left undone. Values are communicated by what is celebrated, by what is tolerated and by what is presumed. These unspoken values that make up the culture of a parish are like the 80% of the iceberg that lurks beneath the surface. Churches may have developed mission statements and may even have published a list of values, but all of these usually make up only about 20% of what a church or organization truly values. Jesus said that building on rock took place only when his words were listened to and acted upon. It is not enough to listen. It is not enough to speak about what is valued. How we act communicates our true values.

If we wish to identify the values of a particular parish, we must look at how it spends its time and money. Look at the parish budget. Look at the staffing positions. Look at what the priorities are, as evidenced by what is done, and not by what is said, and you will identify the values of that particular parish. If a parish says that evangelization is a priority, what is the budget for evangelization? Where I come from, it is more common to see a budget for snow removal than for evangelization. If a parish says that formation of adult disciples is of high value, why then is there no budget and no staff member who oversees this process?

Parish leaders who truly wish to identify the values of their parish communities should look at the parish calendar of events. How are the buildings used? For what kinds of activities? Evaluate the nature and proportion of the uses of your buildings. Look at your parish staff positions. This is a dead giveaway. Do you have more administrative or janitorial staff than pastoral staff? This will tell you that you are a maintenance church. Who are your pastoral staff? How much of your resources go into pastoral ministry, and what is the nature of this ministry? Many parishes have a generic DRE (director of Religious Education) who may have a wide range of responsibilities, including working with children and adults. What proportion of her or his time goes into doing which task? I once did a mission in a parish in the U.S. They saw themselves as a large parish with a school. After seeing the activities and the staffing structure and the use of resources, it seemed to me that this community was really a large school that happened to have a parish attached to it. An honest evaluation of a parish budget will remove any doubts about the true values of any parish, regardless of what statement may be framed on the wall. The sum of what a parish values will constitute its culture.

Common Values

Every parish has a culture, but this often remains hidden, invisible and unnamed. Over the years, I have been fascinated by the question of what makes some parish churches strong and healthy, as opposed to others that are weak and unhealthy. I have studied both Catholic and non-Catholic churches, and it is obvious that there is generally a set of common values among those churches that are healthy and growing. These values are vastly different from those of churches that are in decline, shrinking and dying.

In August 2010, I was named pastor of a relatively new and large parish in our city. This parish had been formed four years before my appointment through the amalgamation of three parishes that were all in close proximity. The pastor at the time led these three communities through a process of union that involved the sale of all three church buildings and the building of a brand new, beautiful, large, state-of-the-art church that would house the newly constituted parish of Saint Benedict in Halifax, Nova Scotia. Three months after the new building was opened and the people moved into the church, I arrived as pastor. If our values are demonstrated by what we do rather than what we say, it was clear that the leadership of this community, not without difficulties, had boldly declared that the mission of the Church was of greater value than the preservation of our buildings: that where we were going was more important than where we had been. After many years of subjecting the mission of the church to the infrastructure, a bold move had been made to rebuild the infrastructure in order to serve the mission. The core values of this community were beginning to change.

As Catholics, our buildings have deep significance. They are not merely functional structures that house the people of God. Our church buildings are consecrated for a sacred purpose and are themselves sacramental, reminding us of the presence of God in our midst, and housing the Eucharistic presence of Jesus himself. As true as this reality is, our buildings, in the end, are always of relative value. Jesus himself, entering the great temple of King Herod, would make the scandalous remark that not one stone would be left standing upon another, that all would be thrown down. (Luke 21:6) We must always remember that this will be the fate of all the buildings we build. The Church of God that will last into eternity is the Church of living stones, built upon the cornerstone of Christ, that must constantly be built up. (1 Peter 2:5) In spite of the great attachments and the sentimentality that the people of Saint Benedict Parish had for their buildings, they participated in the painful process of letting them go and moving into the new, unfamiliar church on May 16, 2010. Three months later, I arrived to a collective sigh of relief. With the arrival of the new priest, surely all the changes would finally be over. Right?

New Wine for a New Wineskin

I am convinced that the primary challenge of the New Evangelization is nothing short of the transformation of the cultures of our churches, which means a conversion of our values. Renewal of our parishes will never be accomplished merely by a change of address and by shifting the furniture. On my very first weekend, I told the parishioners of Saint Benedict that I was haunted by one burning question: What will stop the cultural forces that necessitated the amalgamation and closure of the three previous parishes from continuing to chip away at our foundations so that we will have to repeat the process in another 20 years? The answer to this question, of course, is nothing. Nothing will prevent the continuation of the very decline that got us to where we are now – unless we strive for a deeper kind of change. Our task at Saint Benedict Parish was to allow the Lord to make us into new wine for the beautiful new wineskin we had received.

This necessary change, of course, is one of culture. In the 2007 Aparecida document, which I discussed in Chapter 4, the bishops of Latin America, among them the future Pope Francis, concluded that those who left the Catholic Church to join non-Catholic churches did so not for theological reasons, but for "vivential" reasons. It is not about changing our theology, but about how we live out an already rich theology of the Christian life. This cultural change means a deep, deep change. It means changing what we consider to be normative for the Christian life. It means a total conversion of our lived values, not merely the stated ones. Compared to this change, all others, including closing churches, are merely cosmetic.

In many dioceses across the Western world, bishops are struggling to restructure their local dioceses so that their people can be served by a dwindling number of priests. Sometimes churches are closed. They may be falling apart and may not have the resources to keep their doors open. It does take courage to do this, but closing churches without doing anything else is simply putting them out of their misery. Often parishes are "clustered" (a cluster is when the local priest wakes up in the morning to find out that instead of running one or two churches, he now has three). The expectation that comes with clustering is that everything will continue as before, except that the priest now has two or three of everything. By far, the most sensible option is parish amalgamation. This means that even if two or three parishes come together, they will function as one parish, with one staff and one parish council and one office and one bank account. Churches can exist as an amalgamated parish and continue to worship without any buildings being closed. At the very least, there is a concentration of resources.

The best-case scenario is what I was gifted with at Saint Benedict in the summer of 2010: an amalgamated parish that had just moved into a single new space. It was the best scenario, but was still not enough. It is not enough to pull the trigger on decaying structures. It is not enough to heap more parishes on the shoulders of already discouraged, overworked and frustrated priests, and it is not enough to amalgamate and even build a beautiful new building. None of these actions will suffice unless we address the underlying issue of the culture of our churches that prevents us from becoming healthy. A church that is healthy grows, and a church that is not healthy dies. Even though everything looked great at Saint Benedict, we were still dying.

Living in the Atlantic province of Nova Scotia, we enjoy using maritime metaphors. I think of the three parishes that came together to constitute Saint Benedict Parish as three ships that were drifting towards the rocks. Two small ships and a mid-size ship were caught in a strong current and were all drifting slowly but surely, and it seemed nothing could be done to change this. The current is the cultural forces that have shaped the last three generations. Our ships were not built to sail in these kinds of waters, and none of the three ships had the engine power to turn out of the current. The amalgamation of the three parishes gave us a beautiful new ship with the potential to build a powerful engine, and build it we did. Over the course of my first year, we began to restructure the pastoral team, to add new staff positions and to speak about the vision for our parish (we will consider this stage in more depth in Chapter 7, when we look at the question of leadership). With a new engine, we now had the capacity to do something about this inexorable drift; all that remained was to change the course. A change of course is nothing less than changing the culture of the parish, which ultimately means a conversion of our values.

In a time when the term "New Evangelization" is a kind of buzzword, we often look for a quick fix. We search the ecclesial landscape for the best programs and grab someone in our parish to run them. In the end, no matter how good the program, these attempts will always fizzle and die out. They will not produce the robust flame of authentic renewal in the Church. Any course run in a parish will be only as good as the culture of that parish. Even a very successful tool for evangelization like Alpha will have a very limited impact if the values of a parish are vastly different from the values within a particular program. Alpha places high value on hospitality, great music, amazing and relevant talks, and a transformative experience of community in small groups. Those who are non-churchgoers can come on this course and experience conversion. Then they come to Mass. They taste and see one thing through our program and a very different thing on Sunday morning. Running evangelistic, outreach or renewal programs without addressing the necessary cultural conversion of our parishes will only leave us open to charges of false advertising.

As we prepped for our first full ministry year in the fall of 2010, and as I began to propose new ways of doing things, no one group could say those words that had haunted me ever since I first served in a parish: "That's not how we do things here." What a relief. Due to every parishioner feeling new in this new space, there was a window of opportunity to begin to bring about change. It was about as close as anyone could get to being able to create a parish from scratch. Since that time, we have implemented a focused and sustained campaign to transform the culture of our parish. I have made no secret about this with our staff and ministry leaders that this is our goal and nothing less. I have been clear with them that it will be hard work and that it will take time. Pope Francis, in *Evangelii Gaudium*, speaks of the capacity for the cultural transformation of a parish: "The parish is not an outdated institution;

precisely because it possesses great flexibility, it can assume quite different contours depending on the openness and missionary creativity of the pastor and the community." (EG, no. 28)

Values are also transferable. That means that whatever the context of your church, small or large, urban or rural, these values – if they truly become the foundation of all you say and do – will bring about health, and health will bring about the growth of the parish. The key is that any one value will be manifested differently in different parishes. How a parish expresses a particular value may not look exactly like how we strive to do it at Saint Benedict Parish, but it is the values that bring health, and not the mere imitation of another parish's best practices.

In the remainder of this chapter, I will outline ten common values that are shared by healthy, growing churches, and give examples from my experience at Saint Benedict Parish of how we attempted and are attempting to implement a conversion in each of these values.

1. Giving Priority to the Weekend

This is the day that the Lord has made;
let us rejoice and be glad in it. (Psalm 118:24)

Over the years I have been accused several times of turning the celebration of Mass into a production. As often happens in such moments, what I could have said came to me later – responses that would have been amusing, if not necessarily charitable. To the accusation that everything is a production, I am tempted to say, "Thank you, I'm so glad you noticed."

Duh!

Eleven years ago, after being a priest for six years and a pastor for three years, the obvious occurred to me. The only time we see 80% of our people is on the weekend, yet only 20% of my time in any given week was invested in planning, preparing and executing weekend Masses. It is the classic 80/20 rule. In pastoral ministry, it is easy to expend the other 80% of time and resources on a small number of people. I remember thinking that if the Church was a business, it probably would have gone out of business a long time ago with this kind of strategy. The Church is, of course, not a mere business, it is mystery, but grace still builds on nature and there is an essential truth here. The priority of any parish, and any priest, ought to be about preparing for and celebrating the Sunday Eucharist to make it the best possible experience for the maximum number of people. Too often in my own ministry, and in many parishes, the weekend, and everything that happens, had merely been an afterthought, a mild interruption to the real work of ministry that takes place from Monday to Friday.

Sunday Eucharist ought to be a "production" in the best sense of the word. It deserves to be so. I presume here, of course, a positive connotation to "production." We are not speaking of showmanship, or anything shallow and insincere. We are speaking about being intentional about every aspect of the Sunday celebration. To give our best for the Lord so that people who come to our church can leave with a sense of "Wow!" Why not? If I can go to a sports event or a concert and say "wow," why shouldn't this utterance be genuinely on the lips of those who have been sent from Church to "glorify the Lord with their lives"? The days of the 50-minute get-it-over-and-done-with Mass must end. Jesus told us that the Kingdom of God was like a wedding banquet. (Matthew 22:1-14) The Eucharist is to be a foretaste of this banquet, and so it ought to produce an exclamation of "Wow!" It ought to be "a production."

Many of the values and examples that follow in this chapter do refer to the experience of Sunday morning, so I will refrain from giving any detail here. I do wish to say, however, that if the weekend celebrations are to be a priority, then we must have sufficient time on Sunday mornings to gather, celebrate and connect afterwards. This can be a real pressure on priests as we see the quality of Sunday mornings compromised because of our tight Mass schedules. The parking lot must be emptied on the hour so that those coming for the next Mass can arrive, or the priest must sprint for his car and play loosely with the speed limit to get to the next location for the next Mass. We need to honestly look at our Mass schedules, and ask what we truly value. Do we value meaningful and transformative celebrations of the Eucharist, or is our primary value convenient and static Mass times? Are we willing to change our Mass times so we can have more breathing space during and after each Sunday Mass? In some pastoral situations, due to the size of the building, this may not be an option, but then there is another question: do we value our buildings over a meaningful and transformative experience of Sunday Eucharist?

Saint Paul says in his Letter to the Ephesians, "There is one Lord, one faith, one baptism." (Ephesians 4:5) I sometimes think that the typical Catholic version of this scripture would read, "There is one Lord, one faith, one hour." In all my years studying Scripture, theology, the history of the Church, and canon law, I have not found any reference to Sunday celebrations having to be no more than one hour "or else." Furthermore, in all the times I have crossed over (God forbid) the one-hour mark, I have never seen a single person turn into a pumpkin. Never! Where does this value come from? Sports events are never less than an hour. If we went to a concert that was only an hour long, we would demand our money back. Movies and theatre productions are usually about two hours long, but "Thou shalt not go over one hour for Mass!"

Where Did That Come From?

During my first year of ordination, I was assigned as an assistant priest at the Cathedral. Every other weekend, I found myself filling in around the diocese. I enjoyed this very much, as I was able to get to know the lay of the land. I will never forget my first experience of Palm Sunday as a priest. I was sent on Saturday afternoon to fill in at a local city parish. I was so excited about my first Palm Sunday celebration: a procession of palms, singing, the reading of the Passion and a chance to invite the people to enter into the riches of the Sacred Triduum in the days to follow.

I arrived at the church and was met by a very grumpy usher who told me in no uncertain terms that there would be no procession and that there would be no homily. When I asked him why, he told me that people "were on medication." By the time that liturgy was over, I needed to be on medication! I was the only person in the whole church, other than the cantor, singing Hosannas during the entrance, and in spite of the glares of the usher and his companions, I did dare to preach, even if only for five minutes. So much for my first Palm Sunday celebration, which did conclude, by the way, within the one-hour mark.

My friends from Africa tell me that in their countries, people bring their lunch to Mass, and their celebrations can last well beyond the three-hour mark. I have been to Masses in the Vatican that regularly go beyond two hours. When Eastern rite Christians, Catholic and Orthodox, celebrate Divine Liturgy, it would be unspeakable to even try to bring it to completion before the 90-minute mark. Evangelical and Pentecostal Christians will sing for an hour, and you know that the pastor is not going to preach for any less than half an hour. So why are we so different as Catholics in North America and in Europe? The answer is so simple: habit.

We formed the habit of fast-track Masses due to constrictions of pastoral practice at a time when our churches were full and it was a societal value to go to church. In 1950s North America, it was not uncommon to find urban parishes that had eight or nine Masses on a Sunday morning. These Masses would be on the hour from 6:00 a.m. until noon, often with two different celebrations at once – one in the church and one in the basement. Parishes had to schedule in this manner for two reasons: 1) the sheer number of people who came to Mass, and 2) the discipline of fasting at that time. Before the Second Vatican Council, Catholics receiving the Holy Eucharist were required to fast from food and water from midnight the night before until they received the Eucharist. This explained the prevalence of early morning Mass, after which the faithful could break their fast at "break-fast." It also explains why

Masses did not usually go later than noon. Senior priests who remember those days have told me stories of how fainting and collapsing parishioners were a common occurrence. Today, we have vigil Masses on Saturday evening as well as Sunday evening Masses. The Eucharistic fast is only one hour before receiving Holy Communion, and we do not have the sheer numbers of people attending Sunday Eucharist as we did in the past. The context that conditioned Catholics in the Western world to get addicted to the 45-minute Mass no longer exists, but the practice lingers on.

In the end, it is not really a question of how long the Mass ought to be or could be, but whether this value leads us to health. I believe it does not. It contributes to a "get it over and done with" mentality that turns our Eucharistic celebrations into something to be endured rather than something that endures. Serving the unspoken value of "convenience" may be the reason why, in spite of the change in context, we continue to value the one-hour Mass. I remember as a young teenager going to a Saturday afternoon Mass in town with a friend of mine. This Mass was held in a retirement home and was a Sunday Mass. Presumably, the residents of that home did need food and medication, and somehow the priest was able to move through the entire Sunday liturgy from beginning to end, including a brief homily, in 20 minutes (after being a priest for seventeen years, I still have no idea how he did this). The point of this story is not the amazing feat of rapid worship, but the fact that there were at least a hundred non-residents of all ages who crowded into the small common room and lined the hallways outside in order to avail themselves of the fastest Mass in the West. I cannot be too indignant on this matter as my best friend and I were there for exactly the same reason.

A Culture of Minimalism

The fast-Mass addiction continues to be played out in parish after parish all over the Western world. During my first months at Saint Benedict, I had to address what I considered to be a major problem at our Saturday vigil Mass. We used to get about

99

600 people at this Mass, and at least 25% of them would leave as soon as they had received the Eucharist. That was bad enough, but the back wall of our church is all glass, and you can see the entire foyer from the front of the church. I will never forget the first time I saw this: I could not believe my eyes. Hundreds of people were leaving while I was still giving out Holy Communion. Over the weeks that followed, I addressed this phenomenon in the parish newsletter and during Mass. I was bold enough to say that, although there were indeed exceptional reasons to leave Mass directly after receiving communion, anyone who left at that time every week needed to seriously consider what they were doing. I suggested that they refrain either from leaving early each week or from receiving the Eucharist. This earned me a stream of anonymous letters, including a letter to the bishop and even a letter to the pope (a first).

Some of these letters informed me that if Mass was not so long, then people would not feel compelled to leave early. Two weeks later, the priest who was assisting at the parish was presiding at the Saturday Mass. I was planning to make a few announcements at the end of Mass. I pulled into the parking lot at 4:45 p.m. (45 minutes into Mass) only to see the usual flood of people heading for their cars. That's why I am convinced that this phenomenon has little to do with the length of Mass and more with a desire to just get it over and done with.

The sad truth is that we as pastors have often catered to this minimalist culture, but what other option did we have when we were working within a model of pastoral care that required the feeding of people who had no appetite? Remember that we come from a tradition that would discuss this question: How much of the Mass can I miss and still have it count? A commitment to the priority of the weekend means declaring this frustrating capitulation to be over. Minimalism and convenience cannot be the primary values of a healthy church. Minimalism and convenience have no place in the life of the disciple who is called to save his or her life by losing it. Someone once said that Jesus doesn't ask for much – he asks for everything. If our liturgies are to be meaningful and transformative "productions," they need to be able to breathe and not be constrained by a rigid one-hour rule. Likewise, there needs to be enough time between Masses so that those who are hungry for God are able to linger with one another after Mass to encourage and support one another. We as pastors are called to facilitate this, even if it means – horror of horrors – changing Mass times, eliminating underattended Masses, or even acknowledging that we are being confined by buildings that no longer serve the needs of this new pastoral context.

2. Hospitality

"I was a stranger and you welcomed me." (Matthew 25:35)

Someone once said that the Church is the only organization that exists mainly for the sake of those who do not belong. This is the difference between a church and a club. Clubs exists for the sake of their members. I remember having a conversation with a parishioner who asserted that my job as pastor was to meet the needs of parishioners. I was perhaps too quick to point out that this was *part* of "our" job (the entire community, not just the priest), but that my role was principally to lead an army of missionaries to reach those who were not yet part of our church. This missional orientation is the identity that needs to be embraced in an incarnational manner, and not only in the abstract. It is, again, the difference between what we say we value and what we value deep down. Hospitality, therefore, does not mean being friendly with our friends and all the people who look, think and talk like us, but reaching out to the stranger.

The Eyes of a Stranger

When looking at this value, we need to ask ourselves what the Sunday morning experience is like for the person who does not yet belong. Several years ago, I was leading a parish mission in a neighbouring diocese. After driving for several hours through a snowstorm, I arrived at the parish fifteen minutes before the

Saturday evening Mass. The local pastor and I had exchanged pulpits for the weekend, so he was not around. When I walked into the relatively small church, no one greeted me, even though I was obviously a visitor. When I asked the usher where the bathroom was, I received a grunt and a gesture towards what I eventually found to be the bathroom. I was wearing a scarf that covered my Roman collar, so no one knew I was a priest. The contrast in the way people responded to me after I took off my scarf to reveal my identity was striking.

As a stranger I was Jesus, and no one welcomed me. As a priest, I was just a priest, and it was the "Yes, Father, no, Father, three bags full, Father" routine. I do not want to pick on this particular parish as, sadly, it differs little from what I would have experienced at any other parish. This fact reveals a fault in our culture, and therefore our values, as Catholics. My experience at this small parish was not primarily because I was not *recognized* as a stranger (this is an aspect of church life where smaller parishes have an advantage over large parishes). My experience reflected a value that considers the Eucharistic celebration as a private and anonymous experience, thus rendering the call to welcome the stranger a moot point.

Who's on the Team?

The first step in truly embracing the value of hospitality is to begin with a hospitality team. There do need to be some people who pay specific attention to welcoming at every Mass, and although it seems obvious, we ought to have people on a welcoming team who enjoy welcoming people. We need this ministry to begin before people even enter the building. On Sundays, when it's not too cold, I will often stand outside and welcome our people into the church; when it is really cold, our director of evangelization can often been seen outside, all bundled up in jacket and scarf, welcoming people. Once those arriving are in the foyer, we have two to four people who welcome all comers, as other members of the welcome team hold the doors and are available at the back of the church for anyone who needs assistance. Our welcoming team also includes a team of emergency first responders, appointed for every Mass to be ready in case of any medical incidents. It is surprising to me just how often such a team is needed when about 2,000 people pass through our doors on a weekend. Another vital part of our organized efforts at hospitality has to do with the cleanliness of our buildings, especially the bathrooms. Over the years, I have seen church bathrooms that reminded me of the bathrooms when I was in high school: no soap, no paper towels, no toilet paper, no toilet seat, no lock on the door of a stall, and, once, even no door!

As great as these efforts are, a formal welcoming team can be a double-edged sword, as it can create the impression that hospitality is the exclusive domain of those with official parish name tags rather than being the responsibility of the entire community. Several years ago, I was away on vacation and decided to go to Mass at a local parish with some friends. I was in my "civvies" and did not identify myself as a priest. It was a busy Mass and I was shown about halfway to the front of the church to find one of the few available empty seats. Not only did the elderly lady who was hogging the outside of the pew not move into the centre, she elected not to stand to allow me and my friends to be seated, and glared at us as we gingerly clambered over her. My smiles to the other churchgoers were not returned, and I was left feeling embarrassed and unwelcomed. It was good for me to be reminded about what it feels like to be a stranger in a church.

Pew hospitality is one obvious place to begin when teaching parishioners about their responsibility to be hospitable, but the most simple yet effective way for a congregation to impact the welcoming coefficient of a parish is to remember to smile. Several years ago, Colgate undertook a brilliant advertising campaign on social media to promote the sale of dental floss. Their campaign displayed three photographs of different smiling couples. The man in each photograph had some of his lunch visibly stuck between his teeth. The genius of the campaign is that while the eye is quickly drawn to his afternoon snack safely stowed away between the front teeth, the viewer fails to realize that in one photo, the woman has six fingers, in another, the man has only one ear and, in the third, the woman has three arms. The point is that a smile covers a multitude of sins. Smiling at one another in church is not just a great social practice. It has solid theological grounds, as we are told in Scripture to "rejoice in the Lord always." (Philippians 4:4) Pope Francis, in *Evangelii Gaudium*, tells us that "an evangelizer must never look like someone who has come back from a funeral." (EG, no. 10) So, as someone once said, "If Jesus is in your heart, please notify your face."

Welcoming the Stranger

On November 13, 2013, Pope Francis preached a weekday homily on the parable of the wedding feast told by Saint Matthew. (22:1-14) The pope made two essential points. The first was that when we gather for the Eucharist, or anytime we gather as a Church, we are responding to an invitation to a party, and a party is always a joyful experience. The second point was that in the parable, the servants are instructed to go to the highways and byways to bring in the good, the bad and the marginalized:

> "I go to the feast, but I don't go beyond the antechamber, because I want to be only with the three or four people that I am familiar with …." You can't do this in the Church! You either participate fully or you remain outside. You can't pick and choose: the Church is for everyone, beginning with those I've already mentioned, the most marginalized. It is everyone's Church!

The question of how the marginalized feel when entering our churches is one that haunts me. How welcomed does a person feel who does not look like us, sound like us, dress like us and smell like us? How does the person who is struggling with mental illness feel when entering our churches? How does the person living an alternate lifestyle or struggling with sin and brokenness feel? As my priest friend said, he often felt like the president of an upper middle-class social club. It is not just a question of treating "these people" the same as everyone else; they are the guests of honour. I can recall many occasions at various parishes when I observed someone who does not fit the typical parishioner profile being treated dismissively or as "suspicious" by parishioners. The earliest recorded words for parish hospitality ministers are found in the letter of James, when he chastises Christians for giving preference to those who appear in fine clothes:

> For if a person with gold rings and in fine clothes comes into your assembly, and if a poor person in dirty clothes also comes in, and if you take notice of the one wearing the fine clothes and say, "Have a seat here, please," while to the one who is poor you say, "Stand there," or "Sit at my feet," have you not made distinctions among yourselves, and become judges with evil thoughts? (James 2:2-4)

A wonderful way to measure just how hospitable our parishes are to the marginalized is to measure the sense of security that exists in our churches on a Sunday morning. I once heard a pastor at a conference say that he realized his church had become a safe "club" for a group of like-minded people when he saw parishioners walking around and leaving purses and handbags in the pews. He concluded that if there is no risk that someone might steal your purse in church, then we are not truly welcoming the marginalized. He commented that if there is no one in our churches who drops the occasional F-bomb, then we are not welcoming to the marginalized, but attracting a group of like-minded people. One weekend later, after a particular Mass, a parishioner who is one of God's "little ones" came to me a little frustrated, as she was unable to find the drop-off box for one of our charity drives to help the poor in our area. "Fr. James," she asked in a loud voice, "where the f___ am I supposed to leave this?" I almost had a heart attack. I did gently remind her about where she was, then laughed to myself as I remembered the pastor's words of the week before. Remember what Pope Francis says: that the Church exists for the most marginalized. We are called to be fishers of people.

(Luke 5:10) Anyone who has ever gone fishing knows that there is a big difference between the flapping, smelly, slimy creature that is caught, and the fish that is served up on a plate, complete with a slice of lemon.

The Liturgy

There is one unavoidable difficulty that we must struggle with as Catholics when it comes to being hospitable to those who do not attend church, or those who are non-Catholics, and that is the liturgy. As beautiful as the liturgy is, it is, by its very nature, inhospitable to the outsider. It is so because it is the worship of the initiated. It presumes knowledge of basic theology, gestures, postures, prayers and ritual that are often foreign to the non-Catholic or non-churchgoer. To make matters worse, as Catholics, our actions show that we too often presume that every person in church is a Catholic and knows what to do and what to say.

I was reminded of this recently when presiding at a funeral Mass. One trick I learned a number of years ago for getting a measure of a congregation at a funeral Mass was to take a mental picture at the very beginning when we make the sign of the cross. The number of people who make the sign of the cross will give an immediate sense of at least who the cradle Catholics are and will also identify a few Anglicans. Knowing that in North America the largest religious category is fallen away Catholics, it is generous to infer that less than 50% of those who make the sign of the cross are practising Catholics. At this particular funeral, only one third of the people gathered made the sign of the cross. Immediately, I was struck by the incongruity of the situation. I was assisted by a deacon at that Mass and, as we concluded the Our Father, I somehow wanted to give some explanation for what was to happen next. There was no time. Our deacon eagerly invited the congregation to "offer one another the sign of peace," only to be met with puzzled looks from most of the people present. This let's-all-pretend-everyone-is-a-practising-Catholic attitude remains a significant obstacle to genuine hospitality in our churches.

There is no real solution for this problem as long as the un-churched are going to be present with us on weekends and other celebrations. The first step is to recognize that "the problem" is a great opportunity. The very first thing we can do in situations where there are obviously people from various backgrounds, such as at weddings and funerals, is to acknowledge them, welcome them and invite them to enter into our worship as they are able. Pretending that guests are not really present is extremely inhospitable. More and more, I have found that it is better to presume nothing. Therefore, at appropriate moments, I will often give a brief description of what we are about to do next: listen to readings from Scripture or pray the Eucharistic prayer, "a long and ancient prayer in which we ask God to transform bread and wine into the sacrament of his Body and Blood." I give hints to help people pray the Mass, and I am often surprised by the number of Catholics who approach me afterwards and thank me for helping them to enter into the celebration of the Mass. Brief explanations in the homily or during Mass can help us be more centred on the kerygma or first proclamation and avoid using overly technical and specialized vocabulary. Displaying the prayers of the Mass on a screen or directing our guests' attention to booklets in the pews with the responses can also be a great aid to providing hospitality.

Catching the Fish

The ultimate goal of hospitality is to welcome guests so well that they themselves decide to join the parish and help welcome other guests. During my first year at Saint Benedict, I was struck by the fact that each weekend, at least 30 to 40 guests were "checking us out" to see if, at some level, they could belong in our parish. As wonderful as this was, it was equally clear that we were "catching" very few of them. Another problem was the process in which guests became parishioners. We had the "blue card" option and the "online" option. As the foyer would flood with parishioners at the end of Mass, I would greet as many of them at the door as possible. (I often feel like a hockey goalie getting 600 pucks fired at him in the space of five minutes.) As I spoke to people, I would receive many requests about how to sign up for the parish. This would result in me shouting over someone's head that, if they just pushed through the crowd, they would find a table at the other end of the foyer where there might, or might not, be a blue card they could fill out. This card requested name, address and basic contact information, as well as a box to check if that person wanted envelopes. That was it. The online option was much the same, except you could become a parishioner and never enter the building or speak to another human being.

There were two hospitality-based issues that we needed to address. The first was to make our church foyer more user friendly, not only for guests, but for our own parishioners. We made a move in the right direction by building a mobile welcome booth that would be staffed by parishioners at every Mass. This mobile unit housed a computer and was attached to a big-screen TV that ran friendly and light-hearted slides on upcoming programs and events. The welcome booth also was home to our hearing assistance devices and displayed all of our parish brochures and publications: stewardship booklets, brochures on weddings and baptisms, information on parish membership, etc. It was a point of contact for any questions or inquiries. The key was that it was visible from all directions and staffed by friendly parishioners who were eager to help. Now, anytime I meet new parishioners, I bring them over to the booth right away and introduce them to the welcome team (which is distinct from the hospitality team).

The other question we struggled with was that before we could devise a process for new parishioners to sign up, we needed to know what it meant to become a parishioner. I will say more about this later, but we knew that being a parishioner could not simply mean having your name added to a list. This led us to abandon the "registration card" approach – both the blue ones and the virtual ones. We now invite potential new parishioners to complete a "communication card" and drop it in the collection basket. These cards can be found at our welcome booth, but are also in our weekly newsletter. They are now the first step to make becoming a parishioner a relationship-based process. This way, we reduce the chance of a person being a name on a list. The risk, of course, is that such a process can be interpreted as a kind of obstacle course that makes it difficult to become a parishioner. While one side of the communication card gathers the typical registration information, the other side outlines the process of registering as a parishioner of Saint Benedict. It is intentionally relational and reads like this:

We can't wait to meet you! In such a large parish as ours, we need to be purposeful in being personal. It's important to us that you feel at home here. Our membership process is set up so that we can get to know each other a little better. It's a four-step process. Here goes:

1. *"I like this church!" Complete the Communication Card.*

2. *"But I don't know enough about it." A member of our welcome team will call and arrange to meet with you.*

3. *"Sign me up! I want to be a part of the team." Attend a New Parishioner Welcome Event to fill out a formal registration card.*

4. *"Do they remember me?" Your Welcome Team member will check in with you periodically to see how you are doing.*

After we receive the communication cards, our welcome team swings into action, arranging a visit to the homes of new families to drop off a welcome package that contains, among other things, a DVD featuring the story of Saint Benedict and a visual tour of the church with explanations of the architecture, design and artwork. The welcome package also includes stewardship booklets outlining ministry opportunities, a brochure on expectations, and the latest parish newsletter. In all of this, we are clear that membership in a parish does mean something, and that moving beyond attending to becoming a member ought to be an informed and intentional process.

The final step in this process is something we have struggled to get right. We call it an NPE, or New Parishioner Event.

Its designation as an "event" only happened after failed attempts at having receptions and luncheons. Finally, we believe we have something that works. We host this NPE on a Saturday night every two months, or as needed. As we seek to connect personally with every new member, we limit these events to no more than 20 new parishioners. Attendees are asked to RSVP, and the event is held as a wine and cheese reception lasting no more than an hour, including brief words of welcome by a member of the welcome team, our parish Director of Engagement, and me. The rest of the time is spent mingling, chatting, laughing and enjoying getting to know one another over a glass of wine. Before people leave, they are given an opportunity to fill out a formal registration card at the end of the evening.

Of course, some people find this process overly demanding and intrusive. That cannot be helped. Anyone is welcome to attend our parish. A person can attend our parish every week and not be registered, but when someone decides to sign on, surely it should mean something. Our process has slowed the rate of new names being added to the list, but in the past, most of those names were removed at the end of the year anyway. The real gift of this new process is that it enables us to build relationships – and this is fitting, as relationships and belonging are at the heart of hospitality.

3. Uplifting Music

O sing to the Lord a new song. (Psalm 96:1)

It has been said that Church renewal is all about the three *h*'s: hospitality, hymns and homilies. There is no question that music has the power to reach deeply into our souls and touch us. "He who sings prays twice," said Saint Augustine, and so music and singing songs of praise and canticles to God (Ephesians 5:19) is an integral part of the liturgy. It has been more than 50 years since the Second Vatican Council published *Sacrosanctum Concilium* (Constitution on the Sacred Liturgy) as the first of sixteen documents. This document sounded a clarion call for the renewal of all aspects of the liturgy so that all the faithful could enter into "full, conscious, and active participation." (SC, no. 14) The context of this call to renewal was the liturgical movement that had begun at the end of the nineteenth century and had brought scholars to discover more about the way the early Church celebrated the Eucharist, and how this celebration had developed over the centuries.

What had originally been a unified experience of worship for all the people of God, clergy and laity alike, had, by the Middle Ages, devolved into three distinct modes of participation. First was the person of the priest, whose prayer was almost solitary. He prayed in Latin, which by that time was no longer the language of the people, and he prayed silently. Second was the choir, which sang elaborate versions of the prayers that had once been proper to the assembly. Third were the laity who, removed from the altar, neither sang with the choir nor united themselves with the Eucharistic Prayer prayed by the priest. Those who were literate could attempt to follow the liturgy by using their own missal, but until the 20th century, most Catholics could not read. Instead, the laity were merely passive spectators. Attendance at the Eucharist was often driven by a sense of duty, and the obligation to "hear" Mass was fulfilled by private devotions, such as the rosary, with attention directed not to the altar, but to the presence of Jesus in the tabernacle.

In the years following the Council, attempts were made to call the laity into "full, conscious and active participation," and music was seen as a prime avenue to effect this change. Sadly, what followed in those decades was a wholesale turning away from the beautiful and transcendent to the merely functional. Participation was narrowly defined as "joining in," and the over-all quality of liturgical music was greatly lowered. At this time, a deeply erroneous notion took root in the Church: the old is bad and the new is good. In response to the proliferation of this very un-Catholic perspective, there emerged an alternate perspective that was equally flawed: the new is bad and the old is good.

The Old and the New

Jesus said, "Every scribe who has been trained for the kingdom of heaven is like the master of a household who brings out of his treasure what is new and what is old." (Matthew 13:52) I remember when I was studying theology, a professor wisely told us that the great mysteries of the Christian faith always involved both/and. This both/and approach also has great pastoral merit, especially when it comes to music. The old must have a place in our worship, because the Church is always the Communion of Saints stretched out across history. To be Catholic is to be in the Church "according to the whole" (*kath' holon* in Greek), and this "whole Church" does not permit geographic or chronological limitation. To worship at the Eucharist is to enter into something much, much bigger than ourselves and far wider than one particular cultural expression in one particular time. The old cannot be excluded.

To be Catholic is also to be missionary. While treasuring what is old, the Church cannot be only a repository of ancient things, no matter how beautiful. She must reflect the face of God who, in the words of Saint Augustine, is "Beauty ever ancient, ever new." The worship of the liturgy must also have a missional dimension and must bring ancient and eternal realities to bear in a way that they can be understood and received by the people who gather. It must speak their language. The new is necessary, and even the songs of the Bible command us to "sing a new song to the Lord." (Psalm 33:3, 40:3, 96:1, 98:1, 144:9, 149:1)

For this reason, I believe that the music we experience in the liturgy must strive to embrace both the new and the old, and must resist the temptation to settle for some kind of lowest common denominator. Uniformity is not a Catholic value, and diversity ought to be welcomed into our experience of music at the liturgy without fear of its impact on unity. Imposed uniformity does violence to unity. We should boldly bring the ancient musical treasures from our storehouse and give them a place in our worship. We have a fundamental need to do so, to remind ourselves that the worship of the Church is far greater than our momentary and parochial likes and dislikes. We have a fundamental need to worship with songs that are new and with instruments that are new. We must be prepared to worship with music that speaks to the people who gather, music that is not alien, music that they can even enjoy.

At my parish, we seek to embrace the old and the new by committing ourselves to distinct flavours and experiences of the liturgy at each of the weekend Masses. No one style or flavour is imposed on the whole parish. In this way, we celebrate a diverse experience of music that embraces the breadth of Catholic musical expression, and we leave parishioners free to choose the style of worship that speaks most to them. Our Saturday afternoon Mass features a mid-size choir that sings typical parish hymnbook offerings accompanied by piano or organ. At the Sunday morning 9:00 Mass we have a contemporary band complete with electric guitar, bass guitar, acoustic guitar, keyboard and drums. The sound is professionally mixed to ensure the best quality, and the band plays a variety of old and new hymns, but in a contemporary style. This Mass tends to draw the largest number of young families, and we really do rock the place! I love it.

At the 11:15 Mass, we have a 30-voice choir that sings classic congregational hymns and choral pieces accompanied by organ. This Mass sometimes includes Gregorian chant and Latin Mass parts, and has all the smells and bells. I love this, too! Our Sunday evening Mass features a fifteen-member contemporary choir that sings more contemporary hymnbook music. We are blessed with four unique flavours to choose from, with the entire parish acting as a wise steward, bringing out the old and the new.

Beauty

Another very Catholic value is beauty. Music, as one of the ancient arts, never exists for its own sake, or it can become merely functional. When beautiful, it mediates the divine, because the One who is Beauty is always to be found in the beautiful. It is beauty that contributes powerfully to the wow factor that we ought to be striving for at every celebration of the Eucharist. Beauty often evokes a silent response. This is so when we behold a stunning sunset, or a striking work of art. It can also be our response to wondrous liturgical music, and I find it small-minded to imply that being caught up in listening to something beautiful does not involve "full, conscious and active participation."

There is a place in the liturgy for this type of participation, but the norm for music in the liturgy surely involves opening our mouths and singing God's praises. "I have told the glad news of deliverance in the great congregation; see, I have not restrained my lips, as you know, O Lord." (Psalm 40:9) After almost a thousand years of letting the choir do all the singing, there is still much work to be done in our parishes to call our people to experience the power of singing God's praise.

To Whom am I Speaking?

This task has not been made easier by the types of hymns that are sung in our churches. When I first arrived at my present parish, it was not uncommon to go through an entire celebration of the liturgy, sing the usual four hymns (processional, preparation of the gifts, communion and recessional), and not once sing to God. I have already made a case for diversity over uniformity, so I do believe the liturgy should admit all genres of hymns, and not just hymns or songs of praise. What do I mean? The first question is who are we speaking to, and the second is what are we saying? We can be speaking to God (hymns of praise or petition), about God (confessional hymns), with God (singing the words of God from Scripture) or to one another (exhortation). If we are to take the oldest hymnbook in the Judeo-Christian tradition, the Book of Psalms, as our model, we will see that all these genres of hymns belong in our worship. We ought to sing songs that cry out to the skies about who our God is. The oldest Christian hymn that we know of, recorded by Saint Paul in his letter to the Philippians (2:6-11), is such an example. We ought to take the sacred words of Jesus, spoken to us, and put them to song. Singing "I Am the Bread of Life" helps the living words of Jesus penetrate our hearts as we approach the very mystery through which he gives himself to us. Calling each other to worship, to service, to love and faithfulness also reflects the impulse of many of the psalms.

As right and fitting as all of these genres of hymns are, I believe that hymns of praise ought to have pride of place. They are the most transformative, because they do not just suggest that we pray, call us to pray or tell us how wonderful it is to pray: they are prayer itself. Prayer is talking to God, and is distinct from talking about God or exhorting one another to talk to God. Only in the hymn of praise do we pray twice, because in all other genres, though they have a place in the liturgy, we do not even pray once. It is the hymn of praise that unites us to the Father, Son and Holy Spirit. It is the hymn of praise that can bring about the entirely necessary, intense, personal encounter with Jesus that the New Evangelization calls for. In spite of this, however, if you scan the most commonly used hymnbooks, and drop into the occasional parish celebrations of the Eucharist, the hymn of praise is not as common as it should be.

In my years as a priest, the most sublime moments of the liturgy have been when hundreds of voices are united in praise to God. It matters not if the praise is led by a contemporary band or by choir and pipe organ. There is just something about "Holy God, We Praise Thy Name," or "Joyful, Joyful We Adore You," because we are speaking directly to God. It is also my experience that people are much more likely to cut loose and sing with everything they've got when they are giving praise to God and not just calling each other to go and dance in a forest.

The oldest non-scriptural hymn we have in our tradition is the Gloria. It is so ancient that the oldest manuscripts of the Greek Old Testament, which was the Bible used by the infant Greek-speaking Church, includes the Gloria in a book of scriptural songs and canticles. This most ancient of hymns is pure praise: "we praise you, we bless you, we adore you, we glorify you." This pure praise is followed by beautiful, intimate praise of Jesus: "you alone are the Holy One, you alone are the Lord...." It is the language of intimacy, the language of lovers. It is in praise to God that we move ourselves away from fixating on the *idea* of God to the *experience* of God. Singing *about* God and never singing *to* God is the musical equivalent of only knowing about God and not having any personal knowledge of God. Surely at least once in a while, during Holy Communion, we can sing to Jesus himself rather than singing about him or about "the banquet," or endlessly recommending that we eat the bread and drink the cup. The Eucharist is not an idea. It is not a thing. It is a person. It is Jesus himself, not *in* the sacrament but *as* the Blessed Sacrament.

To be clear, I am not advocating the use only of hymns of praise, or sung prayer (sometimes we sing petitions to God, still better than singing about God), but a return to giving the song of praise a preferential place in Catholic hymnody. It is hymns of praise that move the heart most and help lead those who gather into a personal encounter with Jesus. These are the true love songs, and of all the songs we hear, it is love songs that capture our hearts.

"Praise and Worship"

It is widely known that churches that are healthy and growing are Evangelical Protestant churches that have a strong preference for contemporary hymns of praise. They have produced a huge body of music in the contemporary style known as "praise and worship." There has been much debate in Catholic circles about whether these songs, once described to me as "a bunch of songs about me and Jesus that all sound the same," should be used by Catholics at all, never mind in the liturgy.

Musical preference aside, critics often point out that many of these hymns are overly individualistic, choosing "me" over "we," and tend towards sentimentality. While this is true of some, it is not, in my experience, true of all. The Psalms themselves suggest that there is an ancient tradition of speaking in the first person singular, even in communal worship. While there is a preference for the plural in our hymnody, I do not believe we have any grounds to exclude singular expressions of praise. Regarding the accusation of sentimentality, while some hymns are overly such, I would much rather sing a song with some sentiment than sing some of the sterile, idea-bound hymns of the last decades. Songs move the heart and not just the mind. Love songs are supposed to have sentiment. If the liturgy and our music are to have a missional dimension, our evaluation of music must always include the question of what speaks to the people we are attempting to reach. We live in a post-modern, hyper-individualist culture. Post-moderns do not want to sing about doctrine or theology. Abstractions do not attract them, but authenticity does. As individualists, they relate much better to hymns in the singular, as a sense of collective identity can never be presumed, and young people who do not go to church generally do not have playlists on their iPhones that feature organ music. All this points to the fact that the contemporary "praise and worship" style of music employed by so many churches today does speak powerfully to our culture.

As Catholics, we need to be careful about how we employ such music. An evangelical pastor once told me that he uses the "Brenda Principle" when it comes to evaluating the music sung in his church. When I asked him what that was, he said, "If you can remove the name of Jesus and replace it with 'Brenda,' and it works, it should not be used in church." This approach would address the concern about sentimentality!

Contemporary non-Catholic hymns should also always be reviewed for blatant theological problems. This is rare, and matters little to the average person in church, but the liturgy is the prayer of the Church and pastors must act as gatekeepers. This is becoming less and less of an issue, as many Catholic composers, such as Matt Maher, are writing "praise and worship" material that is gaining wide acceptance in Catholic and non-Catholic circles. In addition, there are a huge number of traditional Catholic hymns that can be successfully set to a contemporary style. There's

117

nothing quite like "O Come, O Come Emmanuel" when played by our 9:00 am band. It is ever ancient and ever new. As already stated, while lyrics that allow the congregation to sing with one voice as "we" are to be preferred, we do not need to be afraid of the occasional "I" and "my" in the great assembly. It is biblical, and it speaks to our age.

But Is It Any Good?

Lastly, when delving into the world of contemporary music, the question of quality must never be forgotten. We have already spoken of the role of beauty in music, and quality is related to this. The human mind and heart are drawn to quality, to things that are well done, and recognize them as beautiful. Contemporary music must be played well to be successful. This requires a level of competency and skill from musicians. It also demands a certain level of technical support so the music will sound right. In many Catholic churches, the sum total of sound monitoring is pushing the on/off button. We have this sense that sound takes care of itself, that it never has to be monitored or mixed and, really, is not that important.

In my previous parish, before we could move to introduce contemporary music, we had to address the fact that the sound system was the very same one that was installed when the church was built in 1959. You could not even plug a single acoustic guitar into the system without overloading it. It is frankly shocking just how sub-standard the audio systems are in most Catholic churches. I believe that installing, maintaining and operating a quality sound system that will highlight the spoken word and allow a full range of music is a better investment for a parish than hiring someone to run Sunday School classes. Hymns, homilies and hospitality are key to leveraging the weekend experience, and a proper sound system touches each of these dimensions.

Putting the V into the A/V

Using screens in churches is indirectly related to the issue of music and helping people feel part of things. When we installed a new sound system in my previous parish (a parish that was housed in two locations), we also installed large screens in both churches. When Saint Benedict Parish was being built, the architect designed the building to allow the use of screens during the liturgy. There is much discussion in Catholic circles about the use of such screens, but I am convinced they can be used in a way that not only respects the dignity and nature of the liturgy, but also adds to it and facilitates that "full, conscious and active" participation we've been aiming for.

Screens allow a diversity of music to be used in the liturgy (requiring that licensing fees be paid), they are cheaper than filling pews with expensive hymnbooks, and they increase participation. I have seen many teenagers in church who would never pick up a hymnbook become drawn to the screens. Even though some of them are not yet singing, at least they are reading the words. Screens also allow us to display some of the key responses in the liturgy and help us extend hospitality to those who may not be familiar with the prayers. Screens give us flexibility to include visual components in the homily, and announcements at the end of Mass.

Arguments that claim this is an innovation foreign to the liturgy do not hold much water. I am sure the same thing was said the first time an electric light or a microphone or even a hymnbook was used in the liturgy. Besides, what is a stained glass window if not a big screen to help people enter into the mystery of the Eucharist? Anyone who has ever entered a Baroque or Rococo (once described by a professor as "Baroque gone wild") church will have to admit that the entire interior of the church is one "big screen." It was also not uncommon in monasteries in the Middle Ages to have a very large hand-copied psalter placed in the monastic choir so that all the monks could sing the chants from one book, or one "big screen."

I have to be honest and say that I have seen some hideous examples of screen use in parishes. Let me offer some principles

119

to follow. The first non-negotiable must be that the screen cannot distract from the liturgy. The focus during the liturgy is threefold: the presider's chair, the ambo and the altar. Any use of screen technology must facilitate this focus and never take away from it. This influences many aspects of screen use, primarily physical placement. I do not believe there is any justification to place a permanent screen in the sanctuary, or even above the sanctuary, as is seen in many non-Catholic churches. The worst example of this I have ever seen was a church that had two big-screen TVs mounted on the wall behind the altar, on either side of the crucifix. Walking into that church was like walking into Best Buy or Future Shop. I'm not sure how they manage to read the Passion each year, especially when we are reminded that Jesus was crucified between two thieves. Screens need to be visible if they are to be of use, yet should not be in the sanctuary proper, but off to the side. This peripheral placement usually necessitates two screens, especially in large churches. Motorized screens, mounted against a wall, are to be preferred, so that outside of the liturgy, they are retracted and become invisible. Projectors should be mounted from the ceiling, so as not to be a distraction, not to mention out of safety concerns, so that no one trips on wires or cords. The physical placement of screens is one issue, but how the screens are used during the liturgy can also be a huge source of distraction.

First of all, please, please, please avoid the ugly white empty screen. This should never be seen by anyone less than 20 minutes before the liturgy. If a church commits to using screen technology, you cannot just use it for the words of a hymn or a prayer. It must be aesthetically pleasing. At Saint Benedict Parish, each week we design a slide that reflects the theme of that particular Sunday; this is the default slide that appears on the screen throughout the liturgy when nothing else is being shown. The theme slide will include the Sundays in Ordinary Time, and will contain a Scripture verse from one of the readings. This verse is carefully chosen and is usually the central theme of the homily (this verse is also on our outdoor electronic sign and is featured prominently in our weekly newsletter). The main focus of this slide is an image that reflects the week's theme. We often use sacred images that blend well with the décor of our church. The theme slides are attractive and provocative.

The background colour of our slides changes from green, to violet, to red or gold to reflect the liturgical season, and during the Eucharistic Prayer the theme slide gives way to a muted and simple Eucharistic symbol so as to minimize any possible distraction from what is taking place at the altar. Animated backgrounds of flowing waters and drifting clouds, sometimes featured in non-Catholic churches, are never used. Likewise, projecting images from a camera onto the screen could be justified only for those who could not otherwise see what is going on in the sanctuary. Even Saint Peter's Square uses screens in this way. We do make an exception to this rule when we baptize during the liturgy, so that those at the front of the church can see what is going on (our font is at the entrance of the church). It is obvious, then, that the decision to use screen technology in our churches is a bit like getting a puppy. They are wonderful and can add to our experience, but they are a lot of work. To install screens means committing to creating content each week and training a team of slide operators. The good news is that this work appeals to many people, young and old, in our parishes, and many will be willing to come forward and be trained in this technology.

Get to Work!

Earlier in this section, I spoke of the need to continue to work to invite our people to know the joy of praising God in song and not just being passive spectators. If we are to grow in this area, regardless of what style of music we use, we must teach and invite. At least once a year, I will preach a homily about the role of praising God in song, but almost every week I will either talk about or extend an invitation to grow in our praise of God. The word "liturgy" comes from the Greek *leitourgia*, and means "the work of the people." Coming to the liturgy means showing up for work.

We need to teach our people that when they stand mute and do not even mouth the words, they are not only not doing their share, but are also discouraging others around them.

Once when I was a seminarian, I was visiting a priest friend for the weekend. I attended the Saturday afternoon Mass at his church and had to bear the discomfort of being one of the only people singing besides the cantor. People were turning around to see who I was. It was not a very encouraging experience. I will never forget what happened at the end of Mass. The priest announced that it was the birthday of one of the altar servers, and the entire congregation spontaneously broke into rousing rendition of "Happy Birthday." I was stunned, but gained a valuable insight that day. Many people in church do not refrain from singing because they cannot sing, or are unwilling to sing, but because they do not know how to sing to God. There are many reasons for this. As mentioned in the previous chapter, perhaps many of them did not know the "joy of salvation," so there was no song in their hearts to be sung. Perhaps this problem was compounded by the type of hymns being used. Either way, we need to acknowledge this and help and encourage our people to sing praise to God.

Often in the liturgy I will take time to invite our people to enter into a particular hymn. At the beginning of Mass, once I reach the presider's chair, if we are singing a hymn of praise and it looks as if half of the church is attending a ventriloquist convention, I will invite the congregation to go back and sing a refrain again. It is important to do this in a way that is not seen as a rebuke spoken in frustration, but as a joyful invitation to "taste and see." It is a word of encouragement, a reminder to be mindful of breaking an age-old habit, and an invitation to prepare our hearts to enter into the worship of the Eucharist. I will sometimes do the same thing as the gifts are placed on the altar or after Holy Communion, when a simple repetitive refrain can be prayerfully sung without a need to look at the screens. This invitation to experience the praise of God generally only works, of course, if we are singing hymns of praise.

4. Homilies

"Woe to me if I do not proclaim the gospel!"
(1 Corinthians 9:16)

We come to the third of the *h*'s. In *Evangelii Gaudium*, Pope Francis made what may be the first official papal joke in writing when he described the state of preaching in the Catholic Church. He said that both the laity and "their ordained ministers suffer because of homilies: the laity from having to listen to them and the clergy from having to preach them!" Sadly, this is often true. Saint Paul says that "faith comes from what is heard, and what is heard comes through the word of Christ." (Romans 10:17) It is the call to faith through the proclamation of God's word that leads those who hear and accept it to the "obedience of faith." (Romans 1:5) The word "obedience" in Greek, *hupakoe*, literally means to be "under hearing."

Preaching is a huge part of the ministry of the priest, and today, more and more, non-liturgical preaching is an essential part of a variety of ministries in the average parish. We need to learn to do this well and give it the best we have. We must remember our context, however. After the theological wars of the sixteenth century, the Protestant Reformers reacted to what they considered to be an underemphasis on the Word of God and preaching. After the Reformation, the sacrament–Word duel continued with the Council of Trent's reaffirmation of the centrality of the sacraments in the life of the Church. (This was, of course, a false opposition. It should never have been an either/or question: both the sacraments and the Word are central.) As a result, solid biblical preaching was not a strong characteristic of the modern Catholic Church and, even 50 years after the Second Vatican Council, we still struggle to implement the clear guidelines laid out by the Council fathers.

Banquet or Fast Food?

As we approach the task of preaching, we must keep in mind that the Word of God is a banquet and not fast food. "Long" and "short" are relative terms and need to be discerned in light of our own church cultures and practices. Not a few jokes were aimed in my direction after the publication of *Evangelii Gaudium* when it came to Pope Francis' comments that homilies should be "brief." I was quick to retort that Pope Francis was saying that the homily should not take the form of a speech or lecture, and that his definition of long was a whole hour!

> A preacher may be able to hold the attention of his listeners for a whole hour, but in this case his words become more important than the celebration of the faith. (EG, no. 138)

I preach on Sundays for fifteen to 20 minutes, and I make no apology for this. The ministry of preaching is key, and we should take it seriously. It's the biggest bang for our buck in ministry and we need to do it well. I do not believe that the people in our pews who are truly hungry for God's Word can get enough nourishment for the week ahead of them if they are only being served up five-minute homiletic hors d'oeuvres. A commitment to more robust and intentional preaching will be favourably received by those who are hungry, but there will be pushback from those who have no hunger. In all of our churches, a portion of the congregation would rejoice if we announced that we were committing to five-minute Sunday homilies. They would rejoice even more if we announced that we were doing away with the homily altogether. But the task of the shepherd is to feed the sheep, and I do not believe the servings for all should be measured by what the non-hungry sheep will receive. From some quarters in the various parishes I have served in, there is almost a sense that the homily is an intrusive add-on to be endured rather than an essential part of the liturgy, and draws out the time it takes to receive Holy Communion and be on one's way.

Perhaps if we paid more attention to the style and content of preaching we could make the homily less of an endurance test and more of a joyous feast of faith. Pope Francis has over and over again reminded us of the centrality of the kerygma, or first proclamation. He reminds the Church in *Evangelii Gaudium* that it is called "first" "not because it exists at the beginning and can then be forgotten or replaced by some other more important things." (EG, no. 164) Preaching, then, will always be Christocentric and evangelical. Saint Paul said, "we proclaim Christ crucified." (1 Corinthians 1:23) Every homily, no matter the setting – Sunday, weekday, wedding or funeral – ought to preach Jesus Christ, his death and resurrection, and the new life found in him through a life of faith, hope and love. Every time we preach, there should be a clear enunciation of this and an invitation to respond to the one who said, "Come to me, all you that are weary and are carrying heavy burdens, and I will give you rest." (Matthew 11:28) In this way, those who hear can be led to that necessary personal encounter with Jesus, which is the starting point of being his disciple.

When we preach, we need to be intentional about speaking to the entire person – mind, heart, conscience and will. Our liturgical and non-liturgical preaching should be intelligent and informative, but not come across as an academic lecture. Preachers will always have to resist the temptation to show how smart they are or to demonstrate all the big words they learned while studying theology. Exegesis should be the foundation of our preaching, and foundations are always hidden. This is a real struggle for us in the Church today, as a result of poor formation in seminaries and schools of theology. These places of formation are academic institutions where one course on preaching, often given by an academic who has little pastoral experience, is but one of about 40 theology courses that will be a part of a priest's training. Seminarians are formed for four to five years, listening to homilies every day given by professors in a hyper-intellectualized environment. It is no wonder, then, that homilies tend to come across as dry and boring to the average churchgoing Catholic. I have often joked that a seminary preaching course could be entitled "Introduction to Boring Preaching" and that the advanced course would be called "How to Put Your Congregation to Sleep in Five Minutes."

Preaching to the Whole Person

Someone once said that one of the greatest distances in the universe is the 8 to 10 inches from the brain stem to the heart. We are very much children of the Enlightenment and are often more at home in the head than in the heart, with the idea of something rather than the reality itself. When asked about the greatest commandment in the Gospels, Jesus refers to the famous passage in Deuteronomy known as the *Shema*: "You shall love the Lord your God with all your heart, and with all your soul, and with all your might." (Deuteuronomy 6:4-5) What is interesting is that in none of the synoptic Gospels (Matthew, Mark and Luke) is the passage quoted as is. In Mark's Gospel, we hear that we are to love God with all of our heart, soul, *mind* and strength. In Matthew, we are to love God with just heart, soul and mind, and Luke gives us the order of heart, soul, strength, mind. We can conclude that while Jesus gives new emphasis to the role of the mind, the heart is first when it comes to love. This is something we already know. This is how it works in any relationship and should be so in our relationship with God.

To speak to the heart means seeking to move people emotionally. We have hungry, restless hearts, and they cry out to be given the rest that only God can give. It is Good News we preach, so the one emotion that should be experienced through our preaching is joy! I always ask myself, and others, if people are experiencing what I say as Good News, no matter how challenging my preaching may be. An indication of whether our people are experiencing joy at what they hear is the presence of smiles or laughter. This is the most human reaction to any good news. I believe that a mark of a good homily is if the people have laughed at least once. The Good News is joyful, life is funny, and there are many great jokes or funny stories that can occasionally be employed by a preacher, providing they have some bearing on the theme of the homily. When people laugh, something happens biochemically in the brain – they relax and become more positively disposed to what you have to say. I think the people of my parish have figured out that if they are laughing a lot at the beginning of a homily, there is probably a difficult and challenging message about to come.

We hear in the second chapter of the Acts of the Apostles that Saint Peter preached a very challenging homily – which began, by the way, with a joke about not being drunk, as it was only 9:00 a.m. At the end of this bold and daring proclamation, or kerygma, in which he told the people, "you crucified and killed [Jesus] by the hands of those outside the law" (Acts 2:23), Saint Luke, who wrote Acts, tells us that Peter's hearers were "cut to the heart." (Acts 2:37) This post-Pentecost sermon is a wonderful example of speaking to the conscience. Peter spoke a difficult message. He was specific about what he wanted people to know. They were convicted and it led them to ask the question "What should we do?" If we are truly to speak to the whole person, we cannot stop at the mind and the heart, but must seek to cut into the heart as well, so that it leads to action. In this, the preacher also speaks to the will, as fruitful preaching will lead people to make a decision, a choice.

To preach to the conscience and the will, preachers must know exactly what they want their hearers to know and what they want them to do. If the preacher does not know this, neither will the people, and the homily will be a nonsensical accumulation of un-related ideas that will not be improved by even the funniest story.

I have found that using Twitter has helped me focus my preaching. I usually communicate the content of my homilies in two tweets: one that sums up the core message of my homily (what I want people to know), and one that describes "what should we do." If I cannot communicate these ideas in 140 characters each, then I, and those who will have to listen to me, am in trouble. If the core message of a homily cannot be summarized in one sen-tence, it probably should not be given. Creating a one-sentence summary is the first thing I do when I begin to build a homily. It is the fruit of reflection and prayer that took place throughout the week, and becomes the centre of the homily-building process.

The What and the How

Pope Francis reminded us in *Evangelii Gaudium* that it is not enough to know "what ought to be said"; the preacher must also be intentional about "*how* it should be said." (EG, no. 156) This is especially true for a difficult message that needs to be preached. The first rule of thumb is always to preach in love. In Ephesians 4:15, Saint Paul says that it is in "speaking the truth in love" that we grow in every way into Christ. If we translate this passage literally, it would read "truthing in love." English does not have the verb "to truth." But we can speak the truth, live the truth or tell the truth, and all of these must be done in love.

Preachers must pay strict attention to their own emotional state when preparing to preach, lest they speak out of frustration or anger. This is deadly. Difficult or challenging truths must be spoken of only out of love – a concrete love for the people themselves, not a love for an abstracted truth. Pope Francis speaks beautifully to this task in *Evangelii Gaudium* (no. 140), where he points out that "the dialogue between the Lord and his people," which is the homily, "should be encouraged by the closeness of the preacher, the warmth of his tone of voice, the unpretentiousness of his manner of speaking [and] the joy of his gestures." He then goes on to reflect on his conviction that what helped people receive Jesus' challenging message was the way he looked at them while he spoke. He looked at them with love, "seeing beyond their weaknesses and failings," and never with judgment or frustration.

The key to speaking about Jesus like this is found in the experience of Jesus speaking to us like this. Pope Francis tells us that "what is essential is that the preacher be certain that God loves him, that Jesus Christ has saved him and that his love has always the last word." (EG, no. 151) Before any preacher can afflict the comfortable or comfort the afflicted, he himself must be afflicted and comforted by the same Word. This is the full meaning of the Word of God being a "two-edged sword" (Hebrews 4:12): it cuts both ways. Those who would dare wield this sword to cut others must first be cut themselves.

When the preacher is cut first, he will preach as one who first hears and believes, before helping others hear and believe. The homily will always be about "we" and "us" and never just about "you." This yielding to the blade of God's Word is *the* most important step in preparing to preach; it demands time in prayer, wrestling with the Word and the core message that must be preached. I have found in my own life that this prayer in preparation for preaching has been my most fruitful. It can be exhausting. How many times have I opened the Lectionary and thought, "Oh no! I hate that reading." Those are usually my best homilies, because they involve my resubmission to an element of Scripture that I find particularly challenging. At these moments, I am profoundly aware that the first person I am preaching to is myself. Pope Francis agrees:

> Yet if he [the preacher] does not take time to hear God's word with an open heart, if he does not allow it to touch his life, to challenge him, to impel him, and if he does not devote time to pray with that word, then he will indeed be a false prophet, a fraud, a shallow imposter. (EG, no. 151)

Ouch!

This vulnerability to the double-edged sword of the Word of God cannot only be present during the preparation process, but should also be evident in the preaching. Pope Paul VI said that our contemporaries no longer listen to teachers, but to witnesses. People desire authenticity. The first question our people are asking when we begin a homily is this: Is he real? If there is any hint that we are not being authentic in our preaching, or are hiding something, or are using the homily as a kind of safe intellectual exercise, our words will not penetrate. Our preaching may be informative but it will not be transformative.

Be Real

We must communicate what the text speaks to us: that we are challenged by it, that we struggle with it, and not speak as if we have it all together. Being vulnerable and real with our people should involve telling the occasional personal story to illustrate a point. This helps people to know (hopefully) that we are real and believable. We should be careful, however, and not overdo this. Referring to ourselves is a necessary rhetorical device in our present climate, a means to better preach the saving message of God's love revealed in Jesus. We preach to lead our people to Jesus, not to ourselves.

Early in my life as a priest, I learned another very important aspect of what it means to be authentic and honest when preaching. It was a Friday afternoon during my first months as a priest. I was late for 5:15 Mass and was not properly prepared for the five-minute homily I would give. I winged it. The next week, I received an anonymous letter from someone who had been at that Mass. This man had been away from the Church for years. That Friday afternoon was his first time back. He noted, although not in an angry way, that I had obviously been rushed, distracted and unprepared. He said that this experience of Mass did not encourage him at all to return to the Church. What made this situation more tragic was that the Mass that day had been offered for the repose of the soul of his recently deceased mother. As you can imagine, I was cut to the heart. The answer to the question "What should I do?" was obvious: be honest, be genuine, be authentic, be vulnerable, and never try to fake it.

Why had I been late that day? That afternoon, I had been working at the local hospital, visiting patients. I had gotten caught up in a pastoral visit and lost track of the time. As I backed out of the hospital's underground parking lot, I ran the entire length of my new car along a concrete pillar, ripping off my front bumper in the process. I was almost sick to my stomach over this. Between car payments and student loan payments, how was I to pay thousands of dollars for repairs? This what was on my mind when, ten minutes later, I arrived the sanctuary to begin Mass. I know I could have been excused for being distracted, but what was inexcusable was that I proceeded to celebrate Mass and preach as if nothing had happened. I tried to fake it and did not succeed.

Some Tips

Here are a few other tips to help preachers give their message meaning and impact. These may not apply to every reader of this book, but you may find something relevant to your ministry.

• Get maximum input for your homily preparation

Theologian Karl Barth once said that preachers should prepare their preaching with the Bible in one hand and the newspaper in the other. Current news stories are always on people's minds, especially those that reveal existential questions, such as natural disasters like earthquakes or typhoons, great evils such as school shootings or 9/11, moral failure or heroism. Pope Francis reminds preachers in *Evangelii Gaudium* to not seek to answer questions that people are not asking. The news evokes questions, and preachers must be aware of the issues their people bring with them. When we fail to address the obvious, we affirm a suspicion that we are ungrounded and otherworldly. Another way to get a sense of the questions being asked is to hear from parishioners. Every week at our staff meetings, we take time to reflect on the readings for the following Sunday; in many instances, one of these gems ended up at the centre of my homily.

• Remember to preach on what has been proclaimed

Preach the Scriptures, and preach the Scriptures that have been proclaimed that week. Do not preach on the previous week's readings, or the version from Luke because you prefer it to Matthew's (I've heard this done). Do not preach on movies, or novels, or sports or the news. These can assist the point of the homily, or be the occasion of a particular focus, but we must always bring the Scriptures of the day to bear.

• Start with a hook and land the d*** plane

This is about the opening and closing of a homily. If a preacher can do this well, much will be forgiven. The opening sentence of a homily is the only chance we have to make a good first impression. Have a catchy, strong opening that connects with life experience in some way. Tell a story or ask a sudden question: "Do you remember where you were when...?" "Have you ever...?"

The ending is all about landing the plane. Once when I was on a flight back to Halifax, we came into land on a really windy afternoon. The plane was about a hundred feet from the ground when all of a sudden the engines kicked in and the plane turned back to the skies. We had to circle for another 40 minutes before the speed of the wind dropped and we were cleared for landing. It reminded me of some homilies I have heard over the years. Land the plane. Do not give the impression of coming into land and then take off again. A good ending can be strengthened by a judicial use of an *inclusio* (ending with a reference to the hook story/image you used at the beginning), but use it sparingly and don't become too predictable. When I prepare a homily, my opening and closing is often the last part of the building process.

- Go text free

One time when I spoke about the time I take to prepare a homily, a parishioner, with genuine surprise, looked at me and said, "You prepare them? I thought you just got up there and did it." I wasn't sure whether to take this as a compliment or an insult. Anyone who has ever prepared to give a homily without a fixed text knows that it takes a great deal of work to make it look like you are just winging it. The extra work is worth it, as our people experience that they are truly entering into a dialogue, rather than listening to a monologue. Even an unpolished homily, delivered without constantly gazing at a text, is much more engaging than the most brilliant oration that is read out loud. Most of my preaching is text free. It is much more exciting and nerve-racking than the safety of a text. I still get nervous before I preach, because as much as I prepare, each time I give the same homily it comes out a little differently. To be sure, there are times when I have used a text, but I limit these to preaching on controversial subjects or at a difficult funeral. There is definitely a case to be made for precision in particular circumstances. When I preach without a text, I generally have a series of simple speaking points that help me stay on track.

- Humble yourself

Approach the task of preaching with fear and trembling (literally), but believe that God is going to use you. As I process to the ambo to proclaim the Gospel, or as I listen to the Gospel being read by the deacon, I always pray the same prayer, over and over again. It usually goes something like this: "Lord, help me not to be a total idiot. Use me. Come, Holy Spirit. Let me get out of your way. Let my only motive be your glory and the building up of your kingdom." I believe and have experienced that God always honours this prayer.

There is a story told from my native land of Scotland of a young minister who walked into his church and approached the pulpit, very sure of himself, if not with a slight air of arrogance. He proceeded to massacre his sermon and withdrew at the end of the service with embarrassment. An old man on the way out said to him, "If ye'd have come in the way ye went oot, you'd have gone oot the way ye came in." When I was a lowly seminarian, the late Bishop James Mahoney of Saskatoon paid us a visit and told a story I will never forget. He told us that one Sunday at the cathedral, he had been preaching what he thought was a very good and powerful homily. After Mass, a young man, visibly moved, came up to him and said that hearing the homily had been a life-changing experience. Naturally curious, the bishop asked which part of the homily had touched him so. The young man replied, "Well, I don't really remember what you were saying, but at one point you said, 'That's the end of the first part of my homily; now I want to move to the second part.' When you said this I just knew that my old life was over and I had to begin anew."

- Don't believe your fans

"Nice homily, Father." It is a refrain heard at the doors of almost any Catholic church as the faithful head for their cars. I once had a little old lady say this to me – and I hadn't even given the homily! The Second Vatican Council told us that the task of preaching the Word of God is the first task of the ordained priest. As with any profession, we can never stop trying to improve. Every preacher can become better. Simple techniques and skills can be used even by preachers who, although they may have the office or task of preaching, may not necessarily have the charism or gift of preaching. Have a group of parishioners who will give you brutally honest feedback about your preaching. Listen to recordings of your preaching. Video yourself. You may be surprised at what you see and what you hear. If secular professions can strive for growth and improvement, how much more should we who have been tasked to proclaim the saving message of Jesus strive to improve.

- Screen your homilies

Many would say that we now exist in a post-aural culture. We are audio-visual learners. We will refrain from entering the discussion of whether this is a positive development. It's just the way it is. It is unthinkable that a lecturer would present anywhere these days and not have something on a screen. No executive would make a presentation to her board without the requisite PowerPoint or Keynote presentation. Young people are constantly stimulated by visuals through their hours in front of a television, computer or smartphone screen. Why then would we not seek to do the same thing when communicating the greatest story and the best news of all?

At Saint Benedict Parish, I prepare eight to ten slides to accompany my homily. I do not use them every week, as I think it best not to become predictable. I preach in what could best be described as a "Ted Talk" style, using the keynotes sparingly. My slides tend to be minimalistic, often containing a single word, phrase or image. At times I may even use a short video clip that assists in delivering my message. I realize that this may drive some liturgists mad, but I will call Saint Paul to my defense: he said, "I have become all things to all people, that I might by all means save some." (1 Corinthians 9:22) It has amazed me to hear parishioners say how much this visual aid helps them – and especially their children – to remember the message of the homily. These images and words serve as great prompts and can also help the preacher get away from using a text.

- Avoid the stand-alones

I really believe that we need to be much more intentional about interconnecting homilies in a parish. Too often our preaching is like those TV shows that have totally independent plots each week. They happen at the same time, in the same place and with the same characters, but are totally unrelated. Our preaching should be consciously building upon previous homilies and be more like TV shows that have a continuous building narrative throughout all the episodes, like *24*, *The Walking Dead*, *Homeland* or *Downton Abbey* – but definitely not like *Lost*.

In parishes with more than one preacher on a given weekend, the homily should not just be the homily for that particular person. It should be the homily that the parish as a whole needs. Preachers need to communicate with one another and agree about what they want people to know and do. The pastor especially needs to preach programmatic homilies on a regular basis that speak about the vision, the plan and the strategy of the parish. He needs to address questions such as where we are going, why we are changing and why we are doing what we're doing. The occasional use of a four-week series that is planned in advance to address particular pastoral concerns can be a real help. The challenge with these, however, is respecting the integrity of the Lectionary.

- Have fun

Lastly, and quite simply, love and enjoy what you do. If it is onerous and unpleasant for you, it will also be so for the people who have to listen to you.

5. Meaningful Community

> Now the whole group of those who believed were of one
> heart and soul. (Acts 4:32)

It was the end of a Saturday evening Mass, and, as I left the entrance of the church to go to the sacristy (located behind the sanctuary), I noticed a young woman sitting in a pew by herself. She seemed upset. When I emerged from the sacristy, ready to go home, she was still there. I went over to her and sat beside her and waited. Eventually, she lifted her head and began to tell me her story. She was a doctoral student at one of the universities within the parish boundaries. She was overcome with stress and anxiety about writing her thesis and had not been eating properly or sleeping. She seemed close to some kind of emotional and physical collapse. Her family lived in a different province and she was alone in the city. I scrambled to think of what I could do to help. I had to be somewhere within half an hour, and it was one of those things I could not miss. I made a phone call to Karen, a young woman in the parish who was also a doctoral student and who lived a block from the church. Thankfully, Karen was home. We quickly concocted a plan – I would drop this young woman off at Karen's before heading to my appointment. Within minutes of arriving at Karen's home, the young woman was sitting in a rocking chair smothered in a blanket, a cup of tea in her hand. While supper simmered on the stove, Karen took out her harp and began to play a beautiful soothing melody.

I will never forget that day. What struck me about this experience was the contrast between the two responses to this person in distress. A relatively full church had emptied out around a person who was visibly in need of help. Those who had lingered in the church after Mass would have seen her, but no one approached her. I do not write this as a reproach, because I do not believe that the issue was that no one cared. I knew some of the people, and they are caring people. Rather, their behaviour was shaped by an attitude that often hinders our ability in the Church to form meaningful community: "it's none of my business."

"Am I my brother's keeper?" (Genesis 4:9)

Experiences such as these beg a question of us whenever we use the term "Christian community" to describe our parishes. Christian community? Really? Does the gathering of a group of often isolated and anonymous individuals under the same roof for an hour constitute a community? I think not. Authentic community is a place where we are known and loved. It is a place where we find others to whom we are accountable and who are accountable to us. This is the heart of Christian community, of *koinonia*, the Greek word that can be translated as "fellowship." When I first arrived at Saint Benedict Parish, I knew immediately that the question of authentic community was going to be a huge challenge. I had never had oversight of such a large parish – large, at least, by Nova Scotian standards, with an average weekly attendance of 2,000 people over four Masses. Someone once said that the larger you are, the smaller you have to become. This is a real advantage that smaller parishes have over larger ones. In the very first months, I began to speak in homilies about Christian community. On one weekend I reminded the people of the words of the theme music for the TV show *Cheers*. I showed the *Cheers* sign on the screens and played a snippet of the refrain.

Sometimes you want to go
Where everybody knows your name
And they're always glad you came
You want to be where you can see
Troubles are all the same
You want to be where everybody
Knows your name.

Is this not the foundation of any human community? If so, how much more should it be true of the Christian community? The following week, a parishioner gave me a small plastic *Cheers* sign that played the refrain when you pressed a button on the side. I keep it in my briefcase and always bring it out to play when I give talks or presentations on community. Everybody recognizes it, and some even sing along.

We have been talking about values in this chapter. Remember that values are manifested by what we do and not by what we say. If visitors from outer space, or from a very different culture, were to come and observe our behaviour, what would they see? What would they conclude? At the end of Mass the priest or deacon says, "Go in peace, glorifying the Lord by your life." He might as well say, "On your marks, get set, go!" The mad dash for the parking lot might lead one to conclude that someone had shouted, "Fire!" or that there was a prize for the first person out.

In the early months of my time at Saint Benedict, at a Saturday evening Mass, I was once overtaken by a little old lady with a cane and dozens of her followers as I processed out. What can be concluded about such behaviour? One could be excused for thinking that most people just could not wait to get out of there. This feeling is tangible at the end of most Masses. When the priest says, "Let us pray," after Holy Communion, listen carefully and you will hear the sound of jingling car keys being made ready for the escape. If the Christian community is to be a place where everyone knows your name, we seem to say to one another, "I don't want to know your name, I don't really care if you came, your troubles are your own problem, now get out of my way."

Several years ago, my Archbishop, Anthony Mancini, wrote a beautiful pastoral letter on the New Evangelization. He addressed this question of community: "The church cannot be a collection of individual believers practicing their faith in private, satisfied with their self-sufficiency." The truth is that the Church can be this, has been this and, sadly, often is this. When the Church is such a sign of contradiction to its own nature, it is a sick and dying Church. If the renewal of our Church is to take place, the question of community will be essential.

Belonging

Social scientists tell us that today, the question of belonging and loneliness is far more crucial than in the past. Fifty years ago, the cultural landscape was very different than it is today.

Fifty years ago, there was still a strong sense of communal morality and social mores. People knew how they were supposed to behave. Most people knew exactly what they were to believe. Sometimes communities were literally divided along belief lines. To mix with the "other" could literally mean crossing the tracks. Fifty years ago, if you behaved properly and believed correctly, you could belong. How things have changed. We now live in a hyper-individualistic post-modern culture. Gen Xers, the generation after the Baby Boomers, and Millennials, or Gen Ys, those born after the early 80s, will not behave in any particular manner just because it is what they are supposed to do. Most people today will behave in a particular way only if it lines up with their personal beliefs. Appeals to authority or tradition hold no water for these generations.

When it comes to believing, a similar dynamic can be observed. Belief systems are of little value. There is no sense of obligation to anything beyond the individual and his or her own personal – and private – beliefs. Most people today are not compelled by a quest for truth, and are largely uninterested in doctrine or any proposal that presents a systematic, comprehensive worldview. Most people today neither join, stay or leave a Church because of belief or doctrine. While this may be distressing to many of us, we must recognize that this is our new reality, and this is the character of a generation to which we are called to bring the Gospel. Most people join, stay and leave churches not because of belief, but because of a sense of belonging, because of community. The old order of behaving-believing-belonging has been reversed. Many are willing to change their lifestyles and behaviours, but only if they truly believe it for themselves. Beliefs are changed not by preaching and teaching, but by building trust through relationships, through caring, through belonging.

The implications of this new reality for us as a Church are huge. First, the state of community in the average parish is an enormous liability when we attempt to attract a younger generation. Second, we must recognize that our pastoral approach is almost universally shaped by the older behave-believe-belong paradigm. How then can we transform the culture of our parish to begin to live out a belong-believe-behave model? Are we ready and willing as a Church to provide opportunities for a real and authentic experience of belonging for those who do not believe what we believe, or do not behave as we believe they should? How will we do this if the only time we gather as a community is at the Eucharist, which by its very nature demands a certain measure of believing and behaving before full belonging can happen? It is the age-old question of whether we are willing to go out to the highways and byways and welcome the "good" and the "bad." It is about going to the margins and the marginalized and shattering the "private club" mentality that is present in most parishes, which are for those who believe the same things and act the same way.

If we get this right, the question then becomes this: "Are we willing to provide experiences of belonging for those who do not *yet* believe, and do not *yet* behave? It is the traditional distinction between the *lex gradualitatis* and the *gradualitas legis*, the "law of gradualness" versus the "gradualness of the law." This was a term used in the pastoral discipline of moral theology. It means that, while we stand by our moral code, our sense of right and wrong, we also stand by the person who is gradually moving, changing and transforming. We love that person into the Kingdom, into the Church, and onto the journey of discipleship. This is a gradual process that cannot be defined or confined, and we must be ready to walk with each person as they move from an experience of community, to reframing their belief systems, to allowing the Lord to change their lives (belonging-believing-behaving).

Evangelii Gaudium tells us that "The Church must be a place of mercy freely given, where everyone can feel welcomed, loved, forgiven and encouraged to live the good life of the Gospel." (EG, no. 114) As I reflect on this truth, it seems almost self-evident now after years in priestly ministry. I must admit that I cringe when I think back on many pastoral situations when I was a young priest ministering out of a behave-believe-belong mindset. I think of the young couples who came to see me for marriage preparation who neither belonged, believed or behaved, and where did I begin? By hammering on their behaviour. They were living together; they were not going to church. No matter how gently or lovingly I did this, for those who had no sense of belief, let alone belonging, it yielded very little fruit.

Beginning with behaviour adjustment was also at the root of my past attempts to labour for the renewal of the parishes in which I served. I was convinced that if I just preached enough homilies on the need to grow spiritually, to serve in ministry and put more in the collection, and if I just provided enough opportunities for parishioners to take programs to help them change their behaviour, then it would all work. I was convinced that if we could just get the right books with the right information into our catechism classes, then we would witness the transformation of belief. After years of working myself into the ground, with a few exceptions, I saw the same 10 to 15% of parishioners taking advantage of these opportunities for growth, and the same 85 to 90% remaining in the pews, unchanged. In the remainder of this section, I will look at some practices and tools that we have employed at Saint Benedict to address this question of meaningful community.

Alpha

I have been a huge supporter of Alpha since I first ran it in my parish in 2001. Remember the story about card socials that I spoke of in the Introduction? After doing the course, I knew that it worked. The hungry were fed, the lukewarm were brought to life, and non-churchgoers and even non-believers were coming to faith in Jesus and returning to church. People were eager to begin serving in ministry, they were hungry for more, the Mass was coming to life for them and the collection was going up! I had never experienced that kind of discipleship fruit from any investment of time and energy in pastoral ministry. It was able to speak and touch people from a variety of backgrounds and levels of faith. How could it do this so successfully? What made this

141

program so different? I was keenly aware that this tool presented the first proclamation in a compelling way, but so did many other programs. On the surface, Alpha is a ten-session process that introduces the Christian faith. Each evening begins with a shared meal, or some experience of shared food, in a relaxed environment. Then there is a talk on some aspect of the first proclamation, the kerygma. After the talk there is a substantial amount of time devoted to small groups of eight to ten guests with at least two leaders. The purpose of the small groups is not to teach, but to listen and facilitate discussion among the guests.

A look under the hood of Alpha reveals that the secret to its success is that it embraces the belong-believe-behave approach to evangelization. It is perfectly suited for the post-modern mindset. The first goal of Alpha is to create a warm, welcoming, non-threatening, non-pressurized and non-judgmental environment where guests are loved and accepted unconditionally. They are given permission, by word and example, to be authentic and real. No one will correct them for their unorthodox (or even crazy) beliefs, their doubts or their struggles. There will be no judgment about their lifestyles. Through the ten-week process, trust begins to build as meals are shared and participants experience being listened to in small groups. As the sense of belonging grows, they begin to let down their guard and receive the message of the talks. At this point, the truth of Jesus and his Gospel begins to knock on the door of their hearts, and by the end of the ten weeks, the process has led many of them to a personal encounter with Jesus and to a decision to follow him. What happens after this transformation of belief is a total re-evaluation of lifestyle and behaviour, as the journey of discipleship begins.

I have been running Alpha in all my parishes since 2001, and I am even more convinced than ever that it is the most effective tool I have found to date. There may be another, but I have not yet found it. I have seen all my parishes transformed by placing Alpha at the centre of our evangelistic efforts, and have even expanded the use of Alpha in my present parish. At Saint Benedict, we are clear that Alpha is not just one of many programs we use, but that it is foundational to our identity as a missional and evangelizing Church. We recently concluded eight different Alphas running concurrently, with over 350 guests, about a third of whom are non-churchgoers. We host daytime Alphas, Friday night Alphas, Thursday night Alphas, Pub Alpha, Sushi Alpha (we take over an entire sushi restaurant), Youth Alpha in the parish and in the local public high school, Alpha in a community centre, Alpha by the Hearth (in homes), and Alpha in a prison. All these courses are run by our parishioners, many of whom have experienced conversion and transformation through their own experience of Alpha. We have a veritable army of evangelizers successfully using this program to create a profound sense of belonging so that guests may hear and receive the Good News of Jesus Christ. To find out more about this, visit alpha.org/catholics.

Pope Francis, through his teaching in *Evangelii Gaudium*, would support the Alpha approach: "All this demands on the part of the evangelizer certain attitudes which foster openness to the message: approachability, readiness for dialogue, patience, a warmth and welcome which is non-judgmental." (EG, no. 165) In spite of this affirmation of the style of evangelization, in some Catholic circles two common objections are raised about using Alpha as a tool for fulfilling the mandate of Jesus. The first is that the course content is limited and leaves out essential aspects of Church teaching. The second is that this course originated in a non-Catholic context and is used by a wide variety of Christians of all expressions and flavours, and that it will to lead to confusion for Catholics.

I have already commented on the need for the kerygma or first proclamation to be clearly articulated, heard and responded to before authentic evangelization can take place. It is therefore necessary to separate the kerygma from the *didache*, the "teaching" or catechesis. Once again, *Evangelii Gaudium* supports this:

Pastoral ministry in a missionary style is not obsessed with the disjointed transmission of a multitude of doctrines to be insistently imposed. When we adopt a pastoral goal and a missionary style which would actually reach everyone without exception or exclusion, the message has to concentrate on the essentials, on what is most beautiful, most grand, most appealing and at the same time most necessary. The message is simplified, while losing none of its depth and truth, and thus becomes all the more forceful and convincing. (EG, no. 35)

Lastly, in the mind of this pope, the ecumenical base that Alpha enjoys is not in any way a liability, but something that will enhance the effectiveness of our efforts:

If we [all Christians] concentrate on the convictions we share, and if we keep in mind the principle of the hierarchy of truths, we will be able to progress decidedly towards common expressions of proclamation, service and witness. The immense numbers of people who have not received the Gospel of Jesus Christ cannot leave us indifferent. Consequently, commitment to a unity which helps them to accept Jesus Christ can no longer be a matter of mere diplomacy or forced compliance, but rather an indispensable path to evangelization. (EG, no. 246)

Sunday Morning

Alpha is a door through which many people can begin to walk the path of discipleship. We offer a wide assortment of catechetical programs to those who have completed Alpha so they can continue their formation and journey towards maturity. Sooner or later, a church that runs Alpha will experience a tipping point when a substantial number of parishioners have been touched by the experience. When this happens, the experience of Sunday Eucharist will begin to change. I would like to speak about three specific changes we introduced to our Sunday Eucharist that, in effect, were an attempt to move a little bit of Alpha from the basement into the sanctuary.

a. Name Tag Sunday

Yes, it is what you think. Name tags for two thousand people! We do this once a month. Parishioners bring their own name tags with them and we set up tables in the foyer where people who didn't bring one can write their name on paper name tags before they enter the church. One of the parishioners inspired me to do this. During my first months at Saint Benedict, I received word that a particular lady was a little upset with me. When I eventually spoke to her, she told me why. "At the end of Mass, you always greet my husband by name, but you never call me by name." I knew exactly who she was. She was Fred's wife, and the reason I knew she was Fred's wife is because Fred wore the same jacket to Mass every week, a jacket that had his name emblazoned on the shoulder. Just like the Cheers theme song says, we really do have a deep desire to go where people know our names.

I am a realist. I know that it is fundamentally socially and psychologically impossible to have warm and fuzzy feelings for 600 people in church. We cannot have meaningful connections with everybody, or know everybody's name, but we can try. We can at least do something about it to show that it really is of value to us, no matter how poorly we may be doing it. We want to go to war with the notion of anonymous Christianity. So everybody gets a name tag once a month.

It has been over three years now since we began this initiative. Resistance has been minimal. In fact, on the very first weekend we did this, I was sure that the usual flow of complaints and anonymous letters would arrive on Monday morning. I received only two complaints, and both were lamenting the fact that we were not going to do this every week. Although we could never know everybody's name, with at least 2,500 regularly attending parishioners (not everyone attends every week), most parishioners do go to the same Mass every week and most sit in the very same pews. As creatures of habit, it is very reasonable that even at Sunday Eucharist we can begin to break through the wall of anonymity and take the first step towards building meaningful community.

b. Prayer Partners at Mass

Since it is the only time the entire community gathers, I have struggled to use the limited time at Sunday Mass to build community over my years as a priest. At the beginning of the liturgy, after the sign of the cross and the greeting, there is a place that is appropriate for a word of welcome before entering into the Penitential Rite. How I have used this time has changed down through the years. A warm welcome, especially to regular parishioners, visitors and guests, is always well received. From there I have moved through the different versions of inviting people to turn and acknowledge those around them. I have moved from a good-morning-to-your-neighbour tack, to the get-your-neighbour's-name approach (this has definitely been made easier on Name Tag Sunday). Both have yielded fruit and have contributed to the defrosting of the church on Sunday mornings.

It does call many parishioners out of their comfort zones. I still remember the looks on people's faces before and after I would extend the invitation. As I would introduce it, I could almost see what they were thinking: "Oh no! He's going to ask us to talk to someone." In spite of this, by the time attention was returned to the presider's chair, there was always a smile on everyone's face, as well as a collective sigh of relief that the exercise was over.

When I came to Saint Benedict Parish, I decided to change this approach. True community is not just a time to socialize. The communion that we celebrate at the Eucharist is not just a smile and a handshake. It is a celebration of our oneness in Christ, in our joys and in our sorrows. Besides, a meet and greet is not really appropriate at the Eucharist. It really needs to happen before we reach our pews. Instead of inviting people to say good morning, or shake a hand or get a name, we invite parishioners at every Mass to find a prayer partner, someone they will pray for, and who will pray for them. We are clear that you do not have to know what you are praying for; God knows. Each week, we take a moment to explain this for the sake of visitors, guests or new parishioners.

We invite people to partner with someone they do not know, if possible, and to pray for that person by name during Mass. Each week, at the end of the Prayer of the Faithful, we pause in silence to pray for the person we met at the beginning of Mass. Small things really can and do make a difference.

Since we have introduced this practice, I have received a lot of positive feedback and stories of encounter and transformation. People have told me in tears that they had come to Mass burdened and wondering if anyone cared, or even if God cared. The experience of being connected spiritually to those around them was hugely significant, and, as most people sit in the same pews week after week, this connection builds as faces become familiar, names are remembered, and people admit to even praying for "that person" during the week.

c. Prayer Ministry after Mass

Several years ago, I made a promise to God that whenever someone asked me to pray for them, I would pause and do it right on the spot. I have not always kept my promise, but more often than not, I do. I did this for a number of reasons – not least of all because I have a terrible memory. How could I keep saying I would pray for people or their loved ones, knowing that I would probably forget? The problem was decisively solved by my saying, "Of course I will. Let's pray right now."

The second advantage is also mostly selfish on my part. The times I am most tempted to respond to a prayer request by promising to pray in some vague, distant future rather than on the spot is when I am feeling spiritually weak or distracted. It is difficult to minister to people in this way if you are feeling not very holy. By forcing myself to pray for them when they ask, I allow my own weakness and sinfulness to be challenged and remind myself that God uses me not because of who I am, but because of who he is.

The third advantage is that the person being prayed for receives not only the benefit of prayer, but of hearing and experiencing the prayer. These moments have led to profound encounters, often with tears and the experience of relief, peace and healing. Every time this happens, I think, "Why don't we do this more often?" One of the limiting factors to this type of ministry is that I am one person in the midst of about 500 to 600 people leaving church after each Mass. But we found a solution. We trained teams of lay people to offer this kind of ministry at the end of each Mass while I am at the door of the church shaking hands.

A key moment of the Alpha experience takes place when team members pray over the guests, that they may experience God's love, the Holy Spirit and healing. The model we use at Alpha is non-intrusive, gentle and respectful. Two team members will ask permission to place a hand on the person's shoulder, then gently pray for them by name. Prayers do not need to be long or eloquent, as God does not only answer the prayers of those with theology degrees. Several things happen in this encounter. First, many, many more people are ministered to in this highly personal way than could be if it were just up to the priest. Second, the team members get to experience the joy of being used by God in this way, and model to others that it is not complicated or difficult to minister to one another like this. At Alpha, teams of men pray with the men, and teams of women pray with the women. This alignment reduces the risk of complications.

In 2011, we brought this experience of praying upstairs to the weekend Masses. Once a month, we have two to four trained teams available after every Mass, and each week we have teams available in the Blessed Sacrament Chapel to pray for those who may need prayer. While I am greeting people at the door, an average of 60 to 70 people each weekend are receiving prayer ministry that has a huge impact on their lives. On weekends when I preach a more evangelistic message that invites those present to offer a response and a decision, I will invite members of the congregation who may have responded in their hearts to the invitation to come forward and receive prayer to take the next step in their Christian lives.

Gallup

The value of belonging is, in many ways, the key to the transformation of culture that needs to happen in our parishes. A key exists not for its own sake, but to open a door, a door that needs to be walked through. If belonging is the key, then it opens the door to faith. Behaving, which is discipleship, takes place when the person walks through the door. We must be clear that we are not advocating belonging for its own sake. That is mere socialization. We are advocating the move towards meaningful community so that the end game of making missionary disciples may be achieved. If the issue of belonging is so central to the process of renewal, surely it is to our advantage to be able to measure it in some way. As Fr. Bill Hanson of Saint Gerard Majella Parish in Long Island is fond of saying, "You cannot manage what you cannot measure." The issue of belonging and the transformation of our parishes can and ought to be managed, so it ought to be measured.

Several years ago, my diocese's stewardship team introduced tools that the Gallup organization had developed for assessing the health of churches. The core philosophy of these tools is outlined in the book *Growing an Engaged Church*, by Al Wiseman. Through research that began in the corporate world, Gallup sought to identify the factors that contributed to excellence in an organization. After great success using these tools in the corporate sphere, they turned their attention to the life of the Church and tried to determine whether the same factors were at work. Gallup found that they were. With some adjustments, they were able to apply these tools to assist churches and church leaders in measuring the health of their churches. Unless something can be measured, it cannot be managed.

For Gallup, a healthy church is a community where people grow spiritually, where people serve others and share their financial resources sacrificially. These are the outcomes that define success, and they are the behaviours so often desired by pastors all over the world. So often we seek to bring about these outcomes by directly focusing on them. We call people to take programs for growth and get the same 20% of parishioners. We endlessly request volunteers to sign up for ministries, with the same rate of success. In terms of financial giving, in spite of appeals, Catholics still give the least out of all other Christian groups. In spite of our enthusiastic efforts, the results have been very limited.

Gallup research indicates that we are looking and working in the wrong place. Rather than focusing on the branches and beseeching them to bear fruit, the research tells us that we ought to focus on the condition of the soil. If the soil is good – and we know the seed is good – then a harvest will be brought forth, thirty, sixty and a hundred fold. The greatest indicator of good soil is what Gallup calls *engagement*. Engagement is not to be identified as busyness or even involvement. Engagement is a sense of *belonging*, a psychological connection to the local church and its mission, and a sense of ownership of what is happening and of where the Church is headed. Engaged parishioners are far more likely to commit to spiritual growth, serve others and give sacrificially. This is the belong-believe-behave paradigm in action. In Gallup's vocabulary, engagement (belonging) drives spiritual commitment (believing), which, in turn, drives the outcomes (behaving) of growing, serving and giving.

Gallup tools enable a church to survey its membership and discover the percentages of 1) engaged members, 2) non-engaged members, and 3) actively disengaged members. Engaged parishioners are described as those who are wildly enthusiastic about their parish. There is a deep sense of ownership and alignment with where things are going. Engaged parishioners serve more, give more and are much more inclined to invite others to their church. Unengaged parishioners are generally happy with their parish, but tend to be passive and uninvolved. The last category is the actively disengaged. They are the parishioners who are deeply unhappy with the way things are, resist any kind of change, and tend to be a negative and destructive presence. I recently saw these categories of human beings summed up by three drawings. The first showed a man building a brick wall, the second showed a man with his feet up on his desk happily snoozing, and the third picture showed a wrecking ball knocking down the wall that the first man had built. The survey developed by Gallup is called the ME 25; it assesses 25 indicators of membership engagement.

In January 2011, over 1,330 parishioners participated in the survey at Saint Benedict for the first time. The results of this survey showed that our parish was composed of 24% Engaged, 47% Unengaged, and 29% Actively Disengaged. Based on Gallup's data from U.S. Catholic churches, these results are slightly better than the average Catholic parish in the U.S. that first uses these tools. Our main area of weakness seemed to be related to our sheer size and our failure to be a parish in which meaningful relationships are built between the people and the leaders of the parish. This placed a demand on us to reshape the perception of leadership within our parish, as one priest cannot have a meaningful relationship with almost 2,500 people. The satisfaction of finding out that we were slightly better than the average Catholic parish at the beginning of this process was short-lived when we learned Gallup's definition of organizational health. For Gallup, a healthy soil condition that will allow a growing spiritual commitment, that will eventually produce the fruit of the Kingdom, is a staggering 4:1 ratio of engaged to actively disengaged parishioners!

This was a sobering insight. It would take four engaged parishioners to neutralize the acidity of every actively disengaged parishioner, and we were only at 0.83:1. More alarming than this was the realization that we were still healthier than many other parishes. I remember having inklings of this when I was at my previous parish. Visitors would remark on how uplifting our liturgies were and how alive our parish seemed to be. My personality is such that I am always focusing on how we can be better and healthier, and I was aware that we were nowhere near being the healthy church that we were called to be. I would often think to myself at these moments that when you visit the hospital, the patients in the intensive care unit look really healthy compared to the people in the morgue.

Many people are reluctant to use tools like those offered by Gallup, and many shy away from anything to do with comparison, but if we do not have a vision for what a healthy church looks like, how will we ever become healthy ourselves? If our lack of health, decline and palliative condition is simply not as bad as in the churches around us, we will still all eventually be dead. Gallup measures essential organizational health. What can be measured can be managed, and if health can be managed, why not measure it?

The results of the 25 questions posed in the ME 25 survey were a significant factor in determining our strategy in the first years at Saint Benedict Parish. We were committed to this process of analysis, and the results have confirmed our experience. Since that time, we have undergone the ME 25 survey twice more, and the results tell us that our management efforts are paying off. As seen in the table below, our latest results have us still short of full health, but we are getting very close.

ME 25 SURVEY

	FEB 2011	MAY 2012	OCT 2013
Engaged	24%	33%	41%
Unengaged	47%	48%	44%
Actively Disengaged	29%	19%	15%

What about those outcomes, those changes in behaviour? Three years after implementing this engagement-based strategy at Saint Benedict, the number of adults in programs of evangelization and faith formation has tripled. The number of parishioners in ministry has doubled, and our weekly collection has gone from an average of $10,000 per weekend to between $20,000 and $21,000 each weekend. This has occurred while the overall number of parishioners in the pews has remained the same. Many have joined the parish, but just as many have left. Health comes through addition and attrition. Our experience supports the theory. Get it healthy and it will grow all by itself.

6. Clear Expectations

"Whoever does not carry the cross and follow me cannot be my disciple. For which of you, intending to build a tower, does not first sit down and estimate the cost, to see whether he has enough to complete it?" (Luke 14:27-28)

Have you ever noticed that most ex-Catholics who have joined another community generally join a church that expects more of them than the one they left behind? This seems counter-intuitive, especially in the face of a secular critique that is continuously telling us that the key to attracting people to the Church is to ask for and expect little. Nevertheless, churches that are healthy and growing are clear about their expectations of members and are not afraid to communicate them. Gallup has affirmed the importance of expectations to organizational health. In the ME 25 survey, the first of the twelve items that directly deal with engagement is to rate one's agreement with the statement "As a member of my parish, I know what is expected of me."

As important as expectations are in any role or organization, well-meaning Catholics start getting nervous when you throw around the "e-word" too much. There is a palpable fear that by communicating in any way that there are expectations to being a member of the parish, we will turn people off. There is a sense that to have clear expectations as a value will clash with the opposing value of hospitality or welcoming. The key is to see them not as opposing values, but as two important values that will have a certain amount of creative tension between them. There are four possible ways that a parish can combine these two values. They are represented below as four quadrants.

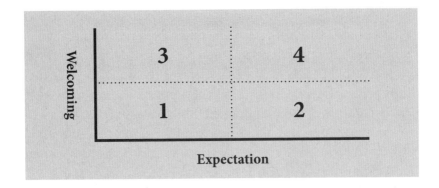

The first option is for a parish to have low welcoming and low expectations. Sadly, this does describe the state of affairs in too many of our parishes. The second option, low welcoming with high expectations, would be terrible. I do not believe that this would exist in any church, as it says, "We do not want you, but we will use you." Option three is found in many parishes that are striving to do the welcoming thing correctly: high welcome, but low expectations. This was the situation when I became pastor at Saint Benedict Parish. Welcoming was a declared value, and the parish was doing a better job than most in living it out. There were, however, no expectations being communicated to actual or prospective parishioners (I distinguish here between those seeking to become members of the parish and those who were simply attending the parish). How could these two things possibly co-exist? Well, they can.

High welcome and high expectation is in fact a more respectful way of responding to people, as what we are saying is, "We believe that God will work in you and work through you; we expect it, and you should, too." This is so much better than saying, "You are most welcome here, and, by the way, we don't expect anything from you at all. You don't have to do anything, give anything, heck, you don't even need to show up if you don't want to, but please know that you are welcome to be a member of our parish." This is but one step removed from saying that we have no expectations of new members because we don't expect God to do anything in and through them. I am fully aware that no welcoming team would ever wish to communicate such things, but is that not what we are saying when we shy away from the subject of expectations?

Jesus

No one has been able to model this interrelationship between welcoming and expectation more than Jesus. He was the epitome of welcome. Just glance through the Gospels. The outcast shepherds at his birth, the lame, the lepers, the sinners, the tax collectors, the rich, the poor – all received the invitation to come to him. He welcomed the woman at the well, Zacchaeus, Samaritans, Romans and Gentiles. Even when children interrupted his break, he told the Twelve to let them come to him. At the same time, this Jesus was clear about what he expected of those who would follow him. "Whoever does not carry the cross and follow me cannot be my disciple." (Luke 14:27) He would go on to exhort the crowds that followed him to "sit down first" and calculate the cost of being his disciple before choosing to do so. He was the one who could look into the eyes of the rich young man with love and issue an invitation saturated in expectation: "go sell your possessions, and give the money to the poor ... then come, follow me." (Matthew 19:21-22)

The expectations of Jesus were not limited to the commitment of becoming his disciple. Once that decision was made, he continued to expect more. He said that "from everyone to whom much has been given, even more will be demanded." (Luke 12:48) Jesus has unreasonable expectations of the fig tree, and curses it for its failure to produce its sweet fruit, even though "it was not the season for figs." (Mark 11:13) Jesus tells us in John's Gospel, "I am the true vine, and my Father is the vinegrower. He removes every branch in me that bears no fruit. Every branch that bears fruit he prunes to make it bear more fruit." (John 15:1-2) Not only does the Father expect fruit – he expects even more from those already producing it. Our God is a demanding God who expects much from us.

In the Parable of the Talents in Matthew's Gospel (25:14-30), we hear again about what God expects of us, individually and corporately. The master who goes on a journey gives his slaves his wealth to manage in his absence. The first receives five talents; the second, two talents; and the third, one talent. I used to imagine this parable as the master giving each man a bag of coins. A talent, however, was a unit of weight – 130 lbs., to be precise. It came in silver or gold. The first point of the parable, which we often miss today, is the sheer value of the treasure that he has entrusted to his slaves. Even the man with the one talent (presumably silver) had, in today's value, about $600,000. His boss was not fooling around. The response of the master when he finds out that the man buried it in the ground because of fear, instead of multiplying it, is harsh. He tells the man that at least he could have invested his money in the bank so he could have collected interest. The point seems to be that God does not expect a moderate return on his investment in us, but a kind of spiritual venture capitalism, even if it means taking a risk.

Parish Expectations

Clearly, Jesus embraced the values of welcoming and expectation, and so they must be part of the life of the Church. How we communicate expectations is paramount. At Saint Benedict, we speak of five expectations of parishioners and clergy alike. All are expected to worship, to grow, to serve, to connect and to give. Our expectations brochure is given to all who show an interest in becoming a member of our parish. It introduces the concept of expectation in these words:

> *Saint Benedict Parish is a Catholic Christian community of disciples of the Lord Jesus. We believe that everyone is called to be on a spiritual journey and what matters is not where a person is on that journey, but that they are actually on the journey itself. Therefore, we seek to welcome all people regardless of the stage of their spiritual life, their struggles and failures. We are a hospital for sinners, not a hotel for*

Saints. We simply ask that you walk with us and be open to what God is calling you to.

To be a member of this parish is to enter into relationship with the other members of the parish who are also on this spiritual journey. We do this together. Clear expectations are at the heart of every healthy relationship.

The brochure then outlines what parishioners can expect from the parish before we speak about what the parish expects of parishioners.

- *Dynamic and uplifting liturgies.*

- *A place where you will experience transformation to become more and more the person God has created you to be.*

- *A place where you will be valued and recognized as having unique gifts and talents for the service of God and others.*

- *A place where you will be given the opportunity to put your God given talents to help others and to make the world a better place.*

- *A place where you will be loved and supported in your spiritual journey regardless of the messiness and struggles of your life.*

- *A place where your needs will be listened to and addressed.*

- *A place where your input is valued.*

- *A place where your financial contributions will be honored and put to work for the building up of the Kingdom of God with transparency and accountability.*

Lastly, we address the five expectations under the heading "What is Expected of you as a Parishioner of Saint Benedict Parish?" These expectations are communicated as follows:

To Worship

We gather to celebrate the Eucharist every Sunday (the Lord's Day). We expect all members of the parish to gather for Sunday worship unless they are unable to do so because of illness or travel.

It is when we gather on the Lord's Day to be nourished by Word and Sacrament that we remember who we are and are given food for the journey. In this task we fulfill our call to worship the God who created us and are given the grace we need to continue to love God and one another.

To Grow

To become a follower of Jesus Christ is to be his disciple. Jesus said, "This is the will of my Father, that you should become my disciples" (John 15:8). A disciple literally means "one who is learning." We believe that learning and growing are lifelong tasks. When we cease to learn and grow we cease to be disciples and will experience stagnation in our spiritual lives. We expect every member of Saint Benedict Parish to commit to at least one program of faith formation each year. We need to remember that our commitment to growth helps those around us to fulfill their own commitment. In this way our Church becomes healthy.

To Serve

Jesus said, "The Son of Man came not to be served, but to serve." (Mark 10:45) The essence of the Christian life is to serve God and one another. The Church is not healthy when it forgets this truth. We are called not just to serve individually, but to do so corporately as the Church. This way we give witness that the Church is the hands and feet of Jesus in the world. We also believe that every parishioner, without exception, has something to offer, something they do well and can do for the sake of the Kingdom of God. We expect every parishioner to serve the parish by being involved in at least one ministry each year.

To Connect

The Church is a community of believers and not simply a collection of individuals who gather for one hour a week. Christian community is one in which we are truly accountable to one another and accountable for one another. This task needs to be taken up with due diligence as the size of our parish makes it a real challenge. We expect every parishioner to contribute to the task of building community by seeing themselves as an integral part of the life of this parish and being intentional about reaching out and connecting with others.

To Give

We expect all parishioners to give generously of their financial resources in proportion to what they have received. We give not to just meet a few basic needs or to pay the costs of maintaining the Church building and a few staff. We give out of gratitude to God, and the more the parish receives, the more we can do for the building up of God's Kingdom, the more we can help the poor, the more programs we can run to help others grow. No one is excluded from this. If someone has less, they give less. If someone has more, they give more. This offering, which we make at Sunday Eucharist, is a key part of our worship.

Perhaps these expectations seem lofty, but as the great artist Michelangelo once said, "The greater danger for most of us is not that our aim is too high and we miss it, but that it is too low and we reach it."

Stewardship

The spirituality of stewardship has been of great assistance as we continue to chip away at the overall culture of our parish and to establish clear expectations as a value. Three annual stewardship initiatives allow us to keep the five expectations before our people and give them an invitation and opportunity to make concrete decisions around them. I have been involved in implementing stewardship in every parish I have served in. The traditional categories of time, talent and treasure addressed the basic demands of being a follower of Jesus, but I always struggled with the seeming absence of a commitment to invest in discipleship, specifically as personal growth and development, as opposed to committing time to serve in ministry according to God-given talents.

Over the years, I had encountered two types of involved parishioners. The first, and most common, were those who constantly served. They served in multiple ministries, would never say no to anything, and just went all the time without ever taking a program that would allow them to receive. All too often, I saw wonderfully kind parishioners like this become burned out and exhausted. In the second, and less common, category were parishioners who would run from one program to another, from one spiritual experience to another, constantly receiving and never giving and serving others. In truth, both options are deadly, although the second may indeed be the deadliest. The Dead Sea is truly dead, because it only has tributaries and no distributaries. It only receives the salt water that evaporates and results in the lethal levels of salt that banish all life. As a pastor, I constantly struggled with how to help my variously inclined parishioners, and myself, find balance in our lives in the parish – to balance serving others with our own need to connect and grow.

In September of 2010, I attended the International Stewardship Conference in San Diego. I had been at Saint Benedict Parish for only four weeks and knew that I had as much of an empty canvas to paint on as I ever would. One afternoon, I wandered into a session that I had not registered for. I sat down. A team from a U.S. parish was presenting on the innovative ways they had adapted the traditional stewardship model to their pastoral reality. They spoke about tweaking the understanding of the traditional three Ts. *Time* was to be understood as a commitment to spiritual growth and discipleship. *Talent* was entirely about serving others. And *Treasure*, of course, was about financial giving. Such a simple distinction! It was a eureka moment for me. I have no idea who the presenters were, or where they were from, but I am very grateful to them to this very day. I returned home eager to share my new insights with our stewardship team.

What followed was a commitment to implement a series of three distinct stewardship initiatives each year. The first, which focused on Time (discipleship), took place in September, at the beginning of the next ministry year. By doing this, we were inviting parishioners to make a commitment to a plan for spiritual growth for the coming year. We were intentional about placing Time before Talent, as we wanted to emphasize the primacy and priority of the spiritual. Our Stewardship of Talent Initiative, focusing on the gifts we have received and the call to share them with others in ministry, took place in early January of the next year, beginning on the Feast of Epiphany, which falls on a Sunday in Canada. Our Treasure Initiative, focusing on financial giving, would take place around May, and has done ever since, depending on the liturgical calendar.

Typical Stewardship Initiative

Week 1: Letter from the pastor to all families

Week 2: Homily on the theme and overview of the initiative

Week 3: Short homily, lay witness and Stewardship Book distributed

Week 4: Short homily, lay witness and Ministry Fair

Week 5: Homily on theme and Commitment Cards brought to the altar

The Stewardship of Treasure booklet was an opportunity to bring together all the typical financial reports presented in a parish in a given year: a year-end report for the previous year, the budget for the present year, and a first-quarter report. This booklet breaks down the information into relevant and interesting facts (the cost of snow removal, toilet paper, etc.). It includes information on legacy giving, on automatic withdrawal, on second collections for the poor, and on the children sponsored by the offerings of the children of our parish on Sunday mornings. It provides a careful breakdown of the average weekly cost of operations. It includes testimonies of changed lives under the heading "The Fruit of our Giving," as well as testimonies of parishioners who had committed to intentional, sacrificial and proportional giving. In this way, we reminded our people that the end result of financial giving, in and to the Church, was changed lives and a transformed world. Yes – we did this for all three aspects of giving, even financial giving, and I lived to tell the tale.

All of these efforts have been an immense amount of work, but they have been well worth it, as we are beginning to see the culture of our parish change. When the Stewardship Team committed to take on this enormous task, we knew from the experience of other parishes that the payload is not usually struck until about the seven-year mark. We knew this when we signed up, and we struggle to keep this before us. We need to be clear that these initiatives are not about data collection, name gathering, financial forecasting or even recruitment. These exercises are an attempt to change the very perception of what is normal in our parish. Everything else is a bonus.

We want all parishioners to see that it is completely normal to commit to spiritual growth, for everyone to serve according to their gifts, and to give a sacrificial and proportional share of household income to the Church. Now into our fourth year of initiatives, we are at about a 40% participation rate. These numbers closely parallel the numbers we have received back from the Gallup ME 25 survey. Parishes that have been down this road testify that it can take five to seven years before a parish will climb beyond the 50% range, and most will plateau in the high 50s or low 60s. This, again, is consistent with the findings of Gallup's measurement of engaged parishioners.

Something for Everyone

There have been many challenges throughout these past years. The first was to create sufficient opportunities for spiritual growth to speak to the diversity of our parishioners, who are of different ages, spiritualities, commitment levels and availability. Opportunities to participate in faith formation activities morning, noon and evening, seven days a week, became our goal. We even presented opportunities such as the Parish Book Club Without the Club, for the really busy person. The various initiatives were so successful that our building quickly became congested, to the point that we were tripping over one another. The resultant stress on the parish infrastructure and staff was not properly anticipated. Now that we have begun to grow a culture of discipleship in the parish, we are moving away from this approach and seeking to streamline our offerings.

When it came to the Talent Initiative, we had to seek to broaden people's understanding of what a talent was, and that there were more ways to serve God than to show up at a commit-tee meeting or sign up for a liturgical ministry. We even created a ministry for the homebound and bedridden called the Blessed Therese Neumann Society. Homebound parishioners would sign up and offer their prayers and unavoidable suffering to God as a form of intercession for the renewal of the parish. In return, a monthly newsletter keeps them informed of what is going on and highlights specific intentions for them to pray for. Other elderly parishioners could commit to pray at home for the parish, or join the parish prayer chain, as a form of service, and the Eucharistic Adoration Ministry took on a new sense of purpose as its primary identity became a ministry to serve others by interceding for them.

The Treasure Initiative was an adventure unto itself. The issue of giving is a very difficult one for us as Catholics, because it is ad-dressed so little, at least in comparison to other Christian churches. The first year we did this initiative, many parishioners thought we were out of our minds. I received no shortage of anonymous phone messages and letters. Some were deeply offended that the subject of giving would be addressed for three or four weeks in a row. Others wrote directly on their Commitment Card that what they would give to the Church was none of our business. I made the case that if public television can ask this of their members, why can't we? If the local children's hospital can ask supporters to pledge a financial gift so that its mission can be achieved, why can't the Church ask the same of her supporters for the mission of Jesus Christ? The second time around was slightly less painful, and the third rendered virtually no kickback. I am confident that in another 50 years it will seem entirely normal!

All of this is a work in progress. Each year, we are realizing that there are ways to improve on reaching our goal of facilitating the cultural change of our parish. The distinction between Time and Talent is still difficult for many of our parishioners to grasp, and even some ministry leaders struggle with it. The leaders of a service ministry will often tell us that their team members always pray together before they do what they do, or that they are the ones who receive whenever they serve. Our response is to remind them that this is exactly how it should be. We must always pray before we act, and "it is in giving that we receive." The question, however, is about the fundamental purpose of a particular ministry. Is it a service ministry or a formation ministry? Does it exist to serve others, or does it exist to build up and feed parishioners? Am I there to give or to receive? Am I investing in others, or investing in myself? It does get a bit confusing, but we are figuring it out, and there is a growing and healthy sense of what is expected of a member of Saint Benedict Parish.

7. Strength-based Ministry

> Whoever serves must do so with the strength that God supplies, so that God may be glorified in all things through Jesus Christ. (1 Peter 4:11)

It was my very first parish council meeting of my very first parish as a newly appointed pastor. We began the meeting with "a quick prayer" and passed out the minutes from the previous meeting, which had taken place under my predecessor. I glanced at the top of the page and saw the names of those in attendance. Beside each name was the number of years and months of "time" left to serve on council. I almost chewed a hole in my cheek to stop myself from laughing, thinking that this was at least an honest depiction of how the average member of a parish council felt. I had been to a few meetings in my day and "putting in time" was exactly how it felt.

Most of the people around that table had been victims of the "warm body" approach to ministry that begins with the need rather than the person. The problem with this "anyone will do" approach is that parishioners end up in ministries that are suited to neither their strengths nor their passions, but "do their bit" out of a sense of duty or even guilt. As a result, many in such ill-matched ministries experience little fulfillment and much frustration. The ministry they serve in also receives little benefit. The experience is life giving neither for the one who serves nor for those being served. The tragedy of this is that most parishioners will never know the joy of being set free in a ministry that takes full advantage of their strengths, talents and passions.

People First

The greatest joy in the world is to know, to experience, being used by the Lord to make a difference in someone's life or in the world. Everyone wins. The one who serves wins, the one served wins, and there is even a win for the Kingdom of God. When I arrived at Saint Benedict Parish and beheld the empty canvas, I wondered what it would be like to attempt to reshape this aspect of parish culture, to begin not with a list of job vacancies or needs, but with people, with their strengths and their passions. What would it be like to not just plug holes, but to sit down first with parishioners and say, "Tell me your story. What are you passionate about? What do you love doing, and what do you consistently do well?"

I knew from my own ministry that while sitting in certain types of meetings was definitely being counted as time off from purgatory, other tasks energized and enthralled me. What if parishioners could be called forth and empowered to step into just such an experience of ministry? My first new staffing initiative, therefore, was to hire a young woman who would take on this task full-time. To my mind, with at least 2,500 regular parishioners, our parish was a huge, unharvested field of trees laden down with fruit. A full-time staff member would barely put a dent in this, but it was a good place to start.

Strengths Finder

The Gallup organization tells us that there are twelve main contributors to organizational health. These are essentially the same whether we are speaking of a workplace or a church. Of these twelve, Gallup says that having the opportunity to do what we do best is the leading contributor to engagement. Remember, engagement is what drives spiritual commitment, which in turn drives changed beliefs and changed behaviour. Gallup employs a tool known as the Clifton Strengths Finder, which is widely used in work environments and organizations all over the world. In recent years, they have developed a Christian version of Strengths Finder called *Living Your Strengths*, and even a specifically Catholic edition.

The basic philosophy is that every person is uniquely made and gifted by God (the Gallup family were and are a devout Christian family, and so was Don Clifton, who developed this tool). They reject a popular theory today that claims that anyone can do anything if they put their mind to it. We all know this from experience. Mozart was a prodigy who was playing the keyboard with great skill by the age of three. I could dedicate the rest of my life to learning to play the piano, I could hire the best teachers and, if I work really hard, I might achieve some level of mediocrity. Although equal in dignity before God, we are all uniquely made, and we fulfill God's plan for our lives when we discover our own uniqueness. It is to our advantage to stop trying to be someone else, and allow God to use us through our own strengths and innate talents.

The traditional mindset, of course, is to identify weakness rather than strength and focus on improving that weakness. Strengths Finder philosophy says: find your God-given talents and invest in them. When we invest in talent by practising and growing in knowledge and understanding, our talent will become a strength – something we consistently and naturally do well. Add to this natural, God-given ability the power and grace of God, and stand back and watch what happens!

Don Clifton identified over 300 unique abilities or talents across the human spectrum, rooted in how people were hard-wired. Whether this is environmental or genetic is not relevant. These talents reflect how we are and the way we generally do things. We are not bound to follow these paths of least resistance, for the human person is never static, but they do reflect a dominant disposition in the personality of every person. Clifton grouped these talents into 34 "themes of talents" and created a survey to help users identify their top five "signature themes." With uncanny accuracy, these themes help a person identify what they may already know; the faith-based Strengths theory invites each person to lean into these talents, to develop them into strengths and to allow God to use them for his glory and the building up of the Kingdom.

Many parishes in North America, including our own, have found this tool to be of great help in fostering strengths-based ministry as a real value. Online Catholic Strengths communities exist, allowing parishes that use this tool to interact and learn from one another. Since introducing this tool to our parish, our staff member who was my first hire, and is now called our Parish Director of Engagement, has been trained to facilitate workshops to help parishioners identify and learn more about their top five themes.

We feature parishioners who have taken Strengths Finder in our weekly parish newsletter, outlining their top five themes of talents and how they use these talents in their ministry. We invite every parishioner to discover their God-given uniqueness so they can truly experience the joy of being used fully by God. We have used this tool to help our staff team and ministry teams work better together, as all 34 themes of talent fall within four broad domains: influencing, executing, relationship building and strategic thinking. The proper mix of talents in any team is necessary for it to function well. It has been an amazing tool for us at Saint Benedict – we use it to help build balanced leadership and ministry teams, even using it as a part of our marriage preparation program... but more about that in Chapter 6.

Some may object and point out that Scripture reminds us that God is more likely to use our weaknesses than our strengths. The fact that our weaknesses generally tend to be the underside of our strengths does not escape the authors of *Living Your Strengths*. The book highlights the negative aspects of each talent and offers Scripture passages and prayer points to consider. If used in a prayerful way, these traits that are called talents can be experienced as the redemption of our weakness.

In the end, this tool drives home that we are "wonderfully and uniquely made." (Psalm 139:14) It's all in the math. The chances of any two people having the same top five themes are 278,256:1. The chances of having the same top five themes in the same order are 33,390,720:1. Unbelievably, the chance of having all 34 themes in exactly the same order is an astronomical 295,232, 799,039,604,140,847,618,609,643,520,000,000:1. Literally, there never has been, nor ever will be, in the history of the world, someone quite like you. The God who has made us for himself wishes to work wonderfully through our strengths and passions. That is something to value. Once we truly value it, it will transform the Church and the world.

8. Formation of Small Communities

When day came, he called his disciples and chose twelve of them, whom he also named apostles. (Luke 6:13)

Universally, churches that are healthy, growing and making disciples embrace a model of the local church as a "community of communities." These smaller communities gather together as one community for Sunday Eucharist. Many distinguish between small groups of eight to twelve people and mid-size groups containing 25 to 35 people. For healthy churches, involvement in a small or mid-size group is not considered optional, but is an integral part of the life of that local church. Imagine bringing Catholic parishes to a place where this kind of community is found!

We have already examined how post-moderns experience conversion and transformation primarily through their experience of belonging. That it is not easy for us as Catholics to reach the unchurched and the fallen away through creating experiences of belonging is no surprise. This creates a challenge for those who have been brought to a personal life-changing encounter with Jesus Christ, whether they were a part of the Church or outside of her. At the point of conversion or awakening, they became aware of their need for meaningful community, a place where they will be known, loved, challenged and supported. This community must be a safe place within which the good work that has begun in them can be brought to completion. (Philippians 1:6) These kinds of relationships are key to a healthy Church. Six of Gallup's twelve ME 25 statements, which measure engagement, speak of this experience of community:

- In the last month, I have received recognition or praise from someone in my parish.

- The spiritual leaders in my parish seem to care about me as a person.

- There is someone in my parish who encourages my spiritual development.

- The other members of my parish are committed to spiritual growth.

- Aside from family members, I have a best friend in my parish.

- In the last six months, someone in my parish has talked to me about the progress of my spiritual growth.

How can an experience like this be possible in an average Catholic parish? Traditionally, it was the parish priest who would give people praise and recognition, care about parishioners and encourage and ask about spiritual growth. This may still work in a small parish where there is a very small priest-to-people ratio, but this is not the case in most parishes today. The bigger a parish is, the smaller it must become. Providing opportunities to experience authentic community must be a priority.

Clerical Culture

The culture that dominates most parishes presents a challenge in making this a reality. Many Catholics place value only on ministry done by the priest, and consider themselves to have meaningful connection with the parish only if they have a strong personal connection to the pastor. If the priest is unable to be at all the gatherings of a committee, team or group, at least he should drop in once in a while. The problem is that if we remain bound to this value, then the number of meaningful communities in a parish will always be limited. This would work in a small parish, but only in a parish that was not healthy. A small parish, if healthy, will grow. If it grows and continues to grow, sooner or later it will be large, and the model will have to change. In a large parish, healthy or unhealthy, this model is already profoundly limiting.

This is a question that haunts me at night when I am trying to sleep. For me, it is not an abstract question, but one that has faces and names attached to it. Sometimes I will think of someone I have not seen in a while, and think, "What happened to her? Where is he? Who is looking out for that person?" It is just so easy for our people to get lost in the crowd and to fall through the cracks, even those who have had authentic experiences of the Lord. I think of the many participants who have come through RCIA in my different parishes, and of the high number of newly baptized and confirmed who have gone AWOL. We bring people to the Sacraments of Initiation through a small- or mid-size group experience. It is transformative and supportive. Participants experience exactly the kind of community reflected in the statements used in the Gallup ME 25 survey, but then the Easter Vigil happens.

The culmination of a lengthy process results in most participants being released into the general population with a slap on the back, a "welcome to full membership in the Church" and a "good luck." Is it any wonder that we have huge casualty rates? The solution is staring us in the face. The very process that brings candidates to faith and to the sacraments is the process that is essential to nourishing the ongoing life of the Church. Meaningful community cannot be part of a program – it must become a normative part of the life of the Church, and the life of the Church must become the program.

"But what are they among so many people?" (John 6:9)

I am also haunted by the question of how the people of my parish can be sufficiently cared for. With so many tasks and responsibilities, with so many staff to lead and guide so that some meaningful degree of ministry can happen in proportion to the number of people in the parish, how can I ensure that parishioners are cared for? I spoke in Chapter 4 about the need to expand our working definition of pastoral care to include bringing our people to maturity. If we wish to move beyond the therapeutic model of pastoral care that dominates most parishes, we will need not only alternate structures, but alternate values.

If a parish priest with just 2,000 families in his parish were to spend ten hours a week visiting families for one hour each, it would take about four years before he could return to continue the conversation. This kind of situation is an unacceptable standard of care. In reality, short of a major catastrophe hitting a family, in most parishes the priest is unable to appear at the door of his parishioners. Caring therefore needs to become the job of all, not just of the pastor. Only then will a Church become healthy. Only then will parish priests be freed from an impossible burden and be able to see it happen. A kind of surrender needs to take place for this to happen, and it is a painful one.

I have struggled so much with feeling like a "bad priest." Often on weekends, by the end of the third weekend Mass, I have seen 1,700 people in church and have greeted hundreds, and still have one more Mass. Dozens of parishioners will ask for prayers for loved ones, and many, on their way out, will say things like, "I know you're busy, Father, but just in case, my husband is in the hospital, on the 7th floor, Room 46." Parishioners give me updates on their health, and their loved one's health, and often communicate out of a presumption that I know exactly who they are and remember every detail of what they told me three weeks ago. Listening and responding is part of my job as a Father of the parish, but how can I *respond* to all of it? By 1:00 p.m. on Sunday, I feel like my brains are oozing out of my ears, and the people keep coming and coming and coming. A very real part of me wants to cry out and say, "Stop! Please stop! I cannot carry this burden. I cannot bear the burden of fearing that a moment's inattention or fatigue may hurt even one fragile person." Too often, I feel that I have been sucked dry, with nothing else to give. One day, after a weekday Mass, I came home and wrote this in my journal:

> *From the back of the church today to the vestry, grabbed a dozen times to hear about nephews' dying dogs and brothers with cancer, illness, sickness. People need to be heard, but is it my role to do so? I didn't become a priest to comfort little old ladies, but to lead people into mission to win the world for Jesus, so that every little old lady can have someone to comfort her in the name of Jesus.*

I hope I don't offend anyone by these words, which were written in anguish. It is not my intent. The truth is that if we are to become a Church where everyone is cared for as they should be, we must acknowledge that this is not the job of the priest. Priests must have the courage to communicate this to their people, and the people must have the courage to communicate this to their priests. It is my conviction that the formation of small and mid-size groups can provide the answer to this dilemma. The good news is that there are many examples of how such a system in a church can operate, even if these examples are not always found in a Catholic context.

Connect Groups

At Saint Benedict Parish, we are trying to implement a system of mid-size groups called connect groups. The model we use comes from Holy Trinity Brompton (HTB), the Anglican Church in London that created Alpha. When Alpha is done right, usually at least 50% of the participants desire to continue in some experience of community. HTB originally attempted to meet this need for community by establishing a network of small groups. Alpha small groups would become church small groups. Over the years, however, they found that small groups would ultimately get smaller and smaller. People would move away or fall away, and the intense and intimate nature of a small group makes it impenetrable to new members that allow it to be repopulated and to continue. Furthermore, when a small group was not working for a new believer, they would often be so embarrassed and self-conscious about dropping out of the group that they would drop out of the church as well.

The solution was to create broader mid-size groups of 25 to 35 people that were both small enough and big enough. They were small enough for people to be known, cared for, loved and called forth. They were big enough for people to sit at the back and not be put under the kind of pressure that might exist in a group of eight. They would be big enough to admit new members and grow. This model, used by HTB and many other churches, allows the movement of parishioners and non-churchgoers from the experience of Alpha into an ongoing community where they will continue their faith development, and, most importantly, not be lost and not fall through the cracks.

These connect groups are led by lay people. Groups meet twice a month in the homes of church members. Each evening consists of a shared meal, a time of singing and praying, a talk by a member and a time of praying for and with one another. The group does

173

not gather as students around a few teachers; instead, all members take a turn to present on a topic or to share their testimony. For many, it is a safe place to give their first talk or to lead prayer for the first time. In this way, members are encouraged, equipped and called forth to exercise their gifts.

The members of the leadership at HTB meet regularly with the lay leaders of the groups and invest primarily in them, equipping them to lead each group so that everybody receives the care they need. HTB has a weekly attendance of over 5,000 people (the average age is 27 years), and has hundreds of connect groups up and running in the homes of their parishioners. In the HTB model, connect groups are also the locus of missional outreach – either evangelistic outreach or work with the poor and marginalized. On the weeks when the connect group does not meet, members meet in small groups that have a specifically catechetical focus, as opposed to the caring and calling forth focus of the connect groups.

At Saint Benedict Parish, we introduced connect groups shortly after our second season of Alpha. After we had finished our first courses, many people had come to faith in Christ for the first time, many had come into personal relationship with Jesus for the first time, and many had had an experience of the Holy Spirit for the first time. But no matter where people had been spiritually before they took the course, those whose lives were touched all experienced a new form of Christian community, and once they tasted it, they wanted more. I had tried to introduce connect groups at my previous parish, but it had not been successful. This time I was determined to make it happen. We have made our share of mistakes, and are still far from getting it right, but less than four years later we now have over 300 parishioners in ten different connect groups.

We started with four connect groups and slowly added to them as we brought more people through an experience of Alpha. This is the one thing we do differently from my previous attempt in my former parish. We ask that all who seek to belong to a connect group go through the experience of Alpha first. This is the only way that members can have a frame of reference for the degree of support and connection that we seek to establish. It was not and is not the only option for people who come through Alpha at Saint Benedict. We encourage the continuation of catechetical formation through a wide variety of adult faith formation programs. These programs, however, are terminal. The groups disband. Parishioners often move from one program to another, but are still left without an essential caring community at the end of the day. It is obvious that we need to care for people by providing temporary community-based faith formation and permanent groups where people truly belong and are cared for.

Once one of our connect groups grew beyond 35 people, our task was to identify, call forth and equip new leaders and split the group into two. Some of the current ten groups are based on age, some are mixed generations, and some are "family friendly," with children and parents gathering together. The best thing about this is that it all happens in the homes of parishioners. People often ask us how we fit everyone in, and the truth is that it is organized chaos, but a load of fun. It is no different than having a party at your house. People do it all the time.

The beauty of the model is that it works. I do not have to be there. Over the last three years, I have visited only two connect groups, but every week I meet parishioners I do not know who tell me they are in a connect group and last week gave their first talk. I love it when I have no clue about what God is doing in my parish. This is the way it should be! How can I even pretend to control the working of the Holy Spirit in a parish of this size? The Spirit blows where he wills, and the job of the pastor is to get out of the way.

At the same time, however, there is a line of accountability to me as the pastor. There has to be. Several of our parish staff meet regularly with the connect group leaders (each group is led by two couples) to coach them and care for them. They report to our parish Director of Evangelization who, in turn, reports to me. All names for potential connect group leaders are vetted by me. Is there a risk that something may happen that may not be totally right? Of course there is, but this is infinitely more desirable than nothing happening at all. As I once heard Pastor Rick Warren say, "Leaders of a Church will either be risk takers, care takers or undertakers." There is always risk in giving up control. It may not be done properly, or, the more common fear, it may not be done as "properly" as I would do it!

But low control is a necessity if the act of caring for one another will become an embodied value and not just be the task of a few ministering to a few more. It is necessary, but it is not enough. The counterpoint is high accountability. (I will be saying more about this principle in Chapter 7, when I speak about leadership.) With regard to connect groups, however, the key is to choose the right people to lead, to trust them with real responsibility, to set them up for success and to constantly be in communication with them. I am amazed and thrilled to see that more than 15% of my parishioners are well protected from falling through the cracks. Our goal is that by 2018, five years after we started, 75% of our parishioners will belong in a connect group, and that such an experience of community will be so normal that no one will think twice about it.

9. Experience of the Holy Spirit

"You will receive power when the Holy Spirit has come upon you; and you will be my witnesses in Jerusalem, in all Judea and Samaria, and to the ends of the earth." (Acts 1:8)

Growing up in Glasgow (my family moved to Canada when I was thirteen), I was vaguely aware that there was another major city in Scotland called Edinburgh. There is a healthy rivalry between these two cities that could lead you to hear on the streets of Glasgow that the best thing to come out of Edinburgh is the last train to Glasgow. I visited Edinburgh for the first time when I returned to Scotland after my first year of university. I spent three days in Scotland's beautiful capital city and even visited its world-famous zoo. There is a well-known story about the Edinburgh zoo that I would like to share.

A number of years ago, the main attraction at the zoo, a gorilla, died a week before the season opening. The management was in a panic, as gorillas were not exactly easy to find in Scotland. Well, at least not in Edinburgh. There happened to be a Glasgow man applying that day for a job at the zoo; the management hired him and talked him into donning a gorilla costume for a few weeks until they could find a new gorilla. The man, being desperate for work, took the offer and was surprisingly convincing in his role of aping the huge primate. As the days wore on, boredom allowed him the opportunity to become particularly adept at swinging on the bars in his cage. This helped him to pass the time and earned him a rather enthusiastic crowd of spectators. One day, he decided to go for the "triple swing" on the bars. He took a run at the bars, grabbed them and went round once, twice, but as he turned into his third rotation he lost his grip and shot through the air. He flew over the fence and landed with a thud in the neighbouring compound, only to realize, to his horror, that he had landed in the lion's cage. He panicked when he saw the lion slowly rise to its feet and begin to pad towards him. At this point he lost all composure and began to scream, "Help! Help! I'm not a gorilla, I'm a man!" The hair on the back of his neck rose as he felt the hot breath of the lion. Then he heard a voice. The voice said, "Shut up, you fool, or we'll both lose our jobs!"

This joke, which I never tire of telling, does ask a rather profound question. Is authenticity related to what is on the outside or what is on the inside? In the realm of faith, are we authentic Christians because of what is on the outside or what is on the inside? Surely, if faith is real and healthy, the answer is both. Faith that is interiorly authentic will also be visible on the outside, but we also know that it is possible for faith to be on the outside only, with no corresponding reality within. This is the age-old dilemma and danger for the Christian faith, stretching back to the time of Jesus himself.

Three Mysteries

In my first days of formal theological studies, a professor told us that all of Christian theology could be contained in three great mysteries: the mystery of God, the mystery of God with us, and the mystery of God in us. The first is the study of who God is, that God is revealed as Father, Son and Holy Spirit, the mystery of the Trinity. The second mystery is the Incarnation, God with us, that "the Word became flesh and lived among us." (John 1:14) The third mystery has to do with the theology of grace and living the Christian life. This mystery is God in us, and is founded on the indwelling of the Holy Spirit.

At the Last Supper, Jesus said many things that would have shocked his disciples. He changed the meaning of an ancient memorial to be about himself, he washed the feet of the disciples, he told them he was leaving them, and shocked them even more by saying that it would be better for them if he left than if he remained. (John 16:7) This seems counterintuitive. I am sure many of us have often dreamed about what it would be like to go back in time and hang out with Jesus, or about if he returned and we could have him with us in the same way as the disciples did. What an exciting experience! Upon further reflection, however, we may quickly realize that this would not be as wonderful as we would think. During his time on earth, Jesus was limited in time and space. The mystery of God "with us" meant that Jesus "emptied himself" (Philippians 2:7) and embraced finitude. Trying to see or be with Jesus would have been much more difficult than trying to see or be with the pope. The best we could do would be to see him at a distance.

Jesus said that it was better for him to go, because then the Advocate, the Comforter or Paraclete, would come. This comforter (*parakletos*) is the Holy Spirit, who will abide with us and be "in" us (John 14:17), bringing about the mystery of God in us.

As great as "God with us" through Jesus would be, how much more profound would our lives be with "God in us" through the Holy Spirit? Jesus confirmed this when he said, "The one who believes in me will also do the works that I do and, in fact, will do greater works than these, because I am going to the Father." (John 14:12) These heretical-sounding words remind us that the very same power that was at work in Jesus when he preached, healed and performed miracles is given to those who believe in him. It is a great mystery, but in his humanity, Jesus "emptied himself" of his "equality with God" while existing the whole time in the "form of God."

We gain this insight from one of the earliest liturgical texts on the infant Church, found in Saint Paul's letter to the Philippians (2:6-11). The Council of Chalcedon, one of the great Christological councils, taught that in the union of the divine and human natures of Jesus, his divine intellect and will and his human intellect and will were unmixed. This means that all of his miracles were done through the power of the Holy Spirit working through his human nature – the same Holy Spirit that he breathed upon his disciples and desires to breathe upon us. This is why Jesus can assert that those who believe in him will do the same works as he, and even greater ones. Indeed, it is to our advantage that God be in us rather than with us.

The Promise of the Father

The key phrase in these Johannine dialogues is "*when* the Advocate comes." (John 15:26) Everything waits on the coming of the promised Holy Spirit. The New Testament does not speak in one voice when it comes to the Spirit of God, nor is there anything that could remotely be construed as a systematic Pneumatology (study of the Holy Spirit), but the New Testament authors are clear about two things: promise and fulfillment. In Luke–Acts, the great two-volume work written by Saint Luke, there is, from the opening, a clear sense that the Holy Spirit is at work. John the Baptist is proclaimed to be "filled with the Holy Spirit" even before his birth. (Luke 1:15) The Angel Gabriel tells Mary that the Holy Spirit will come upon her and that the power of the Most High will "overshadow" her. (Luke 1:35) Elizabeth is filled with the Holy Spirit when Mary visits (Luke 1:41), Zechariah is filled with the Holy Spirit (Luke 1:67), and the Holy Spirit rests upon the prophet Simeon and reveals to him that he will behold the Lord's Anointed. In spite of the activity of the Spirit before and throughout the ministry of Jesus, there is still a sense that the promise of God has not been fulfilled and an expectation that it will come soon. After the Resurrection, Jesus tells them, "I am sending upon you what my Father promised; so stay here in the city until you have been clothed with power from on high." (Luke 24:49)

Volume two of Luke's great opus opens with the Holy Spirit being spoken of twice in the preface, and once the narrative of the Lord's Ascension is taken up, there is an immediate return to the promise of God: "you will receive power when the Holy Spirit has come upon you; and you will be my witnesses in Jerusalem, in all Judea and Samaria, and to the ends of the earth." (Acts 1:8) The fulfillment of the promise is imminent. The clouds burst on the day of Pentecost and those cowering men are transformed by a new Power that will lead to the Gospel being proclaimed to the ends of the earth. The theology of the infant Church develops around this experience of God's power. It is enunciated in Peter's sermon on the day of Pentecost and is entirely about the fulfillment of a long-awaited promise. Peter proclaims to the assembled crowds that what they see is not a drunken spectacle, but the very thing that God has promised. Peter begins by quoting the prophet Joel, that God's promise is to pour out His Spirit "on all flesh":

> … your sons and daughters shall prophesy,
> your old men shall dream dreams,
> and your young men shall see visions,
> Even upon the male and female slaves,
> in those days I will pour out my Spirit.
> (Joel 2:28-29; see also Acts 2:17-18)

Prior to this, in Israel's tradition, the Spirit of the Lord was given to particular people at particular times for particular purposes. A specific judge, king or prophet would be so anointed. At the same time as this limited action of God's Spirit was described, there was in the Old Testament a mounting sense that God would do a new thing. God would put a new spirit in us that would transform hearts of stone into hearts of flesh (Ezekiel 36:26), and there was the clear prophecy in the prophet Joel that the spirit of God would be poured out on all people, regardless of sex, age or status. Peter puts his finger on this tradition, standing before the gathered nations (all people) and proclaims that what they "both see and hear" is the fulfillment of this promise. Peter calls the crowds to repentance and baptism. He promises them that they will receive the gift of the Holy Spirit, "For the promise is for you, for your children, and for all who are far away, everyone whom the Lord our God calls to him." (Acts 2:39)

A Spirit of Power

What follows throughout the Acts of the Apostles is the constant proclamation of Christ, his death and resurrection accompanied with the power of the Holy Spirit. To repent and believe would lead to baptism and to the experience of being filled by the Holy Spirit – which is as tangible as going down into the waters of baptism. This encounter with the Holy Spirit is not abstract, but is truly an experience of God's power (*dunamis*), which transforms the community of believers and the individual believer. It is this same experience of power that Saint Paul speaks of over and over again as giving credibility to his Gospel.

> My speech and my proclamation [*kerygma*] were not with plausible words of wisdom, but with a demonstration of the Spirit and of power, so that your faith might rest not on human wisdom but on the power of God. (1 Corinthians 2:4-5)

> For we know, brothers and sisters beloved by God, that he has chosen you, because our message of the gospel

181

[*euangelion*] came to you not in word only, but also in power and in the Holy Spirit. (1 Thessalonians 1:4-5)

In the early Church, then, proclamation was always accompanied by demonstrations of power through the Holy Spirit. To respond to this Gospel was to receive the proclamation and be filled with this Spirit of Power, which is God in us. This experience of the Holy Spirit was fundamental to the growth of the early Church, and is essential for the Christian life today, especially in the call to the New Evangelization. It is no surprise, then, that churches that are healthy and growing facilitate and encourage their members not just to believe in the Holy Spirit, or to receive the Spirit of God sacramentally, but to truly experience the Spirit of power in their lives. The first wave of evangelization came from a realization of the fulfillment of "the promise" on the day of Pentecost, a realization that was more than conceptual – it was experiential and transformative. So, too, then will the New Evangelization be fulfilled only by a new Pentecost.

In spite of the centrality of the experience of the Holy Spirit in the early Church – and in just about any renewal movement in the history of the Church – today, amidst the calls for renewal, rebirth and re-evangelization, we continue to be more comfortable with the idea of the Holy Spirit rather than the experience of the Spirit who comes in power. In chapter 19 of the Acts of the Apostles, we hear the story of Saint Paul's visit to Ephesus, where he encounters "some disciples." The experience of "receiving" the Holy Spirit is so essential to believing that this is the first question Paul asks. They respond, "No, we have not even heard that there is a Holy Spirit." Further enquiry reveals that they were baptized by John's baptism only. They are given Christian baptism, have hands laid upon them, and "the Holy Spirit came upon them, and they spoke in tongues and prophesied." (Acts 19:6)

Trinitarian, Binitarian or Unitarian?

As strange as this encounter may seem to us, it often reflects the lived reality of so many believing Christians. They may have heard that there is a Holy Spirit, but have virtually no experience of the Holy Spirit and no relationship with the Spirit of Power. Theologically, we are Trinitarian, but too often, in practical terms, we are binitarian, or even unitarian. Some Christians have yet to unpack what the mystery of God as Father, Son and Holy Spirit means. God is no impersonal force or energy. God is not even just a personal God, but a tri-personal God who yearns to be in relationship with us as Father, Son and Holy Spirit. These are not mere modes of being, but three distinct personal relationships. Even those who have had a personal encounter with Jesus that has brought them into relationship with the Father as Father may struggle with being in relationship with the Holy Spirit. Jesus is the way to the Father, the face of God, the icon of the invisible God. (Colossians 1:15) He is the very enfleshment of God, the Sacrament of God, and so is the perfect mediator. What has been seen and touched can be encountered. He brings us to the Father, and our own relationship with our earthly fathers offer us a framework from which to begin to conceive a relationship with the God "from whom every family in heaven and earth takes its name." (Ephesians 3:15) But how do we begin to form a relationship with the Holy Spirit, especially if there has been no tangible experience of the Holy Spirit in our lives?

If the third person of the Trinity has been reduced to a concept, or some abstract thing that we receive at confirmation, with no corresponding experience beyond sacramental gestures, how can we speak of truly knowing the Holy Spirit? It has not helped that it was only recently that the Holy Spirit received a name change. I remember as a child hearing about the Holy Ghost, and struggling to understand. Ghosts were something to be scared of. I had a childish image of Casper the friendly ghost with a halo over his head. I also remember struggling with the word "paraclete." I had heard of a parakeet and, knowing that the Holy Ghost was symbolized by a bird, I concluded that the avian metaphor had been extended. This may sound silly, but I suspect that many people of faith similarly struggle to make sense of this Person of the Godhead. We have a theology that tells us we "have" the Holy Spirit and continue to receive the Holy Spirit, but in a manner that does not in any way translate into a life-altering experience of power. Indeed, this mystery of God-in-us is highly misunderstood in the Church today and remains undiscovered by many believers.

Experiencing the Holy Spirit

When Saint Peter went to speak at the house of Cornelius the Centurion in Acts chapter 10, we witness another stage in the fulfillment of the promise of God. Not only will the Spirit of Power be poured out on young and old, male and female, slave and free, but even upon the Gentiles.

While Peter was still speaking, the Holy Spirit fell upon all who heard the word. The circumcised believers who had come with Peter were astounded that the gift of the Holy Spirit had been poured out even on the Gentiles, for they heard them speaking in tongues and extolling God. (Acts 10:44-46)

Three things happened in this episode. The listeners had an experience of the Holy Spirit, which was visible to those who accompanied Peter; they prayed using the gift of tongues; and they were praising God. This narrative has a familiar ring to it, as it occurs again and again throughout the Acts of the Apostles. It drives home the point that faith in Christ, along with baptism, includes a transformative experience of the Holy Spirit. This experience of having God's love poured into our hearts is moving, it is emotional, and it provokes an enthusiastic response. (Romans 5:5)

This experience of the power of God through the Holy Spirit is foreign to many believing Christians throughout the world. This may be, in part, due to an underdeveloped study of the Holy Spirit in our theological tradition, but is far more likely a cultural intrusion upon historical, biblical Christian spirituality. Anyone who has travelled to Africa or the Caribbean will notice that the fear of emotive spirituality is not a Catholic issue per se, but a Western European Catholic issue that has been affected by post-

Enlightenment culture – in particular, idealism. To dwell in the realm of ideas is far safer and less threatening than to encounter the reality of the idea. This cultural trait seeks pastoral justification in asserting that we must be on guard against emotionalism of any kind. But in the great spectrum of human religious experience, emotionalism generally is not the danger of the North American or European Catholic Church. Compared to our brothers and sisters in the faith who dwell in the southern hemisphere, we are emotionally constipated when it comes to expressing our faith. We draw back in horror, fear or suspicion at anything that appears to be enthusiasm, and quickly label it as "charismatic."

Leaving aside the question of the charisms, which the New Testament takes for granted, the "charismatic" label is often imposed upon any expression of spirituality that touches the affect or emotions. In spite of ancient biblical instructions to raise hands, sing, clap and shout for joy, many of our churches would empty out if this injunction were to be followed. Such expressions of faith too often suffer a quiet intolerance, as people quickly get the message that such behaviours are not welcome in this place.

Enthusiasm

If there was consistency in our culture around the issue of the affect, at least our stoic spirituality would make some kind of sense, but there is not. When we go to the cinema or the theatre, we regard the movie or production to have been a great success if we were moved emotionally. When we go to sporting events, we consider it natural to enter into an almost religious state of emotional rapture. Because I grew up in Scotland, I know what it is like to experience 60,000 men getting intensely emotional at a soccer match. I once went to a Sarah Brightman concert and was fascinated by the reaction of the crowd, and of how no one seemed to mind. People were waving to her, calling out her name, telling her that they loved her at the top of their voices. They cheered and clapped enthusiastically, and no one moved to another seat because they felt uncomfortable with all the emotionalism. Being emotional is a normal and healthy part of what it means to be human, and yet this essential dimension of our spiritual lives is checked at the doors of most churches as we go into pew mode. In church, such displays of emotion leave us fearful, disoriented and threatened. Yet, who is more worthy of our tears and cheers? Who is more deserving of our spontaneous praise and demonstrations of love and devotion than the Lord who has created and redeemed us?

Enthusiasm is the literal response to the presence of the Holy Spirit who is God "in us," as to be enthusiastic is to be *en theo*, "in God." With the Spirit of God in us, the love of God poured into our hearts and God's Spirit speaking to our spirit (Romans 8:16), we cry out, "Abba! Father!' (Galatians 4:6) In this cry we realize, with every part of our being, that we have been adopted by God into the very mystical dance of the Trinity, so that God is truly in us and we are truly in God. The heart, and not just the mind, must be touched.

In order, then, to allow our people to experience the Holy Spirit, we must name and identify this crippling fear of emotional religious experience that isolates those who do not have the cultural church baggage we have. This includes most of the unchurched, whom we are called to reach with the Gospel. In contrast to the dominant Western Catholic culture, post-moderns not only do not fear emotional religious experiences, they welcome them. Just take a look at the "spirituality" section of any bookstore to see that this culture of ours is ready to embrace the most incredible creed, providing there is a corresponding experience to validate it.

A healthy Church is one that does not discredit or exclude experiences of the Holy Spirit that touch the affect. Rather, it encourages such experiences and values authentic diversity of expression, not a pseudo-tolerance that unconsciously demands uniformity of expression. It has a robust respect for how the Spirit of Power is manifested within the community of believers and seeks to evaluate every experience according to the fruits that the experience brings with it. It is a solid rule for anyone in pastoral ministry to evaluate any religious experience, no matter the degree of emotion connected to it, by determining whether the experience has led the person to demonstrate the fruits of the Spirit that are listed in Galatians 5:22: "The fruit of the Spirit is love, joy, peace, patience, kindness, generosity, faithfulness, gentleness, and self-control." These traits are the unmistakable footprint of the Spirit that blows where it will. No matter how powerful or meaningful a religious experience is, if the person involved does not become more loving, joyful, peaceful, patient, kind and generous, then the experience was not authentic. No matter how gentle and un-expressive an experience, if it translates into an increase in these fruits of the Spirit, it is surely of God.

Power in the Parish

How, then, can we introduce experiences of the Holy Spirit into the everyday life of a parish so that it becomes a value that will contribute to the transformation of parish culture? How can we minimize the chance that our own people will feel like their Christian lives are extraneous, with the internal reality absent, like the man in the gorilla suit I spoke of earlier? Pope Francis reflects on this same question in *Evangelii Gaudium*:

> How I long to find the right words to stir up enthusiasm for a new chapter of evangelization full of fervour, joy, generosity, courage, boundless love and attraction! Yet I realize that no words of encouragement will be enough unless the fire of the Holy Spirit burns in our hearts. (EG, no. 261)

Here are a few suggestions from my experience as a pastor of how to help our people experience this burning.

• It is that which is not understood and that which is unknown that causes fear. We need to teach about the experience of "God in us" through the Holy Spirit. We must teach people that there is no single experience that captures how God works in the hearts of believers. We must teach that an emotional response to God is a healthy part of being in relationship with God, just as it is in any other personal relationship. We must teach people that to be Christian is to be "pentecostal." That there is no Christian life or Church outside of the pentecostal experience. We must teach that God gives gifts, including charismatic gifts for the building up of the Church, and that God gives good gifts to his children, and will never give a snake instead of a fish or a scorpion instead of an egg. (Luke 11:11-12) Our disposition ought to be to say yes to each and every "good gift" that God desires to give us. We need not be afraid, even if we may not fully understand.

- Over the years, as I have used Alpha in my parishes, I have found it to be an excellent way to introduce an experience of the Holy Spirit to participants – both regular churchgoers and non-churchgoers. Alpha provides an opportunity to teach about the Holy Spirit and creates an environment in which each participant can have that essential experience of the Holy Spirit. At the heart of Alpha is a weekend or day-long retreat that focuses on the person of the Holy Spirit. It occurs after two thirds of the program has been completed. At this point, participants have had an opportunity to hear the kerygma and respond. Trust has been built with the team members and there is an openness to the experience of God when the invitation is given. The retreat weekend or day usually culminates with a gentle and non-intrusive time of prayer for each participant to be "filled" with the Holy Spirit.

We can argue the relative merit of the vocabulary from a theological point of view, but for the participants, this is about experiencing something: God's love being poured into their hearts. It is often life-changing. Over the years, both in my parish and when I have travelled to speak at national and international Alpha conferences, I have had the pleasure to hear many stories of transformation through the tool of Alpha. At least 90% of the conversion stories are centred on the Holy Spirit day or weekend, when each person was prayed over to be filled with the Holy Spirit. They truly experienced the power of God, and they were transformed.

As more and more of my parishioners have discovered this essential relationship with the third person of the blessed Trinity, the whole tenor of parish life slowly begins to change. Speaking about the Holy Spirit, and praying to and for the Holy Spirit, becomes more natural. We do this at staff meetings and at committee meetings. When we gather our ministry leaders at Saint Benedict Parish for our leadership summits, we always conclude the mornings together by calling upon the Holy Spirit and praying over one another to be filled again. In this we do not settle for a theological conviction that it is by the Holy Spirit that we proclaim "Jesus as Lord" (1 Corinthians 12:3), but we are brutally honest that we seek an experience of God's love and that this is not a sign of spiritual immaturity. We seek God's power because without it, we can do nothing.

In our liturgies, we are conscious of invoking the Holy Spirit in song during the celebration of the Eucharist, and even take extra time after Holy Communion to ask the Holy Spirit to come. After all, as we acknowledge in Eucharistic Prayer III, being "nourished by the Body and Blood of your Son and filled with his Holy Spirit" ought to be a part of every celebration of the Eucharist. We also teach that it is important to pray the ancient prayer of the Church *Veni Sancte Spiritus* (Come, Holy Spirit) with expectant faith. Fr. Raniero Cantalamessa, long-time preacher to the papal household, often tells a story of a custom in his hometown. On Sunday morning after Mass, it is very common to hear invitations to neighbours to come and visit at some point. This invitation, however, is a form of social politeness and includes no expectation that the person will show up. Cantalamessa points out that when we invoke the Holy Spirit and ask him to come, we should do so with ardent expectation. It is only this kind of prayer that will yield the fulfillment of the promise of God in our own time for the renewal of our Church. Only the power of the Holy Spirit will allow us to not only recall our true identity as a missional Church, but to throw off the shackles of maintenance and go out. Pope Francis agrees:

We need to avoid it by making the Church constantly go out from herself, keeping her mission focused on Jesus Christ, and her commitment to the poor. God save us from a worldly Church with superficial spiritual and pastoral trappings! This stifling worldliness can only be healed by breathing in the pure air of the Holy Spirit who frees us from self-centredness cloaked in an outward religiosity bereft of God. (EG, no. 97)

10. Become an Inviting Church

"Come and see." (John 1:39)

If the first nine values that we have reflected on so far come to be valued by a local church, then the last – establishing an invitational culture – will come naturally. If real effort is put into focusing on the weekend as a priority so that the liturgy is uplifting and moving, if there is great music, great preaching, a welcoming environment, then parishioners will naturally desire to invite friends, family and neighbours to come and see.

If our churches become places where there is meaningful community, clear expectations, a focus on gifts, and an intentional system of small and mid-size groups, and an environment in which the Holy Spirit is experienced, then those who come and see will be far more likely to stay and tell. Parishioners will also be more likely to extend invitations beyond Sunday Mass and invite others to experience the life of the parish outside of the celebration of the Eucharist.

Intentionally Invitational

Successful, healthy and growing churches are, however, intentional about creating an invitation culture within the life of their church. To be honest, at this point in my journey with the people of Saint Benedict Parish, we have not yet begun to be intentional in developing invitation as a real value. The key is "not yet." In spite of this, due to work on the other values, our most recent ME 25 survey shows interesting results that back up the claim that this value can take care of itself. Asked to measure their agreement with the statement "In the last month I have invited someone to participate in my parish," parishioners were offered a range from 1 to 5, with 1 meaning "strongly disagree" and 5 meaning "strongly agree." Although we have "not yet" begun to tackle this value, we found that 23% of parishioners strongly agreed and 15% agreed to this statement. That means 38% of our parishioners have invited someone in the last month. This astonishing result placed us higher than the average Catholic response, and higher than the average response for all Christian churches in Gallup's database. What might happen when we become intentional about this?

The first principle to keep in mind when creating an invitational culture is to remind people that it is God who gives the growth. (1 Corinthians 3:7) This means we are responsible for inviting, but we are not responsible for the response to the invitation. In Church circles, it usually takes five invitations to produce one yes, and in spite of the "no, thank you," we will never know how God will work in someone's heart even after the invitation has been turned down. When communicating about inviting others, we need to be clear about this.

We also need to be clear about what success looks like. Anyone who will invite needs to know that they will get a "no" much more often than a "yes." Every time we begin a new Alpha experience at Saint Benedict, we joke about who can gather the most "no"s (conversely, the person who gets the most "no"s is always the person who brings the greatest number of guests with them to the celebration evening at the end of each course). In spite of this, we must be clear that success is in the number of people being invited, and not the number that show up. We cannot be responsible for this. We are called to sow the seeds by invitation and must leave the rest to God.

The second principle is that we need to name and identify the primary factor that prevents 80% of the members of the average parish from inviting others: fear. The fear is real. Fear of rejection, fear of being considered odd, fear of creating discomfort in a relationship, fear of being considered "one of those" people is what most often keeps our lips sealed. There is no shortcut when it comes to fear in our lives. We need to identify it and bring it to the Lord in prayer. We need to hear his voice saying to us continuously, "Do not be afraid."

Awkwardness can also be a factor in preventing invitations being extended. The truth is that many parishioners who do not invite may want to invite others, but do not know how. The key is for the invitation to be natural, as natural as any other invitation to something wonderful that has been discovered. In John's Gospel, this is the exact dynamic that takes place when Andrew, after spending the afternoon with Jesus, goes to his brother Peter and brings him to Jesus. This is the dynamic when Philip goes to Nathaniel, the cynic, and says, "Come and see." Communicating something wonderful and inviting others to it is never awkward, but is often unself-conscious. "Try some of this – it's amazing." The person may say, "No thanks," but the invitation has been made.

The third principle is that nothing inspires people to action like a compelling vision of what can be. For instance, on an average weekend at Saint Benedict Parish, we have 2,000 people in church. If half of them invited one person to church every week, there could easily be 200 new visitors on any given weekend. If even one quarter of these visitors were touched in some way to begin to take another step in their spiritual lives, that would be 50 people each week. The numbers are astonishing, and, best of all, they are realistic. If this ever started to happen, our problem would no longer be about inspiring an invitation culture, but in responding to the people who have taken a step in faith to show up, and even to return again.

A Working Model

Every call to action needs a workable model if it is to be successful. We need to be clear that we are not encouraging parishioners to extend invitations to strangers on street corners. This usually does not work. We wish to begin within the relationships they already have: friends, family, neighbours and co-workers – those already known to parishioners. We need to invite parishioners to take to prayer the question of whom should they invite, to ask God to place names and faces on their hearts. Before the invitation is made, parishioners should be intentional about praying for each person on their invitation list. God's work in our lives is mysterious, and we need to be convinced that the Lord is already doing something in each person's life. We ought to pray for each person before we extend an invitation and afterwards, whether they say no or yes. Depending on the nature of the "no," it may be appropriate to invite again after a certain amount of time, especially if the decline was in the form of a "not right now."

We need to pray for courage before we invite, and then act. We may be as nervous as a high school kid in the cafeteria asking a girl out for the first time, and we may be just as shocked when the response is a yes. Lastly, we need to assist them in following through with their "yes." This will involve laying on extra hospitality, perhaps picking up a guest and driving them to church, inviting them to a coffee social after Mass, and being intentional about introducing them to other parishioners or to the pastor so they can begin to experience a sense of belonging. Lastly, we should assume that they will be open to coming again.

As Catholics, we need to be mindful of the "fit" when we invite non-churchgoers to a parish event. Depending on what Sunday morning is like in your parish, it may not be the best place to begin. If we can be reasonably certain that it will be an uplifting, warm, welcoming, positive experience, we can easily accompany an unchurched person to Mass. At the same time, we must keep in mind that the liturgy is, in many ways, inhospitable to the uninitiated. It presumes a certain level of comprehension of a specialized vocabulary, gestures and symbols that may be foreign to those without a Catholic background.

We have already spoken of the need for non-churchgoers to experience a sense of belonging through meaningful community so they can begin to believe. It is imperative, then, that parishes begin to have a semblance of Christian life outside of the celebration of the liturgy – various events to which the unchurched can be invited and at which they will hear the message of the Gospel. At Saint Benedict, the most obvious place to invite others to is Alpha, but we also have prayer breakfasts for men and women, concerts and events with speakers in a non-liturgical setting.

Alpha

Of all of these opportunities, our Alpha events are the most accessible and the easiest to invite others to. I like to speak about Alpha as "Evangelization for Dummies." We invite people to dinner and movie, and the invitation is always to come and see. The invitation makes explicit that there is no commitment beyond the first week, and that the participant can take the course one week at a time. We are clear that if they decide not to come back, no one will contact them. Alpha is structured so that each process ends with a celebration event to which the "graduates" can invite friends and family members to come and see what they have experienced. Again, it is the most natural thing. Many wish to attend just to see what has affected their spouse, friend or colleague so significantly.

Alpha is designed to run as a rolling program in a church, so that each graduation evening is the first week of the next Alpha. Each "Come and See" event concludes with an invitation to sign up for the next Alpha, which usually starts a few weeks later. After doing Alpha in parishes for more than eleven years, I have learned that it is most common for 80% of the guests who attend a "Come and See" night to sign up for the next time Alpha is offered. Sadly, many churches that run Alpha don't get the invitation momentum going. Rather than having significant numbers of unchurched people attending their courses, each course is mostly made up of active parishioners. This will be of benefit to a parish, as most of these participants will experience renewal and even conversion, but the link to the outside is often lost. Typically, a parish that does not get the invitational dimension of Alpha will experience a plateau after about 60% of its members have taken the program. It will slowly die out, and the committed will say, "That was great! What should we do next?" In many ways, such a parish never really started to run Alpha.

Although we have not yet been intentional about an invitational culture around our weekend liturgies, we have been intentional when it comes to running Alpha. Over the last year, we have seen an increase in the numbers of people taking Alpha at Saint Benedict. We have parishioners who, after experiencing conversion through Alpha, have invited dozens of people to a "Come and See" event. One woman in our parish invited every co-worker in her office: fallen-away Catholics, unchurched people, non-Catholics, atheists, agnostics, Muslims and Hindus. A man who is very involved in our parish and constantly invites others was originally invited by this same woman. After saying "no" four or five times, he eventually said yes to a "Come and See" night, just to make her go away. His life was changed, and through him, the lives of others have been changed.

It is important in every venture in parish life to celebrate our wins. We can do this by telling stories. If invitation is to become a value in any parish, we need to celebrate it. Stories are powerful, but too often we focus on the extraordinary. There is nothing like an amazing story to help us marvel at the way God works, but God most often works in the ordinariness of life. Simple invitations lead to changed lives. The extra spring in the step of a man returning from Alpha each night led his wife to check it out. This curiosity led to an encounter with Christ and entering the RCIA to become Catholic. A co-worker who attended an Alpha "Come and See" just to "shut up" her colleague came to faith and returned to the Church of her childhood. Indeed, there are countless numbers of small miracles, all because someone had the courage to whisper the invitation to come and see something wonderful that they themselves had discovered.

6

THE FRONT DOOR

The Sacraments as Our Greatest Pastoral Opportunity

As Catholics, our biggest pastoral struggle is also our greatest pastoral opportunity. Couples, parents or families who have little or no connection to the Church regularly come knocking on our doors seeking baptism or marriage. Although not as numerous as in previous years, they still come to us. Although their idea of what they are asking for may be very different from the Church's understanding of baptism or marriage, they are coming to us. If we as a Church can navigate these waters well, we will be able to harvest what amounts to be the low-hanging fruit of the New Evangelization.

In Chapter 5, we reflected on the challenge of merging high welcome with high expectation. This is also the case when it comes to responding to requests for sacraments. Let me state a pastoral principle at the very beginning of this reflection on sacraments and the call of the New Evangelization. I believe that it is essential that those knocking on our doors be welcomed with open arms and love, no matter how limited their faith or understanding of what they are seeking.

My last parish was situated near the downtown area, close to hotels and reception halls. One of the churches of the parish was a beautiful neo-classical stone church with a very long aisle. It was a favourite spot for weddings, and it was not uncommon to have up to 30 weddings there each year. Ninety percent of the couples who contacted us would have no real connection with the Church. I would seek to welcome every couple, no matter how weak their connection or how seemingly shallow their motivation. I remember one young woman who, when I asked why she had chosen our parish, responded, "I really like your stage." My response to her was "Fantastic! Let's set up a time to talk."

I strongly believe that our starting point must be that we never say "no" to any request for a sacrament. To do so is to cut off at the heels even the possibility of conversion and transformation. However, this begs the question of what it means to say "yes." "Yes" cannot simply mean the fixing of a date, some paperwork and a quick marriage preparation class.

Our "yes" must be a wholehearted willingness to walk with couples until they are ready to celebrate the sacraments and be accompanied with a clear definition of what readiness looks like. Our "yes" must be an invitation to a process, a journey, as we resist the pressure to provide the church on a certain date. Our "yes," therefore, may also involve a "not yet." The journey must be one of authentic conversion, and not be just a complicated obstacle course that must be successfully navigated in order to get the prize at the end.

Making Disciples, Remember?

The context for the sacramental aspect of the Christian life is found at the heart of the mission that Christ gave to his nascent Church. In Matthew 28:19-20, we are given what has become known as the Great Commission. The wavering disciples are told to "Go therefore and make disciples of all nations, baptizing them in the name of the Father and of the Son and of the Holy Spirit, and teaching them to obey everything that I have commanded you." We saw in Chapter 2 that the task at the very heart of the Great Commission is the making of disciples, and that all the other missionary tasks of the Church revolve around it: the going, the baptizing and the teaching. According to the Great Commission, it is those who have begun to walk the path of discipleship, in the midst of the community of believers, who are to celebrate the sacraments of faith.

As we considered in Chapter 4, one of the basic causes of the lack of spiritual fruit, the frustration among ministers of the Church, is the fact that in spite of our going and teaching and baptizing, our confirming and absolving, we have failed to make disciples of the majority of those who seek sacraments, especially Sacraments of Initiation. To focus on making disciples challenges us to respond to each individual who knocks on our doors as an individual with his or her own history. No one-size-fits-all process will be enough. Rather, we will have to move from programs with fixed starting and ending points, with their respective rewards, to a process more akin to mentoring, walking with those who knock so that they can celebrate sacraments when they are ready.

The *Catechism of the Catholic Church* tells us that liturgy and sacraments "must be preceded by evangelization, faith and conversion." (CCC, no. 1072) No five-month or two-week program can produce these results. If we are to make disciples, we must have models that will move away from sacraments as an age-based reward system to being moments of celebration of authentic faith in the heart of the Christian community. This will take real courage to implement and will require us to overcome several theological biases that are deeply rooted in Catholic culture and consciousness.

In Chapter 4, we spoke about some of the junk that has to be cleared out of the Church before authentic renewal can take place. This junk exists as a kind of unconscious theological consensus that, although in contradiction to our official theology, continues to influence and shape our pastoral activity, how we "do" Church.

Although I focused on the broad themes of Pelagianism and clericalism in Chapter 4, there is much theological junk that needs to be identified around the sacraments when it comes to pastoral practice in most Catholic churches. These are theological positions that unconsciously shape our sense of what is the best thing to do, our sense of what is right, and even what is in the realm of possibility. Although the previous chapter had a more pastoral focus than the earlier ones, I would like now to briefly step back into the world of theology; at the end of this chapter we will turn again to propose pastoral models.

More Junk to Take Out

It is my conviction that traditional Catholic sacramental theology has been disproportionately influenced by Counter-Reformation theology and subsequent doctrinal definitions of the late sixteenth century. The sacramental theology of the Reformers was itself developed in reaction to excesses, perceived and real, in late medieval theology and piety. Post-Reformation Catholic sacramental theology was, in turn, built upon a reaction to the theology of the Reformers.

These perspectives continue to shape our perception and experience of the sacraments to this day, particularly the dogmatic definition that sacraments work *ex opere operato* ("by the action being performed"), and the consequent disproportionate stress on the concept of the *validity* of sacraments, as opposed to their *fruitfulness*. Another post-Reformation focus on how the sacraments communicate sanctifying grace and bring about what is known as *ontological* change (a philosophical term referring to the realm of "being") has led to a de-emphasis on the *existential* or "experiential" dimension of the sacraments. This development particularly affected the ecclesial, communal understanding of the sacraments. Lastly, the predominance of more than fifteen centuries of infant baptism has also had adverse effects on how the sacraments are experienced. This is all quite a mouthful. Let me break it down.

Ex Opere Operato

This Latin term, which literally means "from the work being worked," has to do with the objective validity of sacraments and is widely perceived to distinguish validity from fruitfulness. By a *valid* sacrament, the Church means that what Christ has promised to do through the sacrament has been done. If a marriage is valid, two became one. If a Mass is valid, bread and wine became the Body and Blood of Jesus. If an absolution is valid, a sinner is absolved. By fruitfulness, the Church understands that the footprints of "God in us" will be evident, that the recipient will become more loving, gentle, kind and patient – in short, more like Jesus.

The term *ex opere operato* originated in an early medieval school of theology called Scholasticism, and was clearly enunciated through the theology of Saint Thomas Aquinas. In spite of this, the idea it refers to originates in an earlier period in the history of the Church, in the experience of what is known as the Donatist Controversy. The Donatists, a rigorist sect in Carthage, North Africa, grew out of the experience of the persecution of Christians by the Emperor Diocletian in the year 303. Many in the Christian community failed to live up to their faith promises. Many gave up their beliefs, and some "handed over" the sacred scrolls of Scripture, the sacred vessels and even fellow Christians. The controversy began after clergy who were reputed to be guilty of such failures returned to pastoral ministry. The sect that would be eventually named the Donatists contested the validity of sacraments celebrated by these priests and bishops who had failed and sinned so grievously. This question caused great conflict in the fourth-century Church of North Africa.

Through the intervention of the Emperor Constantine, this question was referred to the Bishop of Rome and was eventually settled at the Council of Arles in 314. The Council decided against the assertions of the Donatists and declared that the sacraments of these clergy were valid sacraments because their efficacy is not rooted in the personal holiness of the minister. Rather, it is found in the faithfulness of the Church as a whole, and, most of all, in the faithfulness of Christ who is *the* priest, as well as the promise of God who can act even through unworthy ministers. The Church found for the efficacy of the sacraments *ex opere operato* and not *ex opere operantis* – meaning from the work itself rather than "from the work of the one working," that is, the minister of the sacrament. Over a thousand years later, the Council of Trent (1545–1563), in response to the Reformers, dogmatically defined this position. Since this time, Catholic sacramental theology has been disproportionately influenced by this question of validity, and the question of fruitfulness has not received the attention it deserves.

It is also worth noting that the Church ascribed the fruitfulness of the sacraments to the realm of *ex opere operantis*, and later included the disposition of the one receiving the sacraments. Fruitfulness of the sacrament, therefore, was dependent on the person of the minister, on his own devotion and holiness, and on the openness of the one receiving the sacrament. Juxtaposed to the question of fruitfulness was the concept of validity (*ex opere operato*), which affirmed that Christ would act in the sacrament in spite of the lack of holiness in the minister or openness in the recipient. A person who receives the Eucharist without faith will still receive the Body and Blood of Jesus sacramentally, even though it may be entirely unfruitful. *Ex opere operato* was originally a justification of pastoral practice in the face of something seriously lacking in the *minister* of the sacrament, guaranteeing the objective validity of that sacrament. Today, however, this concept is used to justify pastoral practice in the face of something seriously lacking in the *recipient* of the sacrament.

Today, therefore, these concepts serve to underline the theological significance of a "valid sacrament" even when the ability of the person to receive it fruitfully is in question. As a result, the issue of sacramental validity has become abstracted from actual human experience, and the *ontological* dimension holds sway over the *existential*. In practical terms, in our contemporary experience, we see the fruits of these theological developments in the all-too-familiar pastoral concern for whether the sacrament was valid, with little or no corresponding concern about fruitfulness. I remember a recent wedding that I presided at outside of my province. I met with the priest before the rehearsal. This priest had meticulously fulfilled all the canonical requirements and had correctly filled out all the paperwork and ensured there were no obstacles to the marriage being "valid." When I asked him if the groom, who was not a Catholic, was a believer, he said, "Oh, that never really came up."

The Concept of Sacramental Grace

By the time the Church clearly understood that there were seven sacraments, Scholastic theology had come to distinguish three ways in which the sacraments could be considered (do not be put off by all the Latin terms; I will explain them):

1. the *sacramentum tantum*: the outward sign (water, oil, bread and wine, etc.);

2. the *res et sacramentum*: the invisible and immediate saving effect;

3. the *res tantum*: the ultimate saving effect (the life of grace).

The second of these aspects, the *res et sacramentum*, had a Christological dimension and an ecclesial dimension: the configuring to Christ proper to each sacrament and the corresponding grace regarding the Church. So, in the sacrament of baptism, for instance, there was the forgiveness of sin (actual sin as well as original sin), the infilling of the Spirit, the configuring to Christ, and adoption by the Father. These all fell under the Christological dimension and are invisible. The ecclesial, and therefore visible, dimension is membership in the Church.

As a result of the focus on the ontological effects of the sacraments and the debate with Luther on the theology of Grace, the ecclesial dimension of the *res et sacramentum* was short-changed. This happened even though baptism was, in the earliest biblical accounts, principally about reception into the community of believers. Today, this ecclesial dimension has slipped so far from the popular understanding of baptism that parents can respond with an "I do" when asked if they clearly understand what they are undertaking by having their children baptized. They declare this with a clear conscience and, all too often, with no intention of being active members of the Church.

Today, the results of this theology can also be seen in the fact that so often we are content with the liturgy of the sacraments, with the *sacramentum tantum*, and the concern for "validity," which concerns itself with the conferral of the invisible grace, even without any visible ecclesial dimension being lived out. As a result, sacraments come close to being magical moments when spiritual vitamins are distributed, through ritual that, although it takes place in the church building, has little or no connection to the Church as the community of disciples. Pastorally, this is rather convenient, because if the essential stuff of baptism is invisible, we can walk away undisturbed by the complete invisibility of any difference our labours seem to make. The one dominant visible demand of baptism, membership in the Church, is considered optional and non-essential. We are left with invisible membership in the visible Church.

Infant Baptism

The practice of infant baptism, although an ancient one, has accelerated the negative impact of the sacramental theology that developed after the Council of Trent (often referred to as "post-Tridentine"). The pastoral normalization of what was originally theologically exceptional has had an impact not only on the theology of baptism, but on the theology of all the sacraments. Here, the saying *lex orandi, lex credendi* (the law of praying is the law of believing) holds true.

That infants were baptized in the early Church is a fact. Although the earliest explicit reference to this practice is not until the Apostolic tradition, attributed to Hippolytus in 215 AD, and in the writings of Tertullian several years later, there are many references in the Scriptures to entire households being baptized. Nevertheless, both the Scripture references and the passage from the Apostolic Tradition allude to, or describe, the baptism of children of adults, who were themselves being baptized. Hippolytus tells us that the children who could not speak for themselves were to be brought down into the water. The norm, pastorally and theologically, was still the baptism of adults. Children were baptized as an extension of the faith professed and lived by the parents who were presenting them. The Scriptures tell us that repentance, conversion and faith precede baptism. Infants were baptized in concert with the professed and lived baptismal faith of their parents.

For obvious reasons, what was pastorally and theological normative (the baptism of adults) eventually became rare and practically non-existent until the sixteenth century, when new mission grounds opened up for the Church. What had been the exception became the norm, and practice shaped theology. Scripturally, baptism was a response to adult faith. Over the centuries, however, as the practice changed, a theology of baptism emerged that had no connection to conversion or personal faith, but rested on the ontological dimensions already discussed. As a result, baptism in particular – and eventually all the sacraments – were disconnected from conversion, from profession of faith and from fruitfulness.

The Challenge

The cultural changes of the last 50 years have revealed existing fault lines in this sacramental system. Because the culture no longer compels people towards a connection with the Church, this connection has rapidly faded. At the same time, our pastoral models are essentially the same as those used before the cultural landslide of the last 50 years. What we are left with is the experience of sacraments that have practically no relation to discipleship, at least for those who have not yet become disciples, yet their original context was that they were rooted in discipleship.

So the challenge before us is not just pastoral, but also theological. Although absent from official Church teaching, these imbalances or biases of Catholic "popular theology" are deeply ingrained in the collective Catholic consciousness and heavily influence our pastoral practice. They need to be addressed and explained to our people before we can present new models to them. Responsible change management means communicating why something is being changed, and must take care that those receiving the explanation are capable of understanding it. Saint Thomas Aquinas told us, "Whatsoever is received is received according to the mode of the receiver." Re-education of our people will be vital so that changes in pastoral practice are not perceived as punishing children and families, as if some essential medicine was being withheld because people were not behaving as we thought they should.

The Cost of Inaction

The consequences of failing to adapt to this new pastoral reality are not declining Church membership, the greying of our parishioners or the lack of ordained ministers. It is not just about the fact that, in most parishes, close to 90% of the baptized under the age of 40 no longer live their faith, or at least not within the community of faith. The issue is deeper than our ongoing decline and the eventual and continuous restructuring of our parishes. The greatest consequence is the toll taken by continuing to settle for external appearances that have little or no connection to the internal reality. How long can a pastor and community joyfully and wholeheartedly celebrate Confirmation as the completion of Christian initiation, knowing all too well that most of the freshly initiated have, in their minds, just obtained a ticket out of the Church? What makes it worse is that the young people know that you know, and, worse than that, they know that you know that they know that you know. At stake is our very integrity as Church.

In my second year as a pastor, I reached a point when I could not do it anymore. I still remember the moment. It was a wonderful liturgy. The bishop was present and all the young people were there with their families, friends and sponsors. During the liturgy, when the candidates were presented to the bishop, a dialogue took place between the bishop and the sponsors, who were told to stand. "Have these candidates faithfully joined the Christian community for worship?" All the sponsors responded, "Yes they have!" I wanted to shout, "No, they haven't, and how would you know because you weren't here either!" Then I was struck deeply by the fact that the liturgy itself is an occasion for people to stand up publicly and tell lies before God and the Church.

What is the cost when a pastor, before the congregation, asks parents of children being baptized, "Do you clearly understand what you are undertaking?" and they say "yes" – and then most never return? How long can we keep this up, when this witnessing of unfulfilled promises begins to make our own "yes" to the demands of Christ and the Gospel more difficult to fulfill? If we get so accustomed to settling for externals, how long will it be before we settle for the externals in our Christian lives, without the corresponding internal reality? Was this not the central critique the Hebrew prophets had about the religious system of their time? Was this not the heart of the conflict Jesus had with the religious establishment of his time, when he accused them of being concerned only with the outside, while they were full of corruption on the inside?

To make peace with this reality is to allow a part of the heart of the Church to die. It also makes peace with compromise and sin. The recent sexual abuse scandals, although of an entirely different order, are extensions of this same malady: settling for the external appearance and the covering up of anything that may reveal an inner dysfunction and making peace with something with which we should wage war. We are one body. The success or failure, joy or sorrow of the other members of the Church truly affects every other believer. If the body is to be healthy, we must demand authentic discipleship of ourselves and of those who seek sacraments of faith, for our own sake and theirs.

New Models of Pastoral Care

I love the story told in chapter 2 of Mark's Gospel about the paralyzed man who is brought to Jesus. The stretcher bearers could not approach Jesus as he spoke from the front door of Peter's house in Capernaum, because the crowds were so big. Undaunted, they outflanked the crowds, climbed up on the roof of Peter's house, dug a hole in the roof, then lowered their friend down at the feet of Jesus. I am deeply struck by the actions of these unnamed men. First they had a deep desire to bring their friend to Jesus. They also had a deep conviction that Jesus would make a difference in the life of their friend. We hear in Mark 2:5 that "when Jesus saw their faith, he said to the paralytic, "Son, your sins are forgiven." The men also had the will to do whatever was necessary to get their friend to the feet of Jesus, even something as crazy as climbing a roof and making a hole in it. They had courage and perseverance. Surely Peter would have greeted their remodelling activities with a few choice fisherman's words. Capernaum was a small town and Peter likely knew where they lived!

This story raises questions that we too must face as we consider how we respond to those who seek sacraments in our parishes. Do we have a desire for every person to truly encounter Jesus in a life-changing way? Are we driven by a conviction that the encounter with Jesus makes a difference? What, then, are we willing to do? What are we willing to change? What obstacles are we willing to climb and even tear through to make it happen? The mission of our Church is to make disciples, not to celebrate good liturgy or keep people happy. Sacraments are given to us to initiate and sustain believers into discipleship. Are we willing to do whatever it takes to make this a reality?

When I received the news that I was to be appointed as pastor to the newly formed parish of Saint Benedict, I met with my Archbishop and asked for his permission to implement new pastoral methods. I asked him to allow Saint Benedict to become a kind of pastoral laboratory. I had been adapting my approach to baptismal preparation, marriage preparation and First Communion and confirmation for years, but, although we had experienced some improvements, we were still falling short. Most of those who received these Sacraments of Initiation into the life of the Church or marriage we never saw again. A new parish and a new church building presented a wonderful window of opportunity, and the permission of the bishop would seal it. Much of what is written in this book had been swirling in my head and heart for years, and the time seemed right to do something about it as I moved to this new parish.

During my entire first year in the parish, we began to implement many efforts, with the broad goal to change the very culture of the parish. The ideas I had around pastoral care of the sacraments, I shared with the pastoral staff, pastoral council and ministry leads. At the end of that first year, I put a basic plan onto paper and submitted it to my Archbishop for his approval. Once I received it, we took the second year to begin to communicate the vision for sacramental practice to our parishioners. We spoke about what exactly we would be moving to and why, and we slowly rolled out changes so they were in place across the board by the beginning of our third ministry year at the new church.

By the time we changed our children's catechetical program and the sacramental preparation for children, the cultural shift that we had been working towards on other fronts had begun to make a real difference. Active parishioners had also been given six months' notice about the impending changes and several explanations about what we were doing. By the time we implemented our approach to marriage preparation and baptismal preparation, we were inviting candidates into a process that reflected what every parishioner was being invited into.

At the time of the writing of this book, we have concluded the second year of our new process with children and youth. We are in the second year of our process for marriage preparation and we have just implemented the model for baptismal preparation.

Already we have had to make several adjustments as we learn from our mistakes or figure out how things can be improved. We implement these changes without any conviction that what we propose is somehow *the* answer to our pastoral dilemma, but with the conviction that it cannot be worse than what we have been doing.

Working with Children

> The new evangelization is the opposite of self-sufficiency, a withdrawal into oneself, a *status quo* mentality and an idea that pastoral programmes are simply to proceed as they did in the past. Today, a 'business as usual' attitude can no longer be the case. (Lineamenta for the Synod of Bishops on New Evangelization, no. 10)

In my part of the world, Nova Scotia, we have never been blessed with a Catholic school system, so catechetics have traditionally taken place in the parish, usually following a classroom model. Here is a summary of our catechetical program and children's sacramental preparation program after we finished our first ministry year at the new church in the spring of 2011.

1. About 70% of the families who had registered in our catechetics program did not participate in Sunday Eucharist.

2. On any given Sunday, only 40% of the students registered were present in class.

3. We experienced a large increase in registrations for the sacramental year and a similar drop-off when it was completed.

4. Mass and class attendance in the sacramental years was no different than in any other year.

5. Of previously non-attending families whose children received sacraments, 95% never returned to church after the program.

During this first year, we had about 80 families for First Communion. It had been the custom at Saint Benedict to do a mini RCIA-style scrutiny with the families during Advent. It was my first year in the parish, so I had not changed anything. After the homily, over 70 families lined up in front of the sanctuary. Most of them I had never laid eyes on. Out loud, before God and the community, parents made a solemn promise to bring their children to Eucharist every week. In spite of this, 60% of them I did not see again until the morning of First Communion, and have seen none of them since. All we had succeeded in doing was enabling these parents, who had no intention or capacity to follow through, to perjure themselves before God. The tragedy here is not just that it likely sounds familiar, but that we did not meet them where they were and, instead, set these families up for failure.

Over the years, I had sought to address this all-too-familiar scenario in the various parishes I served in. When I was first a pastor, and was free to implement change, I was sure that the solution lay in changing the resources being used. I thought that all we needed were solid, orthodox resources that taught the Catholic faith in its fullness. This would surely make all the difference. People would be wowed and compelled by the beauty of the faith. I was wrong. It did make a slight difference, but as important as the right content, the right books and the right programs are, this is still not enough. After years of using various catechetical series, I am now convinced that changing programs, books or resources is the equivalent of putting new tires on a broken-down car. Our problem goes well beyond content, and is inherently a problem with the classroom-based, child-centred model used in most parishes.

The Broken-down Car

Child-centred catechesis presumes Catholic culture and active participation in the Church. But this Catholic culture no longer exists in our society, and most families requesting sacraments are not active members of the parish. The new reality means that no matter how good a program is, its value will be limited unless we work with the parents of the children. Involving parents cannot be an add-on to the classroom model, but must involve the faith formation of adults in the parish as a whole – the kind of culture shift we have been speaking of in previous chapters.

Anyone who has ever flown somewhere is familiar with the safety videos that play before an aircraft takes off. These videos always emphasize that in the case of a drop in air pressure, adults must put on their own oxygen mask before putting one on their children. If something were to happen to the adults, the children could be in trouble. Most parishes focus on the children and neglect the adults. In most parishes and dioceses, the terms "catechetics" and "religious education" mean what we do with children. Adult faith formation too often remains a novelty that a few parishioners may do from time to time. As a result, adults rarely come to maturity in faith. And as soon as children perceive that what they have received is of little value to their parents, the children's own faith yields little fruit. Bringing adults to mature faith is the greatest gift we can bring to our children.

At Saint Benedict, and in the parishes I served in over the years, we always experienced the mad scramble each September to find enough Sunday school teachers for all the grade levels. By trying to provide unique programs for every grade level, our resources were spread too thin, and too often we failed to do anything well. It was unfocused and ineffective. While this may not be an issue for parishes aligned with a Catholic school, there are other challenges in working with the school model, especially in maintaining a vital relationship to the parish and the celebration of Sunday Eucharist.

Lastly, the communication of knowledge alone, no matter how good the content of the program is, will not bring about the desired outcomes of discipleship. Discipleship is far broader than catechesis, and presumes that those being discipled have been authentically evangelized. Remember the words of the 2007 Aparecida document? It told us that unless the kerygma or first proclamation is heard and received, all other steps in the process of making "missionary disciples" are "condemned to sterility."

Attempting to catechize families who have not been evangelized is like trying to plant seeds in concrete. It does not work. Even when we work with families who have been evangelized, a discipleship process must foster real personal growth – not only in knowledge, but in maturity of faith, experience of prayer and discernment of gifts – and "equip the saints for the work of ministry." (Ephesians 4:11)

Catechesis is program based and has fixed start and end points. Discipleship, on the other hand, is a way of life. Several years ago, at an International Stewardship conference, I heard Sister Edith Prendergast give a keynote address. Something she said stopped me in my tracks. It was a quote from Dr. Michael Warren: "Catechesis ought to be occasional and lifelong. We have made it continuous and terminal." It was another eureka moment for me. The simplicity of it was dazzling. Why did we need to cycle children through Sunday school or religious education classes for nine continuous years until it came to an abrupt end with teenage graduates believing that they were now set for the rest of their lives? Imagine that we could move entirely away from a program model and have the Church be the program. Imagine that every parish had a culture of discipleship so that faith formation for all was valued. If it truly became permanent and lifelong, it would not have to be continuous and terminal.

All of these considerations led us to make the following changes to our catechetical and sacramental preparation programs for children at Saint Benedict Parish:

1. Our primary investment of time and resources would be in sacramental preparation.

We knew that our resources were stretched too thin to work effectively with families when we were running thirteen different classes with seven distinct age-based levels. Now, 80% of our energy goes into working with small groups of families who present their children for First Reconciliation and First Communion. Families apply to the sacramental program and must demonstrate their readiness to take this step. Catechists are then assigned to small groups of families as mentors. Each program is eight weeks and takes place three times a year. The average class size is now around ten families. In this way, our director and her team get to know each family personally and journey with them. While each program is distinct, we do ask that families complete the First Reconciliation program before they proceed to the First Communion program. This way of walking with each family has led to a huge increase in families continuing to live their faith in communion with the Church.

The other 20% of our time and resources goes into a bi-monthly program called GIFT: *Growing In Faith Together*. This is an open-ended, all-are-welcome program where no attendance is taken. All families are welcomed, regardless of their faith background or commitment level. Each gathering brings the entire family together for learning and sharing; most sessions also see the parents meet together with a catechist while their children gather in age-appropriate groups for their own activities. This two-tier system allows us to merge the values of hospitality and expectation. There is no real expectation for the GIFT program, some expectation for the First Reconciliation program, and higher expectation for the First Communion program. A family requesting to have their children enrolled in the First Communion program needs to be currently participating in the GIFT program, attending Sunday Eucharist and must have completed our new member process.

2. All catechesis and sacramental preparation would be family based.

We require at least one parent per family to participate in the GIFT program and in sacramental preparation. What a wonderful sight it is to see all the meeting rooms filled with families laughing, learning, singing, playing and praying together between Sunday morning Masses. This is so different from seeing these same rooms filled with children while their parents, whom we didn't know, stood in the hallways drinking coffee and politely declining invitations to go into the hall for the adult catechesis that we would put on each week.

Our sacramental preparation programs involve the parents in two ways: in the classes and in their own participation in the same sacraments. On the day of First Reconciliation, the Catholic parent or parents also celebrate the sacrament. Most of them are returning to the sacrament after many years away. It is a powerful moment when a child, the parents and the siblings all experience the sacrament together. What a difference from the "do as I say, not as I do" mentality of parents who would usher their children to the reconciliation room while saying they would never go in there themselves. For both sacramental preparation programs, the eight weeks are comprised of several morning-long family retreats, home assignments and attendance at Mass together.

3. Reception of sacraments would no longer be based on age or grade.

This change was the most liberating aspect of our new program. Age or grade levels as a standard for readiness to celebrate sacraments is rooted in the days when preparation was done in Catholic schools. It worked when there was a dominant Catholic culture. It was a cookie-cutter model, and it generally made good cookies. By breaking out of the age restriction, we were able to put the focus of readiness on, well, being ready. It underlines that we are not all the same, that we are unique and have a unique faith story as individuals and as families.

With so many families returning to Church after being away, we had continuously been dealing with "older" children needing to be prepared for sacraments. An obviously older child in the midst of younger children on a First Communion Sunday was always a possible source of embarrassment for a parent who might experience some level of social shame for not having brought their children at the "proper age." It could also be a real deterrent to parents coming forward, thinking it was better late than never.

On the other hand, I have met many younger children who demonstrated an understanding of the Eucharist and had an authentic hunger for the sacrament. It never made sense to me that they had to wait because of a one-size-fits-all approach to this sacrament.

Now our First Communion classes have a real mix of ages, from ages six to twelve, and we are cultivating a sense that attuned parents bring their children to the sacraments when they are ready. The other bonus of this model is that it places the decision about taking this step in the hands of the parents. We have turned off the conveyor belt. It is no longer automatic. Parents have to discern not only if their children are ready for this step, but if they and their entire family are ready. Families that requested First Communion for their child but had no habit of attending Sunday Mass would receive a gentle "Yes, but not quite yet" response. They would be encouraged to attend the GIFT program and start attending the Eucharist. When there was some habit formed, they could then consider the next step (First Reconciliation), and so on. Parents with children one or two years apart in age loved this new program, as siblings could participate together. Our approach is more work than the conveyor-belt approach, but much more effective.

4. Sunday Eucharist would be restored to the centre of our programs.

It was ironic in the past that most parents would clamour for their children to become members of the Church and receive the sacrament of the Eucharist, while they themselves were not active members of that Church and never received the sacraments. They would seek to have their children complete most of the program, but never got with the program. Surely the only way to overcome this mentality is to make Sunday Eucharist the program. What we do after Mass is an add-on to what we just experienced. Our gatherings of families always take place after the Eucharist, which means the time can vary. For both the GIFT program and the sacramental preparation program, the families sit together at Mass. For the eight-week sacramental programs, attendance is not so much taken as it is noticed. This is a luxury we can afford when working with smaller groups of families, compared to the days of the 70 to 80 families who remained largely unknown to us.

Although we have only just completed the second year of this new model, two trends are emerging. First, our overall enrolment is down about 50%. In the previous model, however, enrolment did not mean much, as most classes would have only a 40% attendance rate on any given weekend. Second, the impact on the families who do choose to participate is significant. Of the families who did not have a strong connection to the Church before they entered into conversation with us, as many as two thirds of them have continued to be connected with the parish after the sacramental celebrations.

Lastly, and most importantly, I believe that people are being brought to the feet of Jesus through this new process. Parents are taking responsibility and initiative in seeking the sacraments. They are getting reconnected to the parish, and their lives are being touched. Each program ends with conversations about how they can continue their faith formation and be an active part of the discipleship culture we are seeking to establish in the parish.

But what about families who are not in sacramental preparation? What about those weeks when the GIFT program is not on? Are they missing out? Are we being delinquent as a parish for not providing a weekly format? My answer is that only if our catechesis is terminal does it have to be continuous. If it is to be lifelong, it does not have to take place every week. Occasional will do! Besides, the Eucharist happens every week, and that really is the program. For younger children, we have the children's Liturgy of the Word at both morning Masses, so there still is something every week for them. In the end, I readily admit that our particular rending of the status quo is far from perfect. We are still at the very beginning and are constantly learning how to do it better. It is much messier than what we were previously doing, but it is already more than worth it.

5. Confirmation and youth

I have already spoken of the almost universal experience in the Catholic Church in the Western world, when this sacrament that completes initiation into the life of the Church is, in effect, graduation from the Church. What is meant to be a celebration of full membership is a façade covering up systematic apostasy. But surely the sacrament will kick in at some point, won't it? This mindset has kept us locked in a pastoral practice that produces few missionary disciples and is slowly killing us. We have all heard the joke about the priest, the minister and the rabbi who all had problems with bats in their respective belfries. The minister and rabbi tried all the conventional methods and were perplexed about how to get rid of them. The priest, however, had no problem. He just confirmed them and never saw them again. We laugh at this familiar joke, but it is a very sad laugh.

The sacrament of confirmation is not a time-release "grace" capsule, and when we minister it as if it was, the "pill" works by inoculating our young people to the real power of faith in Jesus Christ. By being exposed to such a weak and watered-down version of the Gospel and the radical and awesome demands of following Jesus Christ, it becomes easy for them to walk away and give nothing to a Church that asks nothing of them. The sad reality is that they do not even know what they are walking away from, as they have built up such an immunity to the Gospel message.

The sacrament of confirmation has been described as a sacrament in search of a theology. It has been understood as the sacrament by which a Christian receives the Holy Spirit. In recent centuries, it has come to be seen as a rite of passage into maturity, a moment when the confirmand becomes a "soldier of Christ." In recent decades, it has been presented as a moment for the teenager to make his or her own decision about faith and the Church, a decision that had been made for them by their parents when they were baptized as infants. Although aspects of all these understandings are valid, neither one nor all of them present the primary meaning of confirmation.

218

Confirmation is the completion of initiation into the life of the Church, and brings about the perfection of baptismal grace. The Holy Spirit was received at baptism and has been always present in the life of the Christian. This biblical and ancient understanding of the sacrament of confirmation is much more prevalent today, at least in academic circles. It has led many in the Church to question the present practice of confirming teenagers years after the other Sacraments of Initiation have been received. Some propose that the original order of baptism-confirmation-Eucharist be restored. Others propose imitating the practice of the Eastern Church of giving all three Sacraments of Initiation to infants, in the original order. I will not enter into the question of the order of these sacraments or of the proper age to receive them. These questions will not solve our dilemma. The real questions are the same as those we have examined above: How do we engage the parents of children, and how do we help people become ready to receive the sacraments?

Following the principles outlined above, at Saint Benedict we do not have a conventional confirmation class, and there is no fixed age or grade level for receiving this sacrament. The confirmation "class" is called the Church. It takes place every Sunday at a gathering we call the Eucharist. As we are building a culture of discipleship in our parish where every parishioner engages in faith formation, this also applies to our young people and their parents. This is our first goal.

Our youth ministry program works with young people ages twelve to seventeen in an age-appropriate manner. Once a young person is a part of this program, they may ask to receive the sacrament of confirmation, whatever their age. The key question is not their age, or the order in which they receive the sacraments, but their readiness. Young people who have faith and are part of faithful families who attend the Eucharist can easily become confirmation candidates. They will then continue to do everything they have been doing before. They will keep going to Sunday Eucharist and will come out to the youth group. A member of the youth team will be assigned to them as a mentor; they will be required to come to a few extra classes that explore the theology of confirmation and attend a retreat. Candidates for confirmation in the spring are identified early in the new year.

When parents contact us because their teenagers are at the right age for confirmation, we explain that there is now no specific confirmation program or age, and that the basis of confirmation is about being ready to live out full membership in the Church. Obviously, many parents are not happy with what they hear. Many are looking for the no-strings-attached graduation/apostasy approach to confirmation. We stress that we are here to help them take the steps they need to take and will support them along the way. Most of these young people have neither been to church for years nor have had any connection since they made their First Holy Communion. Many of them have yet to make their Second Holy Communion.

The first thing we do is invite the young person to be a part of the youth group. We use Youth Alpha to expose them to the kerygma and invite a response. This program has been very successful and well received by young people. The teens who participate in the youth group are encouraged to invite their friends, so these groups are always very mixed. Once the stirring of faith begins to take place and a young person seeks the sacrament of confirmation, we begin to encourage them to return to Sunday Eucharist. Once a habit of Sunday worship begins to form, even if the young person still does not attend every Sunday, we will accept them as candidates for confirmation. The celebration of this sacrament takes place once a year in the Easter season. As a result of these changes, we are seeing similar trends to those taking place with our children. The annual numbers of those confirmed are down by 40%, but the numbers of young people who continue to live out their faith in the Church is about 80%. This is a radical shift from just a few years ago, when 75% of the confirmed would vanish and never be seen again.

What a joy it is to see these young people, who have reached some degree of personal faith, come forward and experience the completion of what began for them through the choice of their parents. What a joy it is to see so many parents who have experienced renewal of their faith standing with their sons and daughters as they are sealed with the Holy Spirit. What a joy it is to see such a diversity of ages, from twelve- to seventeen-year-olds, receiving the sacrament of confirmation! What a joy it is to see some of them receiving the Eucharist for the first time on the day of their confirmation, as their families are newly returned to the practice of their faith.

Baptismal Preparation

We have already looked at how the sacrament of baptism has been affected by theological imbalances that grew out of our history as a Church: the focus on the ontological and the neglect of the ecclesiological dimension. That couples can, in good conscience, look you in the eye and affirm that they clearly understand what they are undertaking in having their child baptized, while having no intention of coming back the following week, tells us that we have a real problem. In my first months at Saint Benedict Parish, I met with the members of the baptismal preparation team, a wonderful group of holy and dedicated parishioners. I learned about the process they were using and then asked about the people involved. I asked what percentage of the requests for baptism were from non-churchgoing families. The answer: about 80%. I then asked what percentage of those who were not active members got connected after the process. As they looked over the names of people from the previous years, they concluded that the answer was 0%.

Baptism, for many, has become primarily a celebration of the biological family, a time of thanksgiving for the arrival of a child and an embrace, to some extent, of the faith as some kind of mysterious "good." While it may be these things, for most who contact our parishes for baptism, it is nothing more than these. At

Saint Benedict, we have been working over the past few years to implement a working model to deal with these realities and apply the principles outlined in this chapter. It is still a work in progress, but I will share in this section what we are doing or striving to do to address this pastoral reality.

First, as a Church, we have only ourselves to blame for the average Catholic perceiving baptism as a private rite of passage for the biological family. *Lex credendi, lex ordandi.* The law of praying is the law of believing. In many parishes, baptisms happen early on Sunday afternoon, usually after the last morning Mass. The family and their friends and relatives arrive for the event, since none of them have attended Sunday Eucharist with us, and there are usually no active members of the parish present, other than the priest or deacon. We pay attention to getting the ritual of the sacrament done properly, pose for photographs and then never see the family again. They do not come to us, and we do not go to them. When we celebrate baptism in this way, what right do we have to be surprised that our efforts bear little fruit in the way of discipleship?

I strongly believe that the first and simplest thing we can do to begin to change this mindset is to stop doing "private baptisms." After my experiences of being involved in baptisms in the manner described above as a seminarian, a deacon and a newly ordained priest, I vowed that when I had my own parish, I would never do private baptisms again, except in extraordinary pastoral situations. Over the years, and currently at Saint Benedict Parish, we have a baptismal Sunday once a month (except during Lent). Baptisms take place at the two Sunday morning Masses and I may have between two and six children to baptize. The parishioners have gotten used to it.

If done properly, these baptisms can be celebrated by adding only five or six minutes to the length of Mass. As with the Rite of Christian Initiation of Adults, I do the prayer of exorcism and pre-baptismal anointing before Mass. We have a permanent baptismal font, so I do not have to bless the water (for those who need to do so, this blessing can also done before Mass). When we have baptisms, there is no creed recited by the community; rather, I invite all the baptized, including the parents and godparents, to renew their baptismal vows. With proper assistance, then, it is possible to joyfully baptize two or three or more children and even sing a short litany of the saints and add only a few minutes to the celebration. The family benefits by making their profession of faith standing before and with the community. Their friends and guests benefit from seeing the Church at worship, and the parishioners benefit by being part of such a joyful event. I highly recommend it!

Second, there is a need to reject a one-size-fits-all baptismal preparation program and firmly distinguish between families who have a connection with the Church and those who have none. Why should a faithful, churchgoing, involved Catholic family who bring their third child to baptism go through exactly the same process as a family who attend Eucharist once a year or less, have no real sense of faith, and have no meaningful connection to the Church? Many claim that we cannot ask much of couples who are non-attenders, as we do not want to "punish" them. It seems to me, however, that we are "punishing" the faithful families of our parish and failing to meet the non-churchgoers where they are.

We have an immediate baptismal preparation class and a more remote preparation process. Our immediate preparation takes place on Sunday morning and is based around Sunday Eucharist. A gathering takes place between the two morning Masses, leaving couples free to choose which Mass they will attend. It is a four-week process that includes much the same content as an average baptismal preparation class: an overview of theology, faith witness by a team member, the role of godparents, and a review of the ritual and the details around the baptism. This class presumes basic Christian faith and a meaningful connection with the community of faith. Families who are active members of the parish enroll in this process and can have their children baptized as soon as they wish. Families who have already been through this process need not even take part in it. A simple date is all that is needed. Just like we did it in the "good old days."

For unconnected families who contact us to get their babies "done," we have a remote process that seeks to help them understand what they are truly asking for and we assist them in taking the steps they need to take to be ready. A couple who has no connection with the parish or the Church needs to be reinitiated into the life of the Church either before or as part of the initiation of their child. They need to be welcomed and gradually invited into a process whereby they are reacquainted with Sunday Eucharist and even invited to "second baptism," the sacrament of reconciliation, before they bring their children to the font. The tricky part is how to do this. How do we convince someone who wants to buy oranges that they really want apples? I have no easy answers to this question, but will share what we are attempting to do at Saint Benedict Parish.

The first step is to distinguish between the two groups of parishioners. It is quite simple. We ask, "Are you and your family regular attenders? Have you spoken with Father James?" This is a good question, because before any Mass I always focus on young families, young couples and any pregnant woman who walks into the church. Most families who are seeking baptism for their child will self-identify. Some present themselves as committed regulars even though they are not. Other than asking for some kind of report card, I do not think there is anything we can do to prevent this. Families who are not connected to us are invited to an information evening hosted once a month by a team of young couples.

The goal of the evening is to love them, welcome them and invite them to something bigger. We want to help them to reflect on what they are requesting for their children; if they really want this, they must address their own situation regarding the Church. We invite them to set out on a journey of faith, with the goal of getting ready for the baptism of their child. Just as it is not wise to rush into a marriage because of a child, it is also not wise to rush into a baptism because of a child – at least if there is no or little connection to faith or the Church. One or more of the team members will speak about their own faith journey and focus on the kerygma. No mention will be made of classes, rituals, schedules or dates. At this meeting, our baptismal brochure is given to couples. They are invited to take it home, reflect on it and let us know if they are up for the adventure of stepping forward in faith.

We realize that a good number of the couples who come to this gathering will not be up for the adventure. They want a no-strings-attached private baptism, usually in three or four weeks' time. We need to have the courage to stand our ground and to know that such a version of baptism is false and contradictory to everything we believe about the Christian life. At the heart of baptism is membership in the Church. It is not private, and following Jesus does come with all kinds of strings attached.

When couples are willing to move forward in the process of "getting ready," we welcome and work with them, no matter how messy or "irregular" their lives may be. No circumstance needs to be an obstacle if they are sincere about moving forward from where they are. We commit to accompany them in prayer and assign a young couple to support them as a mentoring couple. Mentoring couples pray for the families, invite them to join them for Mass, and keep in touch with them. These couples make the recommendation for the families in their care to move on to the next step of remote preparation. This will require some established and demonstrated habit of attending Sunday Eucharist. We do not necessarily require weekly attendance, but some kind of "stickiness" to the community. It is important to avoid taking attendance or being overly rigid on this, but we are looking for a connection to be made. Couples also need to go through the welcome process for new parishioners and be encouraged to celebrate the sacrament of reconciliation before their children are baptized.

Will there be mistakes? Absolutely. Will there be discomfort and uncomfortable conversations? Probably. Will people be carried to Jesus and placed at his feet? Hopefully. Will there be changed lives and decisions to become disciples of Jesus Christ? There will be, if we get all the other parts right.

Marriage

Applying these pastoral principles to marriage preparation has an added twist. Since the couple ministers the sacrament to one another through their vows, proper pastoral preparation is not only a question of a fruitful sacrament but also of a valid one. That's why so much ink has been spilled on the canonical issues around marriage and the need for proper knowledge and understanding. In the end, however, the same question applies: How do we help bring couples to the feet of Jesus, and what are we willing to do to support them?

As mentioned earlier, the fact that couples still come to us, unsolicited, to celebrate marriage is an incredible opportunity. There is no doubt that as our society becomes more and more secularized, not only is marriage within the Church diminishing, but so is marriage as an institution. For now, we still have the phenomenon of unchurched, unevangelized, non-attending couples contacting parishes and asking to be married. The first step in responding to these requests is to welcome them with open arms. Over the years, I have heard dreadful stories of priests and parish secretaries interrogating couples over the telephone about Mass attendance and parish boundaries. I believe every parish should welcome these couples in to sit down and discuss their request to be married in the parish church.

As with the other sacraments, our traditional models of marriage preparation presume faith, Catholic culture and even that couples are living the Christian faith in communion with the Church. It is rare for distinctions to be made based on the needs of particular couples and their preparation adjusted accordingly. When I was a young priest at the Cathedral of my diocese, I started a young adult group that lasted for many years. About twelve marriages came out of that group of young people who were seeking to walk the path of discipleship. I remember one year when three of the couples took part in a large district-wide marriage preparation day with about 80 couples from all over the diocese. All of the young adult group couples were almost attacked and mocked because of their faith. They felt persecuted and judged by the other couples at their table because they agreed with the Church's teachings on marriage and faith. How ironic!

Over the years, I always struggled as a pastor with how to meet couples where they truly were. As a young priest, I would require that couples begin to attend Mass at my parish. I would speak to couples who were living together and convince them "by many arguments" that this was not God's plan for them. I would invite all couples to postpone sexual intimacy until they were married, and to move out of a shared home if this was possible, or at least to move into separate bedrooms. All of these efforts met with a limited response. Most non-churchgoing couples would come to Mass until the wedding and then I would never see 90% of them again. I am not entirely sure how my other invitations were received, as I was not inclined to peek through their windows!

In the years since then, I have wised up to a few necessary truths. The key issue here is a change of heart. For most couples, this was not happening by just jumping through the hoops of showing up at the occasional Mass and forming a relationship with a priest they liked. They were not encountering Jesus, and he is the only one who can change hearts. Many of these couples, when invited to speak of their faith, would enunciate a vague kind of theism and would be very sketchy around what they professed about the person of Jesus intellectually, never mind that there was no sense of a personal relationship with him.

Obviously, a bare minimum needs to be established in preparing couples for marriage. It is not enough that at least one of the partners be Catholic: we need to find out whether that person has Christian faith, as this would impact the validity of the marriage. I once took over a new parish and had a wedding the following weekend. The groom was a Catholic and his fiancée was not. I thought I had better meet them before the big day, so three days before the wedding, I met with them in my office. When I asked them about their faith, I found out, to my horror, that both considered themselves to be atheists. I was stunned and stuck (I guess the question of faith didn't come up earlier). As unusual as this example is, finding couples who do not profess Jesus as Son of God is more common than we would imagine.

Basic Christian faith, the intention to lifelong, unconditional, faithful married love, and openness to children are the minimal conditions for validity, but what about fruitfulness? It is no different from the other sacraments. We are called to help these couples encounter Jesus and even have the opportunity to become his disciples.

For this reason, we ask all couples preparing for marriage to take Alpha as the first step in their marriage preparation. I have been asking this of couples for many years now and, although it is not a perfect solution, it has made a difference. Most of the couples have a very positive experience, and some undergo conversion and transformation. After Alpha, we run an evening for engaged couples using the Clifton Strengths Finder, and a Friday evening and all-day Saturday event focused on the sacrament of marriage in particular. It is important for all three aspects to be seen as the preparation process, and not just the immediate preparation. If only 10% of non-practising couples stuck around after their weddings before Alpha was a part of the process, now at least 30% continue to live out their faith, and many are firmly on the path of discipleship. I can choose to focus on those who still do not return, but a 200% increase is not insignificant.

Weddings must be scheduled far in advance. When couples approach us about marriage, they receive a letter from me outlining our process and are invited to consider the invitation to set out on a spiritual journey. If they agree to go forward, they meet with one of our deacons and other staff members to complete the process of preparation. We are now moving towards including mentoring couples as part of this process – married couples who would accompany, support and pray for the younger couple as they journey towards the sacrament.

In the end, if a couple enters into this process in goodwill, then nothing else is demanded of them. Providing they meet the minimum demands of validity, we are bound to celebrate their marriage, regardless of how their hearts are touched through the experience of Alpha and the other programs. We must walk with them, love and support them, always remembering that as a Church, we are in the disciple-making business, not in the wedding business.

Rite of Christian Initiation of Adults (RCIA)

It is no secret that in spite of wonderful sacramental preparation processes for adults in what is known in most parishes as an RCIA program, most parishes also witness a dramatic drop-off of almost 50% of the newly initiated in the first year. Technically, RCIA refers only to the *rites* of initiation and not to the content of catechesis or process of discipleship that is at the heart of the process. While the rites themselves are ancient and beautiful, more attention must be paid to the discipleship process that can make or break a program.

My first experience of an RCIA process took place during my internship year as a seminarian. Although the quality and content of the presentations were excellent, I was struck by two things. The first was that this group was secluded. Each time we gathered, we consisted of a few team members, candidates and their sponsors, with very little exposure and connection to the broader community. The second was that the quality of the formation was of a standard generally not offered to the parishioners at large. As a result, many stood peering through the door of the meeting room, drooling and longing to come in and join us – figuratively, and a few times literally. Why was such great material being kept for a few? It did not make any sense.

When I became a pastor and had my first RCIA process, this is exactly what I changed. The candidates, while keeping their identity as a unique group, were part of a faith formation process that was open to anyone. In this way, they benefited from the connections being made with members of the community, and the parishioners benefited, too – not only from the process, but also from accompanying those preparing for the Easter sacraments.

Another problem around the traditional shape of RCIA programs in our parishes is that the process is often presented as a program or course with a set start date and end date (the Easter Vigil). This is problematic. If the "inquiry" process is truly about discernment, how can it happen within a fixed time frame? Once the candidate discerns his or her willingness to receive the sacraments, how can the catechesis and faith formation leading to election for the sacraments take place in a set period? How can we truly respect the unique spiritual journeys of individuals when this process is overly programmatic? I believe that although the rites of the catechumenate are fixed and on a timeline, nothing else should be. We should be working with potential candidates and helping them to be truly ready to celebrate these sacraments. If a culture of discipleship is present in a parish, then certain candidates could complete several faith formation and catechetical programs before they make their decision to enter into full communion with the Church. Conversely, if the candidate is mature, association with the RCIA group could begin at the approach of the Lenten season and conclude at the Easter Vigil that same year.

Another concern for parish RCIA processes is the centrality of the kerygma, or first proclamation. We remember the words of the Aparecida document, which reminded us that the kerygma must be clearly articulated and responded to for evangelization to take place. Without this, the process of making missionary disciples is "condemned to sterility." Are the members of our RCIA processes truly encountering Jesus and coming into a personal relationship with him? Are lives being changed, or is information simply being communicated?

In response to these challenges, we have developed a new model of an RCIA process at Saint Benedict Parish. To begin with, it is open ended. Candidates for Easter sacraments are not positively identified until early January. Some who come forward may have been in and around the parish for several years, growing and learning at their own pace. We ask that every candidate take Alpha. This is a sure way, as discussed in Chapter 5, to hear and respond to the kerygma, to encounter Jesus, to experience the Holy Spirit and to find meaningful Christian community. In the new year, those who have come forward will begin a more immediate preparation by attending one of our adult catechetical programs that is open to parishioners at large. In addition to this eight-week program, the RCIA group will meet on its own to prepare for the rites specific to the Easter sacraments. After the Easter Vigil, these new Catholics are encouraged to be part of a connect group (see Chapter 5) to continue their yearly commitment to a faith formation program and to see discipleship as a way of life, not a terminal program.

One area of continued weakness that we are currently seeking to address is that, in spite of these changes, we are still losing some of our newly initiated in the first year. The support system that has nurtured them to this point is often withdrawn, and they are left to do it themselves. As we go forward as a parish, we desire to build up a supportive community so that we care for and look out for one another as a fundamental part of what it means to come into the Church. In the future, we plan to assist every person who receives the sacraments to immediately join a connect group where they can be supported and encouraged and can continue a process of discipleship that is occasional and lifelong.

Conclusion

We have covered a lot of ground in this chapter. We cannot propose new models for the pastoral care of sacraments without also addressing underlying theological convictions that shape these very practices. The pastoral section of this chapter describes the very beginning of an attempt to break free from the status quo and the "business as usual" attitude. Much of what is proposed in the pastoral section of this chapter comes out of the experience of a large parish. Some of what is described may not be possible in small parishes, but other aspects may in fact be easier to bring about in smaller, closer-knit parishes.

The proposals in this chapter may not be the best solutions. They may be inadequate, and our implementation of them at Saint Benedict may be wanting, but they are an attempt to do something different. I believe we have pressed the stop button on the conveyor belt and we are moving, with difficulty, into a disciple-making model. It is exciting and scary to have left familiar shores. At times, we have doubts about whether all we are doing is the right thing, but I am encouraged every time a testimony of a changed life comes across my desk or into my inbox or my mailbox. I still struggle with doubts, but when I think about what and how we *were* doing, I am more convinced than ever that we must keep on going, driven by a conviction that Jesus does change lives and by a willingness to do whatever it takes to lower people down to his feet.

7

LEADER OF THE HOUSE

The Essential Role of Leadership

If we are to truly recall the lost identity of our Church, to throw off the shackles of an inwardly focused, self-referential maintenance Church, we need leaders. If the Church has to move, and being missionary demands movement, we need leaders. A missionary Church is one that "goes out from itself toward the existential peripheries," as the man about to become Pope Francis wrote days before the conclave that would elect him. A maintenance Church can do very well by having a manager at the helm, but going from one place to another demands a leader, and a true leader is one not only in name or *ex officio*, but someone who leads. If the primary crisis of the Church of our time is one of identity, then a second crisis is one of leadership.

The Second Vatican Council taught that the priestly ministry exists to preach the Word of God, to celebrate the sacraments of faith and to lead God's people. The Catholic Church has been dogmatically defined as hierarchical. This is not just an archaic formula, but is found at the heart of the teachings of the Second Vatican Council. This means that by office, bishops are the leaders of their dioceses, and priests, in union with their bishops, are the leaders of their parishes. They can neither ignore this responsibility nor give it over to someone else so they can focus just on preaching and sacraments. Still, the question of how a priest will lead is in much need of attention in our Church today.

When I think back to my years of seminary formation, it is safe to say that although I received great training to be a theologian-in-residence, and some training to celebrate sacraments, I received very little training on preaching and nothing about leadership.

Where Is the Puck?

Wayne Gretzky used to say that the secret of his success was that he skated to where the puck was going to be. It seems to me that in many of the houses of priestly formation and seminaries I have visited over the years, we are not even skating to where the puck is, never mind where it will be. If the primary task of renewal is to move the Church from the inertia of maintenance culture, we need priests to be trained as leaders. Many seminaries seem content to focus on producing priests who are holy and orthodox in their theology. While this is necessary for priestly training and ministry, it is not enough. There are many holy priests with solidly Catholic theology who lead unhealthy, dying parishes.

This issue cannot be laid at the doors of those in charge of priestly formation. Dioceses have not adapted to where the puck is, or is going to be, either. Traditionally, new priests would receive on-the-job training as curates for many years; only those with obvious leadership skills would become pastors. Today, almost every diocesan priest will become a pastor, and often very quickly, which means that the period of mentoring that once was assumed does not take place. Even priests who are blessed to be mentored by good pastors are often, at best, being trained to go where the puck is and not where it is going to be.

In my first parish as a pastor, I had two half-time staff, a secretary and a maintenance man. Two years later, after taking over a second small parish, I inherited a quarter-time director of religious education and hired a half-time lay pastoral associate. This was a total full-time staff complement of less than two people. I was able to work with this team fairly well, without any awareness of anything lacking in my training. When I took over the city parish the next year, I had a full-time maintenance man, a half-time cook-housekeeper, a full-time secretary and a half-time director of religious education, for a total of three full-time positions. Two years later, after becoming pastor of the second city parish and working to bring the two together, I was charged with leading a team of eight people, for a total of just over six full-time positions. It was at this point that I realized I did not know how to do it.

No one had ever trained me for this kind of situation. I knew nothing about working with a team or how to lead a team. In addition, I had been charged by the bishop to bring these two very different parishes together to become one parish. I quickly realized that if I were ever going to be able to lead such a change with such a team, I needed to learn how to lead.

Learning Leadership

Everyone has some degree of leadership ability – the ability to influence another person. Most priests have some natural leadership ability. Some are strong leaders and others are weak leaders. A weak leader will rely on his title or office or official authority. This type of leadership in today's Church will not work. This priest will quickly find out that a leader with no one following is just a person going for a walk. What all leaders have in common is that we can learn and grow to become better leaders.

Experiencing this leadership challenge was the best thing that ever happened to me, as it forced me to learn. I turned to the only source of knowledge of Church leadership I could find at the time, and that was from the world of Evangelical Protestantism, and the writings of Pastor Bill Hybels of Willow Creek Church. Watching the videos of its annual leadership summits, I was transfixed and inspired. I found inspiration in the call to dream big and bold dreams through my involvement with Alpha on the national and international level. I began to see clearly that much could be learned from the human art of leadership and that being spiritual was not enough to bring about the renewal of my parish.

Today I pastor a large church with the equivalent of twelve full-time staff positions spread among eighteen people. In addition to the paid staff are the leaders of almost 90 ministries and committees that allow the parish to function. When our staff team began to grow, I quickly realized that everything I had learned about leading a team had to be readjusted to my new reality. I not only had a large team of staff, many of them leaders themselves, but I also had the task of labouring for the transformation of the parish culture, as described throughout this book.

The learning curve has been great, as have the number of mistakes I have made. I have realized that a leader must continue to grow, learn and adapt. In recent years, I have continued to find support in leadership from the Evangelical world, especially from the likes of Sandy Millar and Nicky Gumbel, past and present pastors of Holy Trinity Brompton, a large Anglican church in central London that birthed Alpha. I have been privileged to meet and learn from men like Pastor Rick Warren, author of *The Purpose Driven Life* and, even more relevant to the topic of this book, *The Purpose Driven Church*. I have been blessed to be the lone Catholic participant in facilitated workshops by the U.S.-based Evangelical Leadership Network, which supports innovating pastors. I am thrilled to be among a small group of parishes gathered by the newly founded Parish Catalyst, which seeks to use the model of Leadership Network to work with Catholic pastors and their teams. I have already mentioned the great assistance provided by tools from the Gallup organization, including its Leadership Excellence Course. The writings on organizational health and leadership by Catholic author Patrick Lencioni have also richly contributed to how I exercise leadership in my present situation.

Cultural Obstacles

Over the last number of years, I have been privileged to present workshops to lay leaders, seminarians, priests and bishops in Europe, North America and throughout Latin America on the themes of renewal and leadership. What a joy to meet so many passionate and holy men and women! These leaders who care about the renewal of the Church are crying out for support. In the Evangelical world, the help is out there and easy to find. In most Catholic contexts, it is not.

I have often said when speaking on this topic that I am just a guy with an opinion and a big mouth. Countless Catholic pastors have a track record that is more proven than mine on these issues, and I am indebted to them as well. What I share in this chapter is based on what is called the CASE method of Church renewal. CASE stands for Copy And Steal Everything. We do not have to reinvent the wheel when it comes to leading renewal in our Churches.

Although this question is relatively new in a Catholic context, Evangelical Protestant culture has been actively engaging these questions for decades, and there is much for us to learn. Many of the opportunities for learning come out of the differences in our ecclesiologies. Although the very idea of an "independent church" is an oxymoron, many Evangelical churches function without a local network resembling a Catholic diocese. As a result, these churches literally sink or swim. There is no big brother or "diocese" that will bail them out or prop them up. Everything is on the shoulders of the local church and its leader. Also, the leadership position is often based on the charisms and charisma of a particular person. Pastors who are not strong leaders always run the risk of losing their jobs to someone with greater abilities. For these reasons, Evangelical pastors are acutely attuned to the need to grow and develop their leadership capacities. Not only the life of their churches, but their very livelihoods, are at stake.

By contrast, Catholic ecclesiology places the locus of the local Church in the person and ministry of the bishop and, by extension, into diocesan administration. There are, of course, many advantages to this system, but also many disadvantages. Local parishes that are not healthy will generally be kept on life support by a diocesan structure. In many cases, there are few consequences for doing poorly or failing to grow in leadership. The culture of many dioceses often discourages innovation, and tends to see uniformity as a means to unity. Pastors are appointed by the bishop rather than being called from within, based on leadership ability, and raised up. Generally, as long as a priest can celebrate the sacraments, poor leadership, and even poor preaching, are tolerated. When poor leadership is addressed, it is never proactive, but only takes place after the train wreck has happened.

Another very real problem with the leadership of Catholic parishes is the length of time pastors are appointed. Anyone who studies healthy, vibrant and thriving churches will not only recognize the presence of the ten values outlined in this book, but will see that long-term leadership is essential. Meaningful cultural change in any organization takes time. The churches that have inspired me over the years all had the same pastors at the helm for at least twelve years to lead the necessary change. Most of the churches had the same pastors for eighteen to 25 years.

By contrast, in many Catholic dioceses, priests are transferred every six to eight years. This approach prevents the possibility of meaningful change taking place in a parish. It facilitates the flourishing of mediocrity and the culture of maintenance we have already discussed. Any priest who desires change will be resisted, because he is seen as a transient. He just arrived and will be gone in a few years. Long-time members of a parish are justified in their skepticism. They are the ones who are in it for the long haul. Change is always difficult, but many faithful parishioners will change just enough to adapt so that they don't really have to change. After a few more years, the priest will be gone and everything will just go back to the way it was before.

An even greater tragedy is that priests who labour for mean-ingful change become so dispirited when, just as the deeper change was taking place, they are transferred to another parish, and their successors systematically dismantle everything that they put into place. For this reason, many of our parishes are stuck in the mud – some of them spinning their wheels, and most of them slowly sinking. The very same, of course, can be said about dioceses, as bishops have often been transferred from one diocese to another as often as parish priests are moved. Saint Ignatius of Antioch said, "Where the bishop is, there is the Catholic Church." If, decade to decade, we do not know who our bishop is, how can we know where the Catholic Church is? If we do not know where we are, how can we go anywhere?

Our pastors – bishops and priests – need to be given the abil-ity to lead meaningful change through sufficient terms in leader-ship if our Church is to not only recall but embrace her essential missionary identity. Our current practice presumes a culture of maintenance, and worked quite well when maintenance sufficed. If we continue in this practice today, however, there will be nothing left to maintain in wide swaths of our Church in North America and throughout Europe.

The traditional mindset behind this relatively recent practice of short terms as pastor was to "spread the wealth." Not all priests were equal in their charisms. All we were doing was maintaining a system by managing churches, so it was reasonable to allow par-ishes to have a few years of a gifted priest and then a few years of a less gifted priest. In the end, nothing vital was compromised. The continuation of this practice today, however, will compromise the entire system. The Church is no longer static. It is in decline. By failing to lead meaningful change, the very lives of our churches are at stake.

Many years ago, I witnessed the process of pruning. I came out of the church after a weekday morning Mass and saw one of my parishioners butchering several of our rose bushes. Although she was the leader of our gardening ministry, I still wanted to call the police on her. I was truly shocked. She had chopped off 60% of the roses that had begun to flower. There seemed to be nothing left. Three weeks later, however, I saw the most beautiful, luscious red roses I had ever seen. Before pruning, the limited nutrients were spread out evenly to all the flowers. As a result, all were underdeveloped and, at best, mediocre. By pruning, there were fewer flowers, but they were beautiful and healthy. It is no different in our dioceses. By spreading out the gifts of pastors and constantly moving them, we get, at best, mediocre churches. By keeping pastors capable of leading change in parishes that have the potential to have high impact, we create the opportunity for at least some of our churches to be healthy and strong. The existence of such parishes in every diocese is vital, because without them we do not know what excellence and health look like. When we do not know what this looks like, we easily accept the mediocre as normative. When this happens, we lose our ability to envision anything different. We do not strive for the health and strength of our parishes, for we do not know what this looks like, and eventually we don't believe that it is even possible.

I will return to the need to be inspired by excellence and health later in this chapter, especially when I look at the question of vision. But first, I wish to examine one foundational quality of a leader: vulnerability.

Vulnerability

If I must boast, I will boast of the things that show my weakness. (2 Corinthians 11:30)

"Never let them see you sweat." "Make them afraid of you." These sentiments speak of a model of leadership that is solitary and invulnerable. It generally does not work in the world of business, and certainly does not work in the world of the Church, which functions with the dynamics of a volunteer organization. People make a choice (*voluntas*, in Latin) to belong to a particular church. Even paid staff make this choice, as most of them could be making a better wage working elsewhere. People choose to belong to a parish, and can just as easily choose to belong somewhere else if the leadership is not to their taste.

Leaders who are vulnerable recognize that they are fundamentally limited and incapable of doing it by themselves. In this way, they model for staff and parishioners an essential dynamic that should be at the root of everything we do as a Church. We need one another. We cannot do it ourselves. We need to lay down our masks of strength and perfection and admit that we are not sure how to do it anymore, that we do not have all the answers, and that we need to do this together. An authentic embrace of vulnerability will lead to a more human and humane Church.

As we saw in Chapter 5, a strong leader must be aware of his or her own strengths. Leaders will be most successful when they lean into their natural strengths and talents. At the same time, leaders who know their strengths will be aware of and honest about their weaknesses and deficits. There is no such thing as a well-rounded person. It is a myth. We are all imbalanced. But there is such a thing as a well-rounded team. Leaders who are incapable of being vulnerable will never be totally free to work out of their strengths, because they will never adequately compensate for their deficiencies. The well-meaning pastor who seeks to be well rounded will end up investing huge amounts of energy and resources in self-correction and self-censorship to compensate for his weaknesses. Many, however, choose to ignore their deficiencies and leave behind a proverbial body count in every parish they have served in. I was this type of pastor for many years before I discovered the Strengths Finder tools and philosophy.

I always knew I had the capacity to work hard, had a take-charge personality and was good at getting things started up. I knew that I have the ability to focus on a goal and get it done. It would only be after great strides had been made that I would turn around and see those who had been left behind, many of them casualties of the great progress made. The blessing of having blinders on is that you have eyes only for the goal. By not allowing

241

distractions, you more easily reach your goal. The problem with blinders is that you have no peripheral vision. Time and time again, I have been deeply grieved by the totally unintentional hurt I have sometimes caused to both staff and parishioners in the exercise of my leadership. There were times when people went down around me and I honestly did not see them. I have come to know that I need people around me who have strong relational skills, who can see what I sometimes do not, and who are free to challenge me.

In recent years, I have come to understand that although I have strong influencing strengths, I am weaker when it comes to developing or coaching others. After I had been a priest for eight years, I gave up entirely on the ministry of one-on-one spiritual direction. It was definitely not one of my strengths, and I have literally been fired by every person who asked me to be their spiritual director. I am not good at this aspect of leading, and I have learned that I need others on my team who are. Now, whenever I have staff members who are in need of coaching of some kind, I match them up with other team members who have the gifts to do this. What a relief it was to be vulnerable with my team about this area of weakness. What a relief to them that my particular exercise of leadership was not an expression of disinterest or willful neglect.

Every leader can benefit from this kind of self-knowledge and vulnerability before the people they lead. "Please help me; I cannot do this alone" – this is all we are saying by our vulnerability. The days of the Lone Ranger priest as a solitary paragon of strength are long gone. The do-it-yourself priest will never lead a church from maintenance to mission. No matter how small a parish or ministry is, every leader must develop his or her team. Essential team members in any parish must be the pastoral staff or key ministry leaders, pastoral council members, and competent parishioners with demonstrated leadership ability. Unless a pastor is willing to be vulnerable to this team, it will not be properly composed and will not properly function. A leader without a leadership team to whom he or she is accountable, transparent and vulnerable is a fool and a disaster waiting to happen.

Vulnerability is not only essential between a leader and those who are led, but also among other leaders. We need this not only to maximize our own ministries and to support one another, but also because of our need to model authentically the kind of change we long to see within our churches. I have spoken of meaningful community as a value – of building trust and relationships within our parishes. I have testified to the transformative impact of seeing parishioners praying with and over one another, and how their vulnerability led them to more loving and caring relationships within the parish. This same development must take place within our leadership community, especially among priests.

Sadly, at too many gatherings of clergy, vulnerability is the last thing you would ever witness. Competition, jealousy, suspicion borne of theological differences, gossip and fear prevent many priests from being vulnerable with one another. When it comes to praying together, we can comfortably pray the Liturgy of the Hours, but suggest that groups of priests should be vulnerable about their struggles, lay on hands and spontaneously pray over one another, and many would run for the hills. I have often thought, and experienced, that it is entirely possible to have resentment in your heart for a brother priest before and after praying evening prayer together, but that this is not possible when this same brother is vulnerable and I have prayed over him without using a formulaic prayer. As priests, we are often comfortable ministering in this kind of way with the people we serve. In the end, however, there is always a power imbalance. I have the collar, and you do not. I have the theology degree and the big words, and you do not. I am the priest, and you are not. It can be safe. Remove this safety and it gets very interesting.

In many of my workshops with leaders over the years, I have not just spoken about this kind of spiritual exercise, but have led groups of people to do it. As challenging and uncomfortable as this often is for the laity, it does not come close to the degree of challenge and discomfort exhibited by groups of clergy. Whenever I have led this workshop with mixed groups, I always get lay men to pray with lay men, lay women to pray with lay women, priests to pray with priests, and bishops to pray with bishops (and the occasional Cardinal). When the power imbalance is removed, the mask can truly come down. This kind of vulnerability is at the heart of the meaningful community that will transform our experience of Church, and it must begin with those who lead. I once had a bishop who works at the Vatican sit in the front row of such a workshop. I was nervous about getting the group to "do it," but went for it anyway. Later that evening, visibly moved, he told me that he had never, in his life, experienced prayer like that with a brother bishop.

Vision

Developing a Vision for the Parish

It has been said that the primary role of the leader of any organization is to develop and communicate a vision for what can be. Bill Hybels, the pastor of Willow Creek Church, has taught for years about the essential untransferable duty of a leader to be a vision caster. If the leader cannot do this, he or she will not lead anyone or anything. Hybels defines vision as "a picture of the future that produces passion in us." In previous decades, organizations, including many churches, worked out mission statements. These sometimes lengthy statements, often framed, hung on a wall and forgotten, could easily coexist with a maintenance culture. Mission statements often focused on what was to be done rather than on where we are going. Authentic mission is always about going somewhere, not just about what we ought to be doing. Before we can properly frame what we ought to be doing, we need to know where we are going. Several years ago in London, England, I was navigating to a particular place. I found it on my iPhone map and planned and executed the walk perfectly, saving time through an ingenious shortcut. The only problem was that I had the wrong destination.

Vision is one degree abstracted from what we are doing, and is more about what we dream about being. Any leader who will lead must not only be in touch with his or her dreams, but be passionate about them. This personal vision often begins with a deep sense of discontentment, a conviction that things do not have to be the way they are, that it can be better than this. The only way we can be truly convinced that things can be better is because we have seen it. If vision is about "thinking outside the box," it begins to take shape only after we have looked outside the box and have even gotten out of the box.

Getting out of the Box

In 2005, I travelled to London to participate in the annual International Alpha Conference at Holy Trinity Brompton (HTB). I had decided to attend the Sunday evening service, as Father Raniero Cantalamessa, preacher to the papal household, was to preach. I found my way to the church, passing the beautiful Italian Renaissance–styled Brompton Oratory to reach this comparatively small Anglican church nestled behind it. As I turned the corner, I stopped in my tracks. My first feeling was total confusion and embarrassment. I must surely be in the wrong place. Before my eyes, stretching for 300 metres, was a lineup of 20-somethings waiting to get into the church. But it turned out I was in the right place. At 6:00 p.m., the doors of the church opened, and hundreds of the same demographic poured out. They had been attending the earlier service and were now making room for the next crowd. I had never seen anything like this before. Thousands of young people hungering for the Gospel were lining up in secular London to hear a preacher. This is now a weekly phenomenon at HTB, which hosts eleven weekend services spread over four campuses.

Earlier that same year, I had been appointed pastor of a second church in the city of Halifax. I had been tasked to make it into one parish and at first was convinced that there was no other option than to close the second location, which was smaller, and gather everyone into the older and larger space. Money from the sale of the second church could be used to upgrade the facilities of the first one. I knew the journey would not be easy, but it was necessary. As the days at the conference unfolded, though, I met hundreds of Catholics and non-Catholics who were excited about evangelization. I heard countless testimonies about changed lives. I heard about and witnessed the transformation of churches and communities, and glimpsed the heart of so many on fire with zeal for souls. I also saw a parish church doing what was supposed to be impossible.

That year, HTB was operating out of two locations, the second being about a mile away from the main church. It was one community in two locations, and it was continuing to grow and expand. One afternoon, I escaped from a session and was sitting in the garden by myself, getting some much-needed prayer time, when all of a sudden I was totally convicted about a vision for the future, with my own parish flourishing in two locations. The Lord desires his Church to be healthy. It is possible for it to be so. What difference does it make if a church has two locations, as long as we are growing, developing and being faithful to Christ's mission?

It was a crazy dream, a picture of the future, but it produced passion in me. Many saw it as a pipe dream, but three years later, when our parish legally and canonically became one, it existed in two locations. We had chased away the circling vultures that had been drooling over the prime real estate of the second location. We had placed the parish office in one location and the priest's residence in the other. Weekend Masses were held at both locations. Most importantly, there were activities most days and evenings in both locations, and the parish was growing.

In Chapter 3, we spoke about the crippling effect of grief and discouragement experienced by many leaders in today's Church. It is vital that we address this issue as a Church, and that hope be restored. As we saw earlier, as necessary as it is to "lament," our lament must be done in a truly biblical fashion, and this always embraces hope, a hope that does not disappoint. "A shoot shall come out from the stump of Jesse," proclaimed the prophet Isaiah. (Isaiah 11:1) How many thought him an idle dreamer? Yet, he had a vision for the future that produced passion in him, and it was born of hope. If our leaders are to be people of vision, they must be people of hope. Cardinal Bergoglio wrote in his pre-conclave speech notes that "Evangelization implies apostolic zeal." He developed this theme in his letter *Evangelii Gaudium*:

> One of the more serious temptations which stifles boldness and zeal is a defeatism which turns us into querulous and disillusioned pessimists, "sourpusses". Nobody can go off to battle unless he is fully convinced of victory beforehand. (EG, no. 85)

If leaders are to have zeal and passion to labour for this vision, they must have real hope that the vision of a renewed missionary Church is possible. I have this hope. It is real. I know it, because I have seen it. I have seen it because I got outside the box of my small world.

Scratching the Itch

Ever since I have been a pastor, I have participated in conferences and gatherings within and outside my diocese. When I would listen to amazing speakers talk about what they were doing in their diocese or parishes, or about the call to renewal, I would always walk away with two strong reactions. The first was to be deeply reconvicted. Yes!! Amen!! Absolutely!! I would be once again fired up, and the passion would be stirring. At the same time, I would feel discouraged and overwhelmed. I knew where we needed to go, I burned with zeal to go there, but did not know where to start. I would feel encouraged and discouraged at the same time. Excited and frustrated. I could see the picture of the future one moment, and then would lose it and see only the obstacles and minefields that lay before me.

I once heard a brother priest acknowledge this dynamic at an amazing talk on parish renewal at an International Stewardship Conference. At the very beginning of his workshop, he said, "This is the part where I tell you how great my parish is and how much yours sucks." It was very funny, if a little irreverent, and honest. He went on to say that this is how he always felt when he heard presentations on parish renewal. As difficult as this is, though, it is a necessary experience.

Anyone who has ever scratched a mosquito bite knows the simultaneous experience of relief and frustration. The more you scratch, the more sweet relief you feel. But the more you scratch, the itchier it becomes. Vision begins with a sense of discontent, of dissatisfaction with the way things are. This is not about laying blame or criticizing; this is about theological hope. Things can be better because we worship the God of Jesus Christ, the One who raises from the dead and brings forth springs of water in the desert. The key to being passionate about our picture of the future is to find that dissatisfaction and scratch and scratch and scratch until it drives you crazy. Only when we have crazy passion about the future will we have a vision that inspires others.

Too often, those in leadership positions ignore the itch or seek to medicate it. They seek to live peaceably within their reality. In this way, though they have the office of leadership, they do not exercise it. In the Gospel of John, after Jesus cleanses the temple at the beginning of his ministry, we are told that the disciples remembered the words of the prophet Jeremiah, "Zeal for your house will consume me." (John 2:17) The Greek is *kataphagetai*, and literally means "will eat me up." Does your zeal eat you up?

Someone once said that leaders do not lie awake in their beds thinking about what could have been, but about what could be. My visits to churches like HTB and other conferences have caused me many sleepless nights. The passion is kept alive by a deep conviction that it is possible, that it can happen. The Lord is faithful, and the product, Jesus, is perfect and faithful. This vision has been kept alive because of what I have seen. I have experienced this as deeply essential. We must know that it is possible. We must constantly see others who are doing it better than we are, or else we will stop being dissatisfied and become self-satisfied.

A self-satisfied church is a mediocre church and will never become truly missionary. I spoke in Chapter 1 about the analogy of the photocopier. A photocopier is a wonderful machine when it works. It draws in blank papers, prints and sends them out to do their work. It is analogous to the Church's task of evangelizing, making disciples and sending them out as apostles, or, as Pope Francis has repeatedly said before and after he became pope, to make "missionary disciples."

> Every Christian is a missionary to the extent that he or she has encountered the love of God in Christ Jesus: we no longer say that we are "disciples" and "missionaries", but rather that we are always "missionary disciples". (EG, no. 120)

I have spoken repeatedly of the impact that my visits to HTB have had on me. This is one of the few mainstream Christian churches that is successfully embodying the photocopier analogy. Three times a year, the parish hosts Alphas for young people of an average age of 27. Each course attracts on average a thousand people. At least 20% of them are successfully evangelized, discipled and brought into the life of the parish or join some other church. Several times a year, HTB sends out groups of 30 to 40 parishioners with an ordained staff member to take over a small, dying church somewhere in London. Within a few short months, these "church plants" begin to grow and bear fruit. This enterprise has been so successful that HTB has been asked to make church plants outside of London, in Brighton, Norwich, Lincoln and Kuala Lumpur.

In contrast, the Catholic world of North America and Western Europe, as well as most mainstream churches, seems to be constantly shutting down and shrinking. The experience of what is happening in London seems like a dream, but what a dream!

Holy Trinity Brompton and other churches have proven that it is indeed possible, that our generation *can* be reached with the Gospel. Imagine what would happen in the Catholic Church if we, too, believed this to be possible. In the end, the question of vision asks of us all whether we are capable of being passionate. Those of us who are leaders must face the fact that the vision of what we lead, whether a parish, a diocese, a ministry or a team, will begin with our own personal vision: that picture of the future that produces passion in us.

Charisms

Vision may begin with the leader, but it cannot remain solely in the mind and heart of the leader. It must be communicated and shared in a compelling way that invites others to receive it, take ownership of it and even change and adjust it. Before vision can be shared, leaders must be clear on their own vision for their ministry. Our personal vision will be shaped by our charisms. This is unavoidable. A leader can only be passionate about what he or she is passionate about, and it is no coincidence that strong leaders develop churches that reflect their own deepest passions and convictions. The only alternative is a passionless mediocrity in which business as usual is the way of life.

In his letter to the Ephesians, Saint Paul writes that "The gifts he gave were that some would be apostles, some prophets, some evangelists, some pastors and teachers." (4:11) It is the task of the universal Church to embody all of the charisms, but it is highly unusual for any one leader to be strong in more than three of them. A leader's charisms will shape the very things that he or she is passionate about. The first step in communicating vision to others is an understanding of what your own charisms are.

To be an apostle is to have a passion for going out to reach the "lost," proclaim the Gospel and serve the marginalized. The apostle will not be satisfied in an inwardly focused Church. The prophet will desire to speak challenging words that may not always be welcomed. Pope Francis spoke about this charism in a weekday homily on May 16, 2013. He said, "We can ask the Holy Spirit to give us all this apostolic fervor and to give us the grace to be annoying when things are too quiet in the Church." The prophet will be like Jeremiah, who tried to hold his tongue, but could not do it. "If I say, 'I will not mention him, or speak any more in his name,' then within me there is something like a burning fire shut up in my bones; I am weary with holding it in, and I cannot." (Jeremiah 20:9) An evangelist will be driven by a desire to see people hear and respond to the saving message of Jesus. He or she will be passionate about first proclamation and helping people come into a personal relationship with Jesus. The pastor, on the other hand, will be driven not so much to catch fish, but to tend the sheep, to disciple people into maturity, to visit the sick and the dying. The teacher will be concerned about proper and effective catechesis and faith formation. We need the exercise of all the charisms for the Church to be healthy, but leaders must begin with an honest assessment of their own particular passions, because their vision will be shaped by these, whether they like it or not.

Writing It Down

The next step is to identify the vision of the future that excites us most. Whether we are pastors, staff, ministry leaders or parishioners who care about our church, we all should take the time to write down a one-page description of a future of our diocese, parish or ministry that excites us. Do not be distracted by the obstacles and challenges; just write down your dream. If you seek inspiration, turn to one of the most moving and remarkable vision statements ever written, Martin Luther King Jr.'s exceptional speech and its iconic repeated declaration, "I have a dream." Perhaps this speech was in the mind of Pope Francis when he wrote down his vision for the Church in *Evangelii Gaudium*:

I dream of a "missionary option", that is, a missionary impulse capable of transforming everything, so that the Church's customs, ways of doing things, times and schedules, language and structures can be suitably channeled for the evangelization of today's world rather than for her self-preservation. (EG, no. 27)

I love this statement, for it truly is a vision of the future that obviously produces passion in the heart of Pope Francis, and it is all about the recollection and reclaiming of our missionary identity as a universal Church. In the paragraph that follows, he presents his vision for what every parish should seek to be:

It is a community of communities, a sanctuary where the thirsty come to drink in the midst of their journey, and a centre of constant missionary outreach. (EG, no. 28)

Once you have written down your vision statement, write down your own personal purpose statement that will define your ministry. I did this exercise several years ago, and it was incredibly helpful. After describing my compelling vision of the future of my parish over two pages, I was able to reduce my personal purpose statement to this: "To be a catalyst for the renewal of my parish and of the broader Church."

The next step for the leader is to share this picture of the future with his or her leadership team. The leader's role is to be the primary vision caster, but the Holy Spirit works in the hearts of all people. The leader's vision needs to be communicated with parish staff, with the pastoral council, with every parish leader, regardless of role or office – with anyone who has influence. Listen, discuss, receive their feedback and refine the vision. When these steps have been completed, a parish should take this vision of the future and begin to develop a formal vision statement. This entire process at Saint Benedict Parish, from identifying my own vision to writing a formal parish vision statement, took about two and a half years. Here is our parish vision statement:

Saint Benedict Parish is a healthy and growing faith commu-nity that brings people to Christ, forms disciples and sends them out to transform the world. Every member is com-mitted to worship, to grow, to serve, to connect and to give.

It doesn't describe who we are, but it does describe where we are going. It is a description of the future, and it produces passion in me and in my leadership team. I recognize an echo of my own charisms in this statement, but it looks and sounds very different from what I would have produced all by myself. It is there to remind us about where we are going.

Communicating the Vision

No matter how inclusive the process is for forming a parish vision statement, unless the pastor serves a small parish, the statement will need to be presented to the broader parish. It should be clear by now that the vision for the parish is not the result of a democratic process, but of a consultative and collaborative process led by the pastor. Many parishes are crippled when the leader does not lead, and forming vision is one of the leader's key tasks. When the vision is so broad and vague, it will be both uninspiring and uninformative. If there is more than one vision, there will be two visions, or di-vision, in the parish. Once the vision statement is settled, the leadership of the parish must make a long-term, sustained effort to communicate the vision to all members of the parish, and invite them to embrace it and make it their own. This takes time. There are no shortcuts.

It is said that most pastors overestimate what can be accomplished in one year and underestimate what can be accomplished in five years. Vision processes take years to complete, and the ownership of vision among parishioners can take even longer. This is why long-term leadership is vital for the ongoing transformation of our churches. In Chapter 5, I spoke of the use of Gallup's three categories of parishioners and the ME 25 survey. Engaged parishioners are those who have taken ownership of the vision. Gallup defines organizational health as a four-to-one ratio of engaged to actively disengaged. When this takes place, there is a substantial buy-in and ownership of where the parish is trying to go. Gallup tells us that when engagement reaches about 55%, it begins to level off, and is unlikely to go above 60%. Even the healthiest parish will always have a degree of "naysayers," somewhere around 10%, leaving 30% who are not really invested one way or the other. This kind of embrace takes time and cannot be achieved by posting the parish vision statement on a bulletin board or website or in the parish newsletter.

The late American Vineyard pastor John Wimber used to speak about the need for the pastor to "put the sign on the bus." This is the constant proclamation of where we are headed, done in a way that allows people to decide whether they wish to stay on the bus, get on it or get off it. When waiting for a bus or a subway, the first thing anyone does is look for the sign on the front that tells where the vehicle is going. This is a vital and just task when labouring to move any parish or ministry from maintenance to mission.

The Church of God is missional. It is a bus that is designed to go. For centuries, however, these local "buses" have sat in parking lots. They have been maintained and decorated. People gather to sit in them for one hour a week, and some even drop in during the week, but most of the buses have never gone out. When a pastor starts the engine and calls "all aboard," those who receive the invitation must be told where the bus is going so they can decide whether to be on board. This telling is not just a public announcement, but a process of inspiring and winning people over to be a part of something wonderful. In what follows, I offer a few concrete suggestions for how vision can be successfully communicated. I speak from the context of a parish, but invite you to adapt these ideas to your ministry situation.

Invest in Key People

The key people in your parish are other leaders, people of influence. The word "influence" comes from the Latin *influere*, and also gives us the term "influenza." It literally means "to flow into." Influence, obviously, can be positive or negative. The pastor must identify the influencers in his parish and invest in them. He cannot just choose from the people who agree with him, who like him and whom he likes in return.

There will be obvious key influencers in a parish among the staff and ministry leaders, but such people may also be found behind the scenes, with no formal ministry role, such as members of the ladies guild, or the person who spends much time in prayer before the Blessed Sacrament. Always keep your eyes open for the influencers and *flow into* them so that they can flow into others. A pastor must leave room in his schedule to meet with the people he wants to see. Of those who ask to see me, 99% come with their own agenda. They generally want me to do something for them. By filling every meeting slot with the agenda of others, the pastor will never get to the agenda of the parish. I still struggle deeply with this, but struggle with it I must. Make the time for that cup of coffee with the key influencer. Be honest, and be real. Share your dreams and your passion. Let the person you are investing in know that you regard her or him as a key parishioner who has influence. Speak about your vision and invite that person's feedback, if you have not already done so. Ask for his or her help in making the vision a reality, and be specific.

Preaching

I remember catching myself saying once, "But I spoke about that in a homily last year." It is foolish for us preachers to think that most parishioners are going to remember something we said two weeks before, never mind a year before. In truth, if the sign on the bus is to be plainly recognized, we must speak about vision over and over again. In the last three years, I have committed myself to preaching some form of visioning homily at all the weekend Masses every three weeks. I am convinced that this is necessary. Sunday is the only time we get to speak to the entire community, and if a parish has a Mass schedule that does not allow the pastor to address the parishioners at every Mass, it will be a serious obstacle to communicating the vision.

If a parish is becoming truly missional and is innovating, there will be ongoing change within the parish. Change must always be explained in light of the vision. When explaining the change, we must begin with scratching the dissatisfaction our parishioners are feeling. A simple way to do this is to ask them about members of their families who no longer go to church or have lost their faith. Ask about the absence of young people from our churches. Ask about the poverty and loneliness in people's lives. Ask if the fact that so many parishioners do not receive the care they need is a concern to them. Find the point of dissatisfaction and scratch.

Show that the current situation is untenable, because our society has changed so much. Be careful not to come across as if you are blaming those who went before us or those who are doing their best; instead, blame the changing circumstances and our reliance on the old models. Those who are particularly passionate will have to pay attention at this point. I realized recently that even when I speak to brother priests, I must be careful, as my passion can sometimes be experienced as implicit judgment on them and their ministries. This does not build bridges and will not win people over. Rather, when speaking about change, we must be clear about how the old way of doing things is not working, primarily because of the cultural shift that has taken place in the last 40 to 50 years.

One weekend, I was going to preach on ministering to young people in the Church, as our pastoral council and finance committee had approved the hiring of a full-time youth minister. Our parish had never had a youth minister before. At one point in the homily, I called up ten random young people and stood them in front of the community. They represented the 20% of baptized children who go to church. To demonstrate the attrition rate among our young people through the different stages of First Communion, confirmation and university, I would tell a certain number of them to return to their parents until I was left with one "post university" young person still in church. People were horrified, but it drove home a difficult reality: that if we do not consciously invest in making disciples of our youth, we may lose all of them. This helped rally support for the new youth ministry position.

When communicating about upcoming change, it is not enough to just speak about what we are doing and why we will be doing it. It is always necessary to tie it into the vision statement and invite the parishioners to dream the dream. Vision is communicated when people's imaginations are captured. My favourite words when speaking about vision are "Imagine if...." Imagine if this was a parish that became a place where everyone was loved and accepted. Imagine if this was a parish where all parishioners shared their gifts and talents for the work of ministry. Imagine how our community and our city would be transformed. Imagine if every parishioner gave generously of his or her financial resources: just imagine the good that could be accomplished in the name of Jesus. Imagine what we can do when we pull together. In 2013, our parish donated $38,500 to support relief efforts after Typhoon Haiyan devastated huge areas of the Philippines. In moments like these, it is no longer a question of imagination but a simple pointing and saying, "See what we can do."

Teaching

There is nothing quite like repetition. This is not only necessary in Sunday homilies, but in every gathering of parish leaders. My own staff have taught me this. Again, I too often presume that just because I took time several months ago to reflect on the vision, everyone is still focused and motivated by the vision. This is especially true if a large proportion of staff are from a previous leadership and may have been working out of a different parish culture. The parish vision statement ought to be the focus of off-site meetings and days of reflection with the staff, pastoral council and ministry leaders. At Saint Benedict, we identified this need. We take time at our parish leadership summits to reflect on the parish vision statement and receive feedback and questions about how particular ministries can be better aligned for working towards the vision of the future. As someone once said, "The main thing is to keep the main thing the main thing."

Strategy

Someone else once said that "Vision without strategy is simply hallucination." Vision is fundamental to transformation. It creates a desire and enthusiasm for the necessary journey, but as in any journey, once you have decided where you are going, you must then discern how you will get there. This is strategy – a word that comes from the Greek *strategikos*, the root of which (*strateia*) means "warfare." It reminds us that bringing vision closer to reality by making concrete plans is essentially about doing battle. It is a battle against the human tendency to cling to the status quo and resist change. It is a battle against the many obstacles and challenges that will be in the way of reaching our goal and, in the spiritual realm, we can never forget the principalities and powers that we must constantly do battle with. (Ephesians 6:10-16) There is an enemy, and he is often contented with a church mired in maintenance. The one thing the enemy hates is a church that is starting up its engine with a real intention to go somewhere.

Being Strategic About Being Strategic

When I first arrived at Saint Benedict Parish, I came with a strong vision and enough of an initial strategy to kick-start the cultural transformation of the parish. I am good at activating things, so this has never been a problem. The problem came after two years, as the initial strategy bore fruit and the parish began to transform. All of a sudden there was an entire new set of challenges, the biggest one being that I was no longer certain of what to do next. I had never been that far from the shore, and what had worked was becoming less effective.

Activities had doubled, our building was overloaded, the number of disciples was growing and presenting new pastoral demands, and the existing staff members were beginning to feel the strain. I was absent too often from the parish with my other responsibilities and initiatives, presuming that unless I heard otherwise, everything was fine. It was not. My initial strategy had been to invest in Alpha, connect groups and stewardship, and to use the Gallup tools to help evaluate how we were doing. I sought to establish a culture of discipleship and evangelization in the parish, and it was beginning to take effect. My practice had been to throw every good idea, and a few not-so-good ideas, against the wall and see if it stuck. If it did, we would do it. It was "the more the merrier" model of parish life.

As wonderful as this was, at least for me, it was clear that going around lighting fires was a sure way to eventually bring the entire house down. We needed a new strategy. What also became evident was that our present leadership structures did not allow us to be more strategic. We needed to begin to be strategic about being strategic.

My first problem was a sense that our pastoral council was not working as it should. Although it had ceased to function as a management committee, complete with members who represented constituents, or heads of ministries who reported in on their activities, it was still far from being as productive as it could be. It often felt that by the time the monthly meeting rolled around, we were just meeting so we could say that we had met. I would arrive after a full day at the parish feeling exhausted and with nothing but leftovers to serve. We had only two hours to meet, including time for prayer, and there never seemed to be enough time to sink our teeth into any issue. I would speak about the vision, the big picture, present a few ideas and ask for feedback. As much as the members were in earnest, it felt as if the council was operating as an accountability group that could testify that at least I was not completely off my rocker.

The problem was the growing gulf between this wonderful group of people who were eager to serve and the fact that the key people who were developing strategy, leading ministry teams in the parish and even beginning to lead teams of leaders were staff members who were not around the table. If the purpose of the pastoral council was to counsel the pastor on the big picture of the pastoral life of the parish, these key staff members needed to be there. Around this time, I read a paper by a Presbyterian pastor, Dr. Timothy Keller, entitled "Leadership and Church Size Dynamics: How Strategy Changes with Growth." It was a eureka moment for me, as it identified a dynamic I had sensed but had been unable to put my finger on until then. This dynamic is almost never discussed in Catholic circles: the fact that churches or parishes of different sizes have very different cultures and need different models and styles of ministry and leadership to function properly.

I had inherited a Church that had blended two smaller parishes and one mid-sized parish into one large parish. We had not stopped to acknowledge the real trauma that was caused to parishioners by this sudden change – not just in location and leadership, but in size. Although I had made some additions to parish staff, we were essentially trying to run the parish with the same staffing, leadership structure and expectations that we had had before.

Keller's article is open source and can easily be found on the Internet. I cannot recommend this paper highly enough for anyone interested in the future of his or her parish. It is written from an Evangelical Protestant perspective, but other than some terminology and his description of how small church "boards" operate, all his insights can be applied to a Catholic context. These insights are vital for many Catholic dioceses as we go about restructuring dioceses and closing, clustering or blending parishes, but never addressing the need to change leadership and ministry styles and philosophies to fit the size cultures of the new communities.

Let's review some of his main points.

A. Church Size

Keller has five categories of churches:

1. House Church (up to 40 members)

2. Small Church (40 to 200 members)

3. Medium Church (200 to 450 members)

4. Large Church (400 to 800 members)

5. Very large Church (more than 800 members)

We can see that the average Evangelical "small Church" is very different in size from the average "small" Catholic parish. Saint Benedict had, in actual fact, been an amalgamation of two large parishes with one very large parish to create a new very, very large parish, or a mega church. The irony was that the leadership structure was still that of a medium-sized church, according to Keller's definition. It was no wonder that, in spite of ourselves, we were finding it impossible to be strategic.

B. Size Dynamics

Keller points out that the move from smaller to larger churches will mean experiencing 1) increasing complexity, 2) shifting lay-staff responsibilities, 3) the need to be more intentional about assimilation of new members, 4) the need to be more intentional about communications, 5) increasing expectations about the quality of "production," 6) increasing openness to change, and 7) the shifting role of ministers.

These realities will demand the following changes, if parishes are to remain healthy and not stifle:

- Smaller decision-making bodies: In smaller churches, decisions are made by many people, and ministry is done by few people, relative to the size of the congregation. In larger parishes, decisions must be made by relatively fewer people, and ministry is done by many people. In really small parishes, a parish council may successfully run as a management committee, but this will not work in a mid-sized parish. In a mid-sized parish, a parish council may become a "pastoral council." It does not attempt to manage every aspect of Church life, as this would involve meeting for about six hours a week, every week. Instead, it is charged with "the big picture," and can operate successfully if it is composed of ministry heads and a few staff. It will exist primarily as a "reporting in" mechanism and will give the pastor a place to seek advice and input on difficult situations. In a very large parish, however, strategy will be developed more and more by parish staff and a small number of parishioners gifted with strategic abilities. Pastoral council meetings are no longer about reporting in on tactical matters, but are purely concerned with the broad strategy and future direction of the parish. Tactical matters and more precise strategy become the stuff of staff meetings and specialized committees.

- Decentralization: As a parish grows in size, the pastor should not only have increasingly less direct oversight of ministries, but eventually even less oversight of ministry leaders and even staff. If this leadership change is not addressed, the life of the parish will stagnate and be bottlenecked by the limited time and energy of the pastor. In very large parishes, the pastor will meet directly with staff and ministry leaders who are themselves overseeing other staff and ministry leaders. We explored this dynamic in Chapter 5 when we looked at the development of mid-size communities in a parish.

- More specialized staff: In a smaller parish, it is typical to have some theologically trained ordained or lay staff, in addition to the pastor. These staff members will be generalists and will oversee teams of workers. The larger a parish, the more it will need staff to be trained specialists who lead other leaders. To quote Keller, "Very large churches do not need theologically trained people to learn a specialty so much as they need specialists who can be theologically trained." Staff in large parishes must be self-starters and be capable of leading ministry without close supervision. They will be responsible for making decisions that affect their particular ministries without always seeking the ear of the pastor. They must be able to move from being leaders to being leaders of leaders. In larger churches, understanding and buying into the particular culture of each parish becomes essential when hiring new staff. Larger churches often benefit more from raising up staff from within rather than bringing people in from outside. When bringing a staff member in from outside, proper attention must be given to training that staff member in the history, culture and values of that parish.

- The changed role of the pastor: This element has a huge impact on the health of a parish and the health of a pastor. Both the pastor and the parishioners must adapt their expectations of the pastor's role as a church moves from small to large. Sociologists tell us that most pastors can directly care for up to 200 people. When people expect instant access and a personal relationship with a pastor, regardless of the size of a parish, heartbreak and burnout are inevitable. In a large parish, the pastor will not spend most of his time doing ministry, but will delegate this work so that he can spend more time on preaching, leading, developing and communicating vision, and overseeing strategy. In our Catholic context, at the heart of the pastor's role will be sacramental ministry.

At Saint Benedict Parish, based on our frustration and the insights we gained from the likes of Keller, we knew that the first strategy to develop involved changing the staffing and leadership structures to reflect the new size culture of our parish. We had to do this before we could become strategic about our mission.

Changes to Pastoral Council

As I mentioned, pastoral council was no longer operating as a management committee or a reporting body, but was attempting to be about broad strategy. In spite of the excellent and gifted members and leaders of the pastoral council, we were struggling.

Two key changes were made. First, we expanded the number of pastoral staff members on the council, adding staff who had the most strategic gifts and who oversaw ministry teams. This meant increasing the general membership of the council so there would be an even number of staff and parishioners. We did this by introducing a five-step discernment process that began with broad nominations from all parishioners but gave us excellent new members without having elections of any kind. These new members helped to allay any concerns about staff dominating pastoral council.

Second, we stopped having monthly two-hour meetings. We now meet every two months for at least four hours, often on a Saturday morning. The agenda is set well in advance, and members are expected to come prepared, having read and reflected upon resource material. Since this change, the focus of our pastoral council has been entirely on developing the parish vision and purpose statements, aligning and evaluating ministries against the vision statement, and working out the broad strategy for a five-year plan.

Staffing Changes

The demands of the culture shift that was taking place at Saint Benedict Parish required us to hire a full-time director of communications. We hired from within, choosing a qualified person who was already aligned to the vision of the parish. This change meant hiring another staff member to move into the vacant position and realigning job descriptions.

One final change was required. After my arrival at Saint Benedict Parish, we quickly discovered that weekly meetings with all hands on deck were vital. With so much activity, how quickly the wheels would begin to fall off the wagon if people missed staff meetings. We always spent at least 20 to 30 minutes in prayer, and would go around the table and report in. The meetings would often be a deluge of information, an attempt to deal with problems specific to different ministries, and sporadic wanderings into big-picture strategic questions. (The latter was necessary, because it had not been happening at pastoral council.) After two years of working this way, staff members were often frustrated. Many would be silent at meetings and allow others (including me) to dominate discussions. Tensions among staff were obvious, and for the most part remained unaddressed. Then I discovered the writings of Patrick Lencioni.

Death by Meeting

Patrick is a founding member of The Table Group, an executive consulting organization that addresses leadership and organizational health. He is also a devout Catholic and has a huge desire to see parishes become healthier and parish leaders lead more effectively. Patrick has written many books, including *The Five Dysfunctions of a Team* and *The Advantage*. But the book that had the biggest impact on our parish staff was his bestselling *Death by Meeting*. Judging this book by its cover, one could be forgiven for concluding that it recommends reducing, if not getting rid of, meetings. We have all been practically bored to death in meetings that seem to go on and on and on. That is his hook.

Through a parable, Lencioni poses this question: Why are we so bored at meetings and so unbored watching movies? Both last for about two hours, and while a meeting is about reality and directly impacts our lives, movies are an escape from reality and have no direct impact on our lives. His answer: the presence of drama and conflict. Conflict drives drama and keeps our interest. Our meetings are boring not because we have too many of them, but because real drama is often absent. Too many of our team members never say what they really think within the group, and when they do, it's only to select team members at the water cooler. As a result, the staff culture of our parishes is often unhealthy. Members do not give their input into significant questions because of their fear of open conflict. Yet opposition and disagreement can be a very important dynamic. If it is not allowed to be expressed in a positive and healthy manner, it will manifest in an unhealthy manner.

For Lencioni, the problem is not that organizations have too many meetings, but that they do not have enough of the right kind of meetings. He encourages four different kinds of meetings: the daily check in, tactical meetings, strategic meetings, and quarterly off-sites. We took his insights to heart and implemented a number of changes. We are still learning the best way to embody his principles, but it has already made a huge difference to how we work together as a team.

Developing Strategy

With the changes to how our pastoral council and staff teams functioned, we now had the capacity for rich and fruitful strategic planning. As I outlined above, low-level strategy is worked out by the parish staff. Broad strategy is the domain of the pastoral council. Here are five possible activities for parish pastoral councils to sink their teeth into: vision and purpose statements; values analysis; five systems analysis; SWOT analysis; and the five-year plan.

1. Vision and Purpose Statements

If a parish does not have a vision statement, that is the place to begin. Remember, a vision statement does not describe the Church as it currently is, but what it seeks to be. Ask the leadership of your parish if they know what the vision is. If they give you blank stares, ask where you are going as a parish. If they look at you as if you are crazy, then you need to begin a process of developing a vision statement, as described earlier in this chapter. Be patient in this process, as it can take a minimum of six months.

In the 1980s it became trendy for organizations to develop mission statements. They were usually some blend of vision with a list of organizational values and stated priorities for action. They tended to be overly long, convoluted and so vague that they were virtually meaningless to the average person. Many organizations no longer bother with mission statements. Instead, they have a simple and clear purpose statement. If the vision statement is the compass of the parish, the purpose statement is the needle that tells you if your actions are aligned with the direction you wish to go in.

Purpose statements are short and specific. They define the primary purpose of the organization, against which all activities can be measured. The purpose statement of Saint Benedict is "To raise up disciples who joyfully live out their mission." At Nativity Parish, of *Rebuilt* fame, it is to "Love God, love others, make disciples." Holy Trinity Brompton's is "to play our part in the re-evangelisation of the nations and the transformation of society." Saint Monica Catholic Community's is "To form loving disciples who will transform the world." Downtown Chicago's Old Saint Patrick's Church's statement is "to serve the life and the work of the laity on the world."

2. Values Analysis

In Chapter 5, we discussed values as being what our actions profess rather than what our published statements say. A vital responsibility of a pastoral council is to undertake a brutally honest assessment of what the parish truly values at present. This can be done by looking at the parish schedule to see what type of events take place in and through the parish. The parish budget will reflect exactly what a parish values, as will the staffing structure and job titles. What the parish celebrates and what kind of complaints are listened to will help fill in the picture. Finally, a thorough breakdown of how the pastor spends not only his time but his energy in ministry will reveal what is valued by the parishioners and the pastor.

An honest assessment of real parish values of a church may look something like this.

1. Preservation of buildings

2. Child-centred catechetics

3. Convenience

4. Minimal expectations

5. Stability

6. Caring for our own members

7. Parish as a social hub

The next task is to evaluate on a scale of one to ten how your parish is doing in living out the ten values common to healthy and growing churches (see Chapter 5):

1. Giving priority to the weekend

2. Hospitality

3. Uplifting music

4. Great homilies

5. Meaningful community

6. Clear expectations

7. Strength-based ministry

8. Formation of small communities

9. Experience of the Holy Spirit

10. Become an inviting church

If a parish worked through one of these value conversions every year, the parish would begin to experience real transformation by developing the first four items. Remember that with values, what matters is that they are truly valued and not just stated. This requires authentic conversion of heart. In January each year, a pastoral council could begin to develop a strategic plan to grow in a particular value and begin to execute it the following September. Execution would involve a communication plan, through teaching and preaching and concrete changes in the life of the parish. The gains would be cumulative. How these values are lived out in different contexts may look different, but what matters is that the values, when truly embraced, bring a church to a place of health; healthy things grow and produce fruit. It may take time, but once a church truly begins to experience value conversion, it will begin to move and gain momentum.

3. Five Systems Analysis

Pastor Rick Warren of Saddleback Church often speaks of the five systems of Church life. He has also referred to them as the five New Testament purposes for the Church. When speaking of them as systems, he compares the Church to the human body. The human body has ten systems – the skeletal system, digestive system, nervous system, reproductive system, etc. All ten systems need to be working properly for the body to be healthy. If all of these systems are working properly, the body is at ease. If even one of them is not working properly, the body is at "dis-ease." The Church also has systems, and all must be functioning well for the body to be healthy. The five systems of church life are worship, evangelization, discipleship, fellowship and ministry. As in any body, these systems cannot exist in isolation from the others. The proper functioning of each is indispensable for the health of the body. We need to have a clear understanding of what each system entails or we will not perceive our lack of health and will misdiagnose our ailment.

- **System 1: Worship**

This is an obvious one for us as Catholics. Our primary act of worship is the celebration of the Eucharist. Worship can include prayer meetings and times of praise experienced in small groups.

- **System 2: Evangelization**

This is the proclamation, or kerygma: the Good News of God's love revealed in Jesus, and the salvation offered through his cross and resurrection. It is proclaimed to those who do not know Jesus. Evangelization brings people into an encounter with Jesus Christ and leads them to a decision to trust, follow him and become his disciple. Evangelization will seek to bring those who respond to that encounter to the sacraments of baptism or reconciliation. It is directed to those outside of the Church, but may also be aimed at those within the Church who know about Jesus but do not know him personally.

- **System 3: Discipleship**

Discipleship is the lifelong process of growing, maturing and learning that the believer eagerly enters into if truly evangelized. It includes catechesis, but cannot be reduced to it. It includes growing in faith, knowledge, prayer and identifying one's God-given gifts.

- **System 4: Fellowship**

Fellowship is community – what the New Testament calls *koinonia*, the common life. It is meaningful community where people are known and loved, called by name and supported in their call to holiness. It may include socializing, but cannot be reduced to it. Fellowship happens when parishioners are accountable to and for one another.

- **System 5: Ministry**

Ministry is service to others. It includes essential ministry within the life of the parish so that it can function and form its members, but exists, in a missionary culture, to go out and serve those who do not belong. The true measure of the life of ministry in a parish is not how many lectors a parish has, but the proportion of ministry that is going out to the "existential peripheries," as Cardinal Bergoglio called them. He restated this rather forcefully in *Evangelii Gaudium:* "I prefer a Church which is bruised, hurting and dirty because it has been out on the streets, rather than a Church which is unhealthy from being confined and from clinging to its own security." (EG, no. 49)

These five systems overlap and cover the same dimensions of church life as do the ten values. Analyzing the overall health of the parish through an honest evaluation of the health of these systems is another means to arrive at a starting point of developing a strategy for renewal of a parish.

4. SWOT Analysis

Once the parish leadership has made an honest assessment of the health of the parish, then the real strategic work begins.

Whether a council uses the ten values to measure health, the five systems, or some other standard, a simple second step is to conduct a SWOT analysis. SWOT stands for Strengths, Weaknesses, Opportunities, Threats. This can be an energizing and exciting process to conduct with your leadership team. They will pinpoint present weaknesses, the opportunities to grow and the threats to that dimension of church life. This is a fantastic process that provides a leadership group with all the elements it needs to form a strategic plan.

5. The Five-Year Plan

Becoming strategic means making a plan. When we want to meet a friend for coffee, we make a plan. If we want to organize our finances, we make a plan. How is it that we automatically plan so many things in our lives, but when it comes to the life of the Church, most parishes, and some dioceses, have no plan. They literally exist from moment to moment, being reactive rather than proactive. This is, of course, symptomatic of a maintenance culture. But if the bus is to leave the parking lot and know its destination, there must be a plan – unless "the plan" is just to drive in a general direction of something, hoping for the best. Most organizations never plan beyond a five-year mark, as so much changes during that time that cannot be anticipated.

The key points in a five-year plan are at the six-month, one year and three-year mark. These are the chapter markers and can be the framework upon which a parish will build its plan. The degree of detail of the strategy will depend on the makeup of the council and the size of the parish. In a smaller parish, the pastoral council will work out a detailed strategy and may even be involved in the execution of it. In a larger parish, the council will paint with broad strokes and leave the lower strategy to the pastoral team and other committees, to those on the ground in that particular area of parish life.

At Saint Benedict Parish, we have used all five of the above approaches. Our current plan has been developed by going through a visioning process based on the five systems of church life. Having completed a SWOT analysis of the health of our parish based on the five systems, we asked our leadership team to dream about where we would be in five years' time. What would worship, evangelization, discipleship, fellowship and ministry look like in our parish in the year 2018? After working through the responses, we were able to develop five one-sentence vision statements that would serve as the basis of a five-year plan. This plan would be a synthesis of five individual plans, reflecting each of the five systems. Each plan would have a series of goals to be achieved on a timeline. These goals were S.M.A.R.T.: specific, measurable, attainable, realistic and timely. Once each plan was outlined, they were synthesized and all the goals were put into priority within an overall timeline.

Executing the Plan

Three frogs sat on a log. Two decided to jump off. How many are left?

The answer to this riddle is obvious, is it not? There would be three left, because deciding to do something and doing it are not the same thing. We have all had experiences in our lives when, in spite of our good intentions, we lack follow-through. Sadly, in many churches, parish plans and diocesan plans are produced with great effort and sacrifice. They are polished and published and then sit on shelves, often unread and forgotten within a few years. By that time, a new bishop or priest arrives, and we begin all over again. One can put the sign on the bus, plot the route and turn on the engine, but at some point the handbrake must be released and the gentle dance between the brake and the gas pedal begins.

There is no question that when it comes to executing the plan, the driver is the pastor. His task, in consultation with the staff and pastoral council, is to know when to step on the gas, when to brake and when to turn a corner. Every development along the way will be felt by the passengers, and when the bus stops, some may decide they have had quite enough, and get off. Other passengers will get on.

Leading change within an organization is the essential task of any leader today. Leading change in a volunteer organization is the most difficult kind of leadership. No one is compelled to be a part of the volunteer organization. They are always free to take their marbles and go home. If the fragile interplay between gas and brake is not done wisely, it can cause severe damage to the bus. The driver must know when to go slowly and when to speed up, conscious that the bus is a fragile thing. This is where the true test of leadership is found.

The pastor may ultimately be the lone driver, but if he has a healthy and balanced leadership team where honest and open exchanges can take place, he will not be lonely. If he has a competent and capable staff who work well as a team and trust and care for one another, they will be the ones who will take responsibility for executing the details. In the midst of the fun, the role of the pastor will be to keep the team and the functioning of the parish healthy.

Volumes have been written on executing plans by men and women who have much more knowledge, wisdom and experience than I do. In what follows, I will share how I have invested my time in overseeing the execution of our strategic plan.

- **Low Control, High Accountability**

I spoke about this principle in Chapter 5. In anything larger than an 800-member church, the pastor and the parishioners will have to embrace this principle. The pastor must give up control and the temptation to micromanage. Likewise, the people must let go of the model of parish in which the only way that gatherings, ministries and activities are validated is by the presence of the priest. Sheer size may mitigate against this, but practicality is not the only reason for the pastor to exercise low control over ministries. The positive principle of subsidiarity applies here. Subsidiarity means that as much as possible, decisions that affect people should be made by the people being affected. In this way, people have ownership of their particular ministries. Unless a parish ministry is about to drive off a cliff, the pastor need not interfere in its decisions. He can give gentle guidance and suggestions, but may have to live with decisions he disagrees with. (I am speaking, of course, of aspects of parish life that would not touch upon issues of faith and morals.)

In some ministries, the demands of subsidiarity will place the pastor at the heart of the decision-making process. Decisions by the pastoral council, finance committee, stewardship team, and so on are much closer to the vital organs of a parish, and the pastor should be involved. Decisions of pastoral council, ultimately, are the decisions of the pastor in consultation with his council. At the same time, a pastor must be wise in recognizing that if an entire group of competent lay people who care for the parish and buy into the vision recommend against a course of action in a meeting of the pastoral council, he may need to give up control.

The only way a low-control culture can thrive in a parish without everything eventually falling apart is to balance it with the value of high accountability. Every ministry must report in and be accountable to a staff member or a ministry leader who in turn reports to a staff member who reports to the pastor. Another aspect of high accountability is buying into the parish vision and culture. If ministries are led by competent lay people who totally agree with where the parish is going, you have a winning combination.

- **The Push Out Factor**

Low control requires the empowering of lay people in ministry. If a pastor is going to delegate real responsibility to a parishioner, real authority must also be delegated. This authority and responsibility will lead to the multiplication of ministry within the parish and of parishioners who take real ownership of what they do, and are not doing it as a favour for Father. The push out factor refers to this empowerment. The discernment, calling forth, equipping and empowering of leaders is vital to the growth of a parish church. This means that the pastor must always, as a matter of principle, push out to competent parishioners the elements of his ministry that are not essential to his role as priest and pastor. Someone once said that the mark of a great leader is not the number of followers he or she has, but the number of leaders he or she has raised up.

This principle does not apply only to the pastor, but to all the staff and, indeed, to all ministry leaders. I tell our staff all the time that their job is not to do the job, but to call and empower others to do it. Our staff and ministry leaders should be leaders of leaders. Pushing out enables a parish to grow, and the more a parish grows, the more the pastor, staff and ministry leaders will have to push out.

- **Leadership Summits**

I have already spoken about the role these gatherings play in helping parishioners fully embrace the parish vision statement. In any large parish, investment in leaders is critical. Leaders need to be affirmed, supported, listened to, equipped and encouraged. This is why, three to four times a year, we gather all parish ministry leaders and their heir apparents to gather with the pastoral council and stewardship team for a morning of prayer and reflection.

These sessions include an opportunity to unpack the parish vision, hear feedback, have leaders speak to one another and teach on some aspect of leadership. We may present to ministry leaders about how to evaluate their ministries, how to be true leaders and not just schedulers, how to push out and work themselves out of a job, and how to plan for the succession of a new leader. At Saint Benedict Parish, we have identified the raising up of leaders as the most pressing and crucial task ahead of us. All the threads of the strategic plan cross over on this issue.

Leadership summits also provide a mechanism for real accountability. If a parish ministry wants to experience low control from the pastor and the staff, its ministry lead must attend the leadership summit. The dates for these events are planned a year in advance, so ministry leads have plenty of notice. We always conclude these gatherings of leaders by calling on the Holy Spirit and having a time of prayer ministry, laying on hands that our leaders may once again experience the infilling of the Holy Spirit. These events have been a significant factor in keeping that fragile bus together and not falling apart through the twists and turns, lurches and bumps along the way to our destination.

- **Team Composition**

"Beggars can't be choosers" goes the saying, and in many parish cultures this is definitely the mindset that is often found in ministry groups and teams. A pastor has a sphere of influence and must play a more direct role in the formation of particular teams while encouraging health and balance in every ministry team in his parish. The first team the pastor is responsible for composing is his own staff. This task cannot be passed on to anyone else in the parish. The pastor will evaluate the character and competency of his staff, or those who would apply for a staff position, but also of extreme importance is the fit of that person into the culture of the parish and the buy-in to the vision. If there is no real unity on these essential issues among the staff, there is little likelihood that the parish will ever be free of di-vision and become healthy. Trust will never take root within the parish staff and, as a result, will not be able to flourish in the parish as a whole. A pastor who ignores staff who are disruptive or "actively disengaged" seals his own fate by his inaction.

Other teams that the pastor should pay close attention to are obviously the pastoral council and finance committee. Parishes have many different processes for selecting members for the parish council. Whatever the process, it must involve the broader congregation, giving them the opportunity to put names forward. At the end of the process, however, there should be no one on the parish pastoral council whose presence is not supported by the pastor. This does not mean that the council is composed of mere "yes men (and women)." It is healthy and beneficial to have mature parishioners who can freely disagree with the pastor from time to time and are not afraid to express this disagreement.

However, disagreement or healthy conflict must take place within the context of full agreement with the parish vision statement and culture. One of our requirements for membership on pastoral council at Saint Benedict is that all who are discerning a place on council must have attended Alpha and read a certain number of books and articles that have affected and shaped the culture of the parish.

The general wisdom about the membership of finance councils decrees that its ranks be filled only with bankers and accountants. This can be disastrous. It is the job of the pastoral council to dream about what could be done and the finance committee to define what can be done. But if all the members of the finance committee are number crunchers with no pastoral imagination or no passion for evangelization, discipleship and mission, then the missional culture of the pastoral council will be on a collision course with a maintenance culture of the finance committee. A good smattering of passionate, faith-filled business entrepreneurs can provide balance against the necessary skills of the financiers on the committee. At Saint Benedict, we ask all members of the finance committee to also attend our leadership summits so they can continuously reflect on the parish vision statement.

- **Staff Team Health**

If a parish is to execute strategy and help the bus to move, the most important team of all is the parish staff. If a parish is smaller, the "staff team" may also include some key parishioners who function as volunteer staff. Just as a parish has a culture 80% of which sits below the surface, unseen, so does a parish staff. If what is under the surface is ignored, it can lead to a breakdown in the team that will be felt throughout the parish. Remember, it was the part of the iceberg below the water that struck the *Titanic*, and it was the breach in the hull below the water level that sank her. Our struggles in team building over the last number of years at Saint Benedict forced us to place high priority on identifying the kind of culture we would strive to create as a staff. The process of teaching, reflection and discussion led to the creation of a formal staff ethos statement. We revisit this statement each month by reading it before we begin our strategic meetings.

Saint Benedict Parish: Staff Culture Ethos

We value each other and build interpersonal trust by:

1. Caring for the well-being of the whole person.

2. Intentionally investing in the interpersonal relationships within the office.

3. Engaging in open, honest communication with each other and refraining from gossip and detraction.

4. Fully and attentively listening to others with ears and hearts to deeply understand the other person, not just respond to what is being said.

5. Choosing healthy conflict over tension.

We value parish ministry with excellence and empower leaders by:

1. Having a clear mission statement for the parish, a compelling scoreboard to track progress and clear job descriptions for every staff member.

2. Assigning roles and responsibilities to staff that are: 1) important because they meet the identified needs/opportunities of the parish and 2) life-giving because they put the leader's strengths and passions to work for best results.

3. Having a bi-monthly leadership in-service (lunch supplied).

4. Celebrating team and individual 'wins' and affirming personal contributions made by staff.

5. Giving staff permission to invest some time on new projects that are approved by the Pastor.

We value the work we are called to do and align for execution by:

1. Having a clear, one-sentence summary job description for every staff member that is aligned to the parish mission statement and rooted in their full job description.

2. Growing in our understanding and practice of the new meeting rhythms.

3. An annual in-depth evaluation of ministries to ensure alignment to the parish mission/purpose.

4. Bi-annual performance discussion with every staff member and direct supervisor.

5. Monthly reading and re-committing to the Staff Ethos (before strategic discussions).

Having a Thick Skin

I have a plaque in my office that reads, "Change is good, as long as I don't have to do anything different." The processes of creating vision statements and strategic planning will raise the curiosity of some, but most passengers wake up with a start when the bus begins to move – that is, when things start to change. A leader must be prepared that as soon as he or she begins to lead, there will be unpleasantness.

This is so because leading, by its very definition, means making decisions, sometimes difficult ones. Whenever any decision is made in an organization, there is some disagreement, and even more so in a church community. Where there is disagreement, there will be criticism. Leading means moving others from one place to another. Moving means change, and change is always resisted and the leader always criticized by some. Anytime this kind of criticism wears me down or weighs heavily on me, I always think of poor Moses and the endless complaints he endured as he sought to lead the Israelites from Egypt to the Promised Land. At least I have not yet asked God to kill me.

Constructive criticism about how something is being done by those who are invested in the parish, and are passionate about where the parish is going, is very different from hostility rooted in fundamental disagreement with where the parish is going. The pastor must be attentive to the former and listen carefully. He also must be equally prepared for the latter, and set his face like flint. In truth, those who are actively disengaged are very difficult to win over. If they are won over, it is rarely by the one who is the symbol and source of the change they so ardently resist, but by a peer. The wisest response to the latter form of criticism is to ignore it. Gallup tells us that giving substantial amounts of energy to the actively disengaged will make virtually no difference. Some passengers will choose to get off the bus, and while some may quit peaceably, others will make noise.

The most painful kind of noise is the anonymous letter. During my first two years at Saint Benedict Parish, I received anonymous letters once or twice a week. I have had letters of complaint written to the bishop and even to the pope himself criticizing my preaching style, the speed at which I process into Mass, my height (or lack thereof) and, my favourite, being a "holy roller." Hallelujah! The pastor who wishes to lead must be prepared for these kinds of attacks.

Saint Paul tells us to "take up the whole armour of God" and to "take the shield of faith, with which you will be able to quench all the flaming arrows of the evil one." (Ephesians 6:13, 16) The leader must know that when he or she begins to lead in the world of the Church, they are not dealing with a human reality, but with a spiritual reality. The enemy is very content for the Church to be maintenance focused and to continue to sink into the mud. He need pay no attention to it, if it is so. A Church that begins to recall its lost identity, step out in faith and move from the safety and comfort of maintenance to a life of mission is suddenly a threat.

The most painful aspect of the anonymous letter is not the cruel things that are often said, the fact that you are unable to respond or that the writer claims to be speaking for some silent majority, but that the writer did not feel comfortable bringing their concerns to the leadership of the church to discuss in a healthy manner. After my first year at Saint Benedict, I told the parishioners I would not read unsigned letters. I also spoke to them about the obligation to dissent. Not only are they allowed to disagree with the pastor, and to communicate this disagreement, but they have an obligation to do so.

I am not speaking here about public dissent from Church doctrine, but disagreement about what we are doing and how we are doing it. I am the first to assert that the only certainty I have about the changes I have introduced is that they cannot be worse than what we were doing before. I make no claim that we have the best models or that we have perfected them. A parishioner who disagrees may have something of value to say. This is especially the case if it is someone who is invested in the parish, who fulfills all of the expectations to worship, to grow, to connect, to serve and to give.

Expanding the Vision

It is too light a thing that you should be my servant to raise up the tribes of Jacob and to restore the preserved of Israel; I will give you as a light to the nations, that my salvation may reach to the end of the earth. (Isaiah 49:6)

In Chapter 1, we reflected on the identity crisis of Israel during the lifetime of Jesus. They had forgotten their missionary identity to be a light to the nations. Instead, they had settled for something much too "light" or "small": only raising up and restoring their own. We reflected that this same identity crisis is the root cause of the ill health that afflicts much of our Church in the developed world. We have forgotten our essential missionary identity: that the Church does not *have* a mission but *is* a mission.

Over the past number of years, I have had the pleasure to encounter many Catholics who yearn for the missionary identity of the Church to be reclaimed. They yearn for it and labour for it. On many occasions, however, I have found myself reflecting on the words of Isaiah when the conversation of missionary-minded Catholics seems to focus only on restoring fallen-away Catholics. This is a huge mission field, but I truly believe that the Lord's words through the prophet Isaiah speak to us today and tell us that such a vision is too small a thing. The Lord wants his Church universally, and locally, to be a light to the nations.

I once heard the U.S. pastor Steven Furtick say that if our vision is not so big that it scares the living daylights out of us, it may be insulting to God. I once heard Rick Warren say that unless our vision stretches us beyond what we are capable of, we may be being unfaithful. Faith requires that we truly trust in God. Most often, however, our pastoral plans remain entirely in the realm of the safe and what we think is possible. The truth is that it requires no faith at all; we are just trusting in our own strengths and resources. In this way, we truly are being unfaithful, because we do not need faith to achieve those goals.

Conclusion

As this book draws to a close, I invite you, as a leader, to ask yourself if your own vision is too small. Is it big enough for God? Rick Warren once said, in authentic humility, "God has used me to do great things, because I expected Him to do so." This expectation, of course, is not rooted in who we are, but in who God is. Our Lady said, "The Mighty One has done great things for me, and holy is his name." (Luke 1:49) Do you believe that God can do great things in and through you? Do you believe that when you stare at your paltry loaves and fish and hear the Lord speak in your heart, "You give them something to eat," he will multiply the little that you have?

I have been a priest for seventeen years. I began my formation for the priesthood 25 years ago. A lot of water has passed under the bridge since I first gave up running from a strong and urgent sense of a call to priestly ministry. When I stopped squirming before the Lord's call, there is only one word to describe the calling I felt. It was a passion. A passion to make a difference. A passion for people to experience the love of God in Jesus Christ the way I did. A deep passion and conviction that, if only the world knew, heaven truly would come down to earth. I had a fire in my bones. I experienced zeal that "ate me up."

Then I studied theology.

Don't get me wrong. I loved studying theology, and I had wonderful professors and classmates. I had excellent theological formation during my years in the seminary. But my passion took a double hit during those same years. The academic atmosphere of the seminary did not lead me to do "theology on the knees." My love of the scriptures was eroded by a universal and overabundant application of historical-critical methodologies. My image of Jesus was bruised and confused by Christologies "from below" that overshadowed everything supernatural and never seemed to arrive at the higher realms.

The second passion hit came through the experience of my own brokenness and sinfulness. My spiritual honeymoon was over. Prayer did not come naturally to me, as I had once thought it did. It was difficult, and was often dry and painful. It was hard to admit, but I began to recognize that much of my early passion seemed to have been a thinly disguised egotism. Several months before I was to be ordained a deacon, I was praying one night in a small chapel with the lights out. I was alone and prostrated myself before the Lord in the Blessed Sacrament, when I suddenly had a realization that caused great panic. I was out of time! Six years earlier, I had begun my journey of formation for the priesthood. It had not been without its bumps and twists and turns. Still, I had been very confident that in spite of all my weaknesses and sinfulness, by the time my seminary formation was over, the Lord would have perfected me, or at least removed my biggest flaws.

As I lay there in the darkness, I felt two things. First, not only had I not been perfected, but I was in worse shape than when I started out. I felt further away from this elusive perfection, and less holy than at the beginning of my journey. I had started with a conviction and a passion to change the world for Jesus. By the end of my first year of theology, I thought that perhaps I could have an impact on my diocese. After my pastoral year, I thought I could maybe change a parish. Now, as I was about to be ordained, I realized I was incapable of changing myself! Second, I had a deep conviction that God's call was still there – not in spite of my weakness, but because of it.

Every person who has ever been ordained has been asked, "What was the most memorable moment of the ordination liturgy?" I know my answer. I will never forget it. It came after the laying on of hands and the prayer of consecration. I had just been vested by a priest whom I loved and admired. With everything in place, I turned towards the altar with an overwhelming sense of purpose that can only be summed up by the words "Let's do it. Let's get to work." Seventeen years later, I still remember the moment and how it felt.

In the months that followed, I sped from ordination into parish life, where I learned very quickly not to rock the boat, upset the apple cart or make waves. It was as if I had slammed into a brick wall going 60 miles per hour. The passion and zeal that had brought me into and through the seminary had never dreamed that a culture of complacency, mediocrity and minimalism could be so determined and resilient. Face to face with this reality, it was all too easy to lose sight of the vision that God gave to me when I was first called. The fire in my bones was slowly dying. The spirit that animated me was dissipating, and dry bones were beginning to be visible under my priestly garments.

"Mortal, can these bones live?"

"O Lord God, you know." (Ezekiel 37:3)

God does indeed know. Dry bones can live because it is the Lord's desire to breathe new life into his people, into his Church! There is only one person who is able to put the fire back into our bones: the One who came as tongues of fire on the day of Pentecost. Only when we experience the absolute dryness of our bones can we fully submit to God's Spirit, who speaks to our spirit so that we cry, "Abba! Father!" (Romans 8:15) It is not we who change anything – the world, our diocese, our parish or even ourselves. It is God's Spirit who renews the face of the earth, who first birthed the Church and continues to bring her to new birth. It is the Holy Spirit of God who brings us to embrace our true identity as a missional Church. It is God's Spirit, poured out in a New Pentecost, who gives us the ability to bring about a New Evangelization.

I think back to my youthful yearnings that God would use me to change the world and realize that they were not foolish after all. It is a constant theme in the Scriptures that God chooses what is foolish and weak to shame the wise (1 Corinthians 1:27), that God almost shouts at every one of us, "I want to make a difference in and through you. Your vision is too small. It is too small a thing…."

So I ask you, my brother, my sister, whatever your ministry is or your leadership consists of, how can the vision for your ministry be expanded? Do you realize that you are weak and foolish? Then you are ready to be used by God. Does your vision for what God can do through you make you tremble? Is it truly big enough for God? If you lead a ministry within your parish, how can you impact your entire parish? If you lead a parish, how can you impact your diocese? If you are working within your diocese, how can you impact your region, your province or state? What about your country? Could God not only impact a nation through you, but even change the world?

Jesus made a promise to his apostles: "But you will receive power when the Holy Spirit has come upon you; and you will be my witnesses in Jerusalem, in all Judea and Samaria, and to the ends of the earth." (Acts 1:8) This is God's call to each and every one of us. It is not rooted in ordination, but in our fundamental identity in Christ as baptized believers. Our calling is to not just impact our immediate community. That is "Jerusalem." It is not just to impact our region or province. That is "Judea." It is not even to impact our nation, "Samaria," but to go to the "ends of the earth."

Jesus promised that we would receive power when the Holy Spirit comes upon us. That power is there for the asking – from the same Spirit who reminds us that we are the very mission of Christ, the Spirit who brings a revolution of life even to a valley of dry bones. What a moment! What a time! What a privilege to play a role in the renovation of God's Church!

God knows! God knows that these bones can live.

Hallelujah!

Do you?